T0383878

Dynamic Competitive Strategy

Dynamic Competitive Strategy by best-selling author Dr Tony Grundy casts a radically new light on competitive strategy by showing you the dynamic dimension of existing strategy tools and new ones created to deal with rapid innovation and turbulent change.

He shows us refreshing and challenging ways of developing strategy, including:

- Agile approaches to strategy and planning
- The art of the Cunning Plan – with 101 ways to be innovative
- The alien approach: how might an alien see your industry and business?
- A whole new set of dynamic strategy tools
- Scenario storytelling and the art of mental time travel
- How emotional value can leverage competitive advantage
- Dynamic stakeholder analysis and influencing

He also includes case studies of Arsenal, Brexit, Dyson, Metrobank, Tesco, the infamous honey badger and others from everyday life.

This book provides an overall theory and a wealth of practical guidance based on 30 years of Strategy Consulting and Management Research and Teaching that will transform your thinking about strategy. Tony truly "turns strategy upside down," as he does on the cover.

Dr Tony Grundy is Director of Strategy and Corporate Development, and has lectured at leading Business Schools such as Cranfield, Cambridge, CASS, Durham, Henley and Warwick. The author of 21 books, he works globally across all industries to design and facilitate strategy process, and train or coach senior executives in Dynamic Strategic Thinking.

Dynamic Competitive Strategy

Turning Strategy Upside Down

Dr Tony Grundy

Routledge
Taylor & Francis Group

LONDON AND NEW YORK

First published 2018
by Routledge
2 Park Square, Milton Park, Abingdon, Oxon OX14 4RN

and by Routledge
711 Third Avenue, New York, NY 10017

Routledge is an imprint of the Taylor & Francis Group, an informa business

British Library Cataloguing-in-Publication Data

A catalogue record for this book is available from the British Library

Library of Congress Cataloging-in-Publication Data
DataNames: Grundy, Tony, 1954- author.
Title: Dynamic competitive strategy : turning strategy upside down /
    Dr. Tony Grundy.
Description: Abingdon, Oxon ; New York, NY : Routledge, 2018. |
    Includes bibliographical references and index.
Identifiers: LCCN 2017029095 (print) | LCCN 2017040887 (ebook) |
    ISBN 9781315113036 (eBook) | ISBN 9781138081086
    (hardback : alk. paper)
Subjects: LCSH: Strategic planning. | Competition.
Classification: LCC HD30.28 (ebook) | LCC HD30.28 .G784 2018
    (print) | DDC 658.4/012—dc23
LC record available at https://lccn.loc.gov/2017029095

ISBN: 9781138081086 (hbk)
ISBN: 9781315113036 (ebk)

Typeset in Bembo
by Apex CoVantage, LLC

Contents

Figures

1 Introduction

What is this book all about?

Strategic thinking and planning should move from being 80% static and 20% Dynamic to 20% Static and 80% Dynamic.

– Tony G.

Every book needs a rationale *d'etre*. This one has one in spades.

It was more than 35 years ago that I first became gripped by the concept of "Corporate Planning," conceived of as a theory of corporate development and change that would steer a more complex business through new and uncharted waters. New concepts at that time were things like life cycle analysis, environmental analysis and capability (strengths and weaknesses) analysis.

At that time I was in my first "real" job in BP Group Internal Audit, at a time when BP basked in two massive fountains of oil from Alaska and the North Sea. As a newly qualified Chartered Accountant I had signed a two year deal mixing work and an endless sequence of serial package holidays that took me to five-star hotels globally. In those comfortable days I used to read a new book on Corporate Planning at least every other week!

Planning appealed to me as a way of overviewing a business, especially as I regarded the financial training that I had received. It did seem to me that the Corporate Planning discipline was far more interesting than following a purely financial career. But whilst the new discipline was for sure more holistic, it was framed in a more or less steady-state universe, maybe with the exception of the scenario storytelling that was being done by Shell.

But looking back at these first generation planning systems, particularly those of one of the founding gurus of Corporate Planning, Igor Ansoff himself, the models were very static. "SWOT" (strengths and weaknesses, opportunities and threats) analysis was portrayed as a snapshot, or X-ray picture of the current situation, not an evolving capability. "PEST" (political, economic, social and technological) analysis, although naturally a more dynamic tool for charting organizational shifts, was used much the same.

By looking at the historical context we can better understand how the strategy models of today are by and large, dynamically stillborn. Equally, if we look at the business context of that time, with the exception of the economic cycle and balance of payments crises the UK (and most of the EU) was in during generally stable economic growth, competition never quite had the cutting edge of today, which is often ferocious. Looking back, one can only think one thing: *How things change!*

Whilst contemporary strategy claims to deal with "99% of known strategic germs" about today, I feel it is stuck between its original first generation model, or "paradigm", and the much more agile kinds of processes that characterise the present business world. This is manifest in:

- the fact that almost universally the tools in regular use by managers have only static application;
- the fact that there were very few tools to capture the dynamics;
- the fact that managers primarily construct the future through projections from the present and the past; sometimes I call that "T-1 thinking";
- the fact that, with exceptions, the "environment" is seen as bit of a nuisance in planning – addressed by either static PEST analysis, or if you get really lucky, with Porter's Five Competitive Forces – but again from the present perspective rather than future.

In addition, probably 90% of plans are really very average in their thinking and do little to add any innovative or "bendy" contribution to the business model and to the economic performance of the business.

I feel that many plans are akin to having a plan for Christmas which is "get a Christmas tree, some decorations, roast a turkey and consume a lot of alcohol and food and invite family around." *That is so very average.* We need a lot more from strategic planning! What about getting the best value for money in the market for the bird, some Italian sparkling wine that outdoes champagne at half the price, and deflecting your mother-in-law from making negative comments about the newly fitted kitchen? A strategic plan worth its stuffing needs to be clever enough to handle dysfunctional behaviours, random upsets and sudden new opportunities arriving (let's abandon the burnt goose and just go out to the pub!).

In this chapter I look at:

- Deficiencies in the traditional models
- Dynamic competitive strategy from previous theory
- How is this book different?
- The Evolution of my thinking
- Here's what you will get out of this book
- Who is it aimed at?
- Content of the book
- Chapter summary of key points.

Important note on style

I write in a lively way, as if we were in the same room. *I don't do boring.* I use little twists and my unusual humour to carry you with me. It will not just be reading a book; *it will be an experience* – and it will stick!

Deficiencies in the traditional models

We now look at a number of the more popular models in traditional strategic planning. This will show that these models are at least 80% static but can be made far more dynamic. These include:

* SWOT analysis
* PEST analysis
* Porter's Five Competitive Forces
* "GE" (General Electric) Grid
* Competitive positioning.

> *"How is a threat an opportunity and the weakness a potential strength?"*
> *—Tony G*

SWOT analysis

First, let's take "SWOT" analysis:

> "SWOT" (or Strengths and Weaknesses, Opportunities and Threats) analysis is a quick and dirty brain dump of the things that determine a company's position internally and externally. Typically a SWOT picture (Figure 1.1) is drawn as four quadrants on a page. "Strengths" include the things that the company is good at, and the test should be only when it is better than the average competitor. Weaknesses are the corollary of this. Typically we would include things like brand, technology, leadership and management, unit costs, customer service and innovation.

"Opportunities" would be things like new markets, products, channels, alliances and technologies. "Threats" would arise from competitors, entrants, regulations, economic uncertainty, substitutes, technology and the internet, market maturity and commoditisation.

Strengths and weaknesses, opportunities and threats, are all likely to shift over time. For instance, Tesco PLC, the international supermarket retailer, boasted superior customer service from around 1997 through to 2007, then started to slip. This relative decline accelerated from 2010 to around 2014 to a point where it would be fair to say it had dropped from "strong" to "weak" (see more on Tesco in Chapter 7).

A new CEO, David Lewis, was then brought in in October 2014 from the FMCG Company Unilever to turn it around. Even so, there seemed to still be huge issues in turning the company around, which had lost its direction in many ways. By late 2016 there were some marked improvements. By that point, for example, Tesco was now gaining relative market share and not losing it (an important but not the sole indicator). David Lewis's magic was beginning to work, which is not bad after just two years. The point here is that *a strong position*

Figure 1.1 SWOT Analysis

(*and the various strengths within that) can go from being really strong to weak, and then back to a bit stronger in only around eight years: a true, very dynamic rollercoaster.* (See more on Tesco in Chapter 7).

External opportunities and threats are even more volatile. Picture January 2016. Except for a small number of commentators, "Brexit" was never going to happen. But after the referendum, where that was all upset, by January 2017 the battle was really heating up to try to get the best possible deal for the UK both outside the EU and with the EU without being saddled with the burdens of Brussels and what had been seen to be an open border for migrant workers.

A relatively simple way of making a SWOT analysis more dynamic is to identify the interrelationships within the dour elements of the SWOT, in particular where:

- a strength is offset by a weakness, or a weakness is compensated for by a strength
- there is a strength which makes it easier to exploit an opportunity
- there is a strength which makes it easier to deal with a threat
- there is a weakness making it harder to exploit an opportunity
- there is a weakness making it more vulnerable to a threat
- there is a threat that undermines an opportunity.

These interdependencies are shown as arrows on Figure 1.2

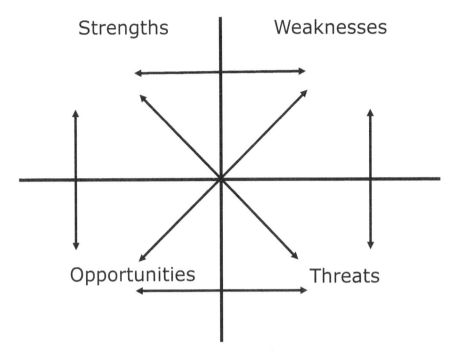

Figure 1.2 SWOT Analysis – with Cross-Impact Analysis

PEST factors

PEST factors are the Political, the Economic, the Social, and the Technological factors that shape the industry environment (Figure 1.3). Again, this technique as generally practised is no more than a listing of the factors that people see around them. This is a bit like the experience of flying when you look out of the window sideways from the plane and see some brightness and clouds. But this sideways out picture could be horrendously misleading. For all you know you might be hurtling towards a terrible storm, a mountain or into a new dimension!

At minimum, the PEST should be done as a time series, say of short term, medium and longer term – if you choose to do it like a series of black and white stills. But it is always better if you can stretch to do it more as a cine film with a proper, dynamic flow featuring a chain of events. For example:

> The complacency of the conservative party and the disinterest of the labour party in the UK (political) in 2016 allowed Brexit champions to mobilise the fear of working class and provincial families of inward worker migration and the threat to jobs (social and economic) to result in a finely balanced and surprising "vote out" for Brexit…

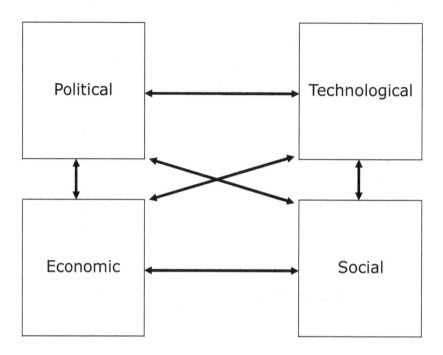

Figure 1.3 PEST Analysis

This threatens foreign interests in investing in sterling resulting in an effective devaluation (economic factor), a surge in share prices (inflating the value of UK corporate overseas earnings-economic factor) and thus paradoxically stabilises the economy. This dampens the fear amongst the electorate that Brexit will be very damaging (social factor), so that any unexpected turn down in the economy from a "hard Brexit" will then result in a big shock (social and economic factors). The stock market might then crash triggered by a wave of automatic selling of shares (technological factor).

Notice here a systemic picture over two to three periods of time has been created for a dynamic PEST with an interlinked chain of events. How many "PESTs" have you seen with such systemic qualities, if any?

Another way of making it more dynamic is – just like we showed with the SWOT analysis earlier – to look at the interactions of the forces with each other. So we should look at how:

- the political environment shapes the economic (for example with the uncertainty that Brexit caused for the UK economy);
- the economic environment shapes the political environment (so a recession may make voters believe the government's management of the economy is bad and threaten re-election);

- the political environment may impact on the social environment (for example, Brexit may encourage migrant workers to leave, actually shrinking the population);
- the social environment may influence the political (through shifts in attitudes towards politicians overly overtly and obviously pursuing their self-interests cause political alienation causing abstinence from voting, and thus greater political volatility);
- technological factors impacting on the economic (for example through the threat of higher unemployment and major structural change in employment patterns through the increasing exploitation of artificial intelligence [e.g. in service industries]); and
- technological factors that have, are, and will continue to reshape our social lives through changing the way we think, communicate and behave socially (through internet, texting and the centrality of the ubiquitous mobile phone that is to people today what the handgun once was to the cowboy).

Indeed, it is the interactivity of the PEST factors that has made PEST not only more important but also faster changing than in previous decades post-2000. But it isn't the only essential tool for analysing the external environment – to do that properly you need at least one more thing: Porter's Five Competitive Forces (see Figure 1.4).

Sometimes, however, it is thought that only PEST matters. I once had a client who wanted just some input on what was an already elaborate PEST when its take on competitive structure and dynamics was little more than some fragmentary analysis of a few of its competitors. I'm really sorry, but that's not the same as a Five Competitive Forces analysis! Neglect Porter's at your peril.

Porter's Five Competitive Forces

Now let's turn to Porter's Five Competitive Forces (Figure 1.4). This is a slightly complex picture depicting four forces driving a fifth towards the centre, called "Competitive Rivalry." The others are made up of:

- bargaining power of the buyers (customers): if low it's a good thing, if high it's a bad thing;
- entry barriers: the higher the better;
- supplier power: the lower the better; and
- substitutes: few, or ideally, none.

This model has been displayed in countless strategy books again and again as a model in stasis. Rivalry is likely to go up when any of the other factors are negative (e.g. bargaining power of the buyers gets worse or there are new entrants). And that's it – the model is finished – there is no more to say by Professor Porter. Essentially his end product is thus a singular and a static picture of the five forces.

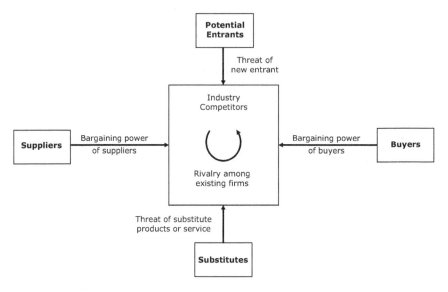

Figure 1.4 Porter's Five Competitive Forces

Porter (1980) has embellished the model a little with some qualitative characterisations to reflect, for example, that these forces will vary in their attractiveness between the emergent, growth, maturity and decline phases of the competitive lifecycle of a market. But what about how they are changing? Which is going better or worse? Which is most important and why? The Five Competitive Forces model – were I to misquote the estate agents' cliché that a house is "deceptively spacious" (bigger inside than it looks) – is "deceptively static" (appears to be static but isn't at all). But it really doesn't have to be! And that's not to mention the question of whether – and if so to what extent and how – these are impacted dynamically by the wider PEST factors.

We will soon see that Porter's is one of the most dynamic models of all.

As an example of the dynamic interaction of these factors I will go back to the very first book I wrote on strategy (Grundy 1994) called *Breakthrough Strategies for Growth*. In it was a future-looking case study on the retail supermarket business in the UK. This was drawn from my teaching on the Strategy MBA course at CASS Business School, where I used this market as a case study from 1993–1994. A recurrent theme that the students brought up, which I captured in the case, was that there was a price war in the industry very likely to emerge.

Around that time the UK supermarket industry was very different than today. UK supermarkets made very good margins and price competition was modest by today's standards. In the early 1990s, the UK was hit hard by a deep recession caused in part by unsustainable economic growth fuelled by monetary stimulation, and the PEST factors had deteriorated greatly. But the retail supermarket market was inevitably going to be the last UK market to be hit, as spending on foods and regular items was the least sensitive to falls in income per capita. But, sure enough, it would be hit, and hit hard.

Whilst the entry barriers to the market were considerable, three overseas niche players – Aldi, Lidl and Netto – entered the UK market all around the same time, attracted by that market's superior margins. This, combined with the decline in retail supermarket spending generally, triggered a very fierce price war. The threat of the entrants and increased buying power of the consumers (due to a squeeze on incomes leading to more shopping around) squeezed competitive rivalry, showing the interdependency of three of Porter's forces, which I call the "hot triangle":

- Entry threat and barriers
- Buyer power
- Competitive rivalry.

In my 1994 book I wrote that up as a case study which in part anticipated the future (1995).

Around 1996 I had begun to do some consulting work for Tesco and attended a learning event where I met then CEO Terry Leahy, who was in his early 40s. I gave him a copy of my book with the case study on Tesco in it.

About a week or so later I got an anxious call from Learning and Development triggered clearly by Terry reading the case study asking:

> "Did you base your case study on your work with Tesco or on something else?"

I laughed and pointed out that I had not consulted for Tesco at that time I wrote it, to which the reply was:

> "Well, Tony, that's even more embarrassing then, as it seems that you know us a lot better than we know ourselves."

Indeed, at the time I was writing the supermarket majors seemed quite oblivious to the fact that this crisis was happening to them, and the price war was a very big shock! Indeed, the effect was a drop in margins of 1%, which was £1billion of industry profits! (See the longer case study in Chapter 7.)

Another important thing to realise is that sometimes models are incomplete and stillborn – for example, Porter's own model, which can be refined in many ways. I believe that the model becomes far richer with the addition of a sixth force: the "industry mind-set" (Grundy 2002). I defined this as "the assumptions, the beliefs, and the expectations in an industry about how to compete and succeed." In my view this shaped the behaviour of the more tangible forces like buyer power, entry barriers, rival competitors and also substitutes. The industry mind-set is very much about the shared mental map and model of how the industry is and what it is becoming.

Interestingly I had been aware of J.C. Spender's work on strategy and recipes (1980) for nearly 30 years. But I hadn't associated his "industry recipes" as closely as I might have with my "industry mind-set" until I found myself reading his published PhD thesis as research for this book. Spender's idea is that to make sense of an uncertain environment, managers need to make judgements about potential outcomes that don't follow sufficiently from known facts. So they bridge the gap between deductive rationality and what is needed to actually make a strategic decision by relying on what they know are the shared recipes (or "rules of the game") for competing that are prevalent in the industry (Spender 1989).

Spender's work was done in the 1970s, when industries were a lot more stable and far less exposed to disruptive change than they are now. This suggests that strategy and strategic thinking is harder than ever now. Internet technology and newer, more agile entrants can wreak havoc with the "recipes" as described by Spender that previously helped maintain continuity, stability and commitment to stay in markets which were in secular decline. So "strategic decisions" become at the very least, very fraught. *And that's exactly the thing from which this book springs.*

Next, let's look deeper at the "GE" or the "General Electric Grid (Figure 1.5).

The "GE" Grid

The GE Grid distinguishes between the external attractiveness of external markets and competitive position (Figure 1.5). "Market attractiveness" can be supported by second-tier techniques, such as 'PEST' factors (Figure 1.3) and Porter's Five Competitive Forces (Figure 1.4). "Competitive position" can be tested by customer value analysis, by competitor profiling or with both plus an analysis of relative costs.

In a conventional GE Grid, different businesses have static positions, which is a very big limitation. In reality they will tend to shift considerably over time. For example, as a market matures and becomes more competitive, there will tend to be a downward shift in market attractiveness. Also, if a particular player harvests its position and doesn't refresh or rethink its current way of competing then it can slip from being to the North-West quadrant to the centre, or even to the East, either way coinciding with a decline in financial performance.

In the example of Tesco from 1995 through 2016, I would say that it started off in a market afflicted by a price war whose inherent attractiveness was medium to low. Its relative competitive position was average, as around that time it was on parity with Sainsbury (position "A").

By 2000 to 2008, its core market grew particularly through non-food and financial services, and through an easing of competition, resulting in a positioning of higher-medium attractiveness; Tesco's position in the UK became very strong indeed (position "B").

As the UK economy ground to a halt and incomes were severely squeezed following the credit crunch, Aldi and Lidl stepped up their very successful attack in the UK over 2009 to 2014, and market attractiveness fell severely, probably below the 1995 levels. Meanwhile Tesco had lost its way in customer service, management and leadership, and they had slipped back from "very strong" to "weak" (position "C"). But by 2016, Dave Lewis seemed to have pulled them back to a more average position (position D).

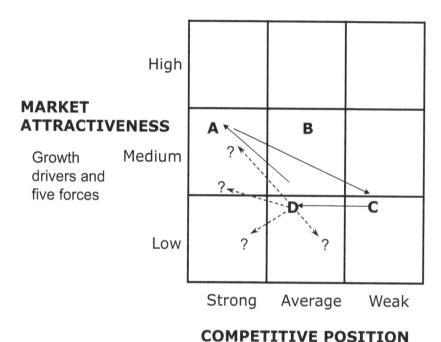

Figure 1.5 The "GE" (General Electric) Grid (Showing Tesco UK 1995 to 2016)

Dynamic competitive positioning

We have already seen one technique that purports to give us an overall competitive positioning – the strengths and weaknesses of "SWOT." This tool can be represented alternatively by picturing relative strength and weakness on a picture, which I call "competitor profiling" (Figure 1.6). This typically has a number of sub-areas of possible competitive advantage. Some generic ones include:

- Brand strength
- Product performance (value relative to price)
- Service quality
- Innovation (external and internal)
- Cost base (relative unit costs)
- Systems (IT and non IT processes)
- Skills (General Management, Sales and Marketing, Operations and IT, HR).

And each of these is rated on a 1-to-5 scale:

- 5 is "very strong."
- 4 is "strong."
- 3 is "average."
- 2 is "weaker."
- 1 is "very weak."

	Very strong 5	Strong 4	Average 3	Weak 2	Very weak 1
Brand image					
Product performance					
Service quality					
Innovation drive					
Cost base					
Supporting systems*					
Support skills*					

* These are both within & cross-functions

Figure 1.6 Competitor Profiling

In its most basic form, you simply draw a cross on the column from 1 to 5 of where you think your own position is against the criteria, with a view to justifying what this is based on – for example, who you are better than or worse than in that particular respect. You draw a line through the crosses to give you your profile. You do the same for a key competitor, and when that's done, another sheet for yourself against yet another competitor. It is probably best to do this repeatedly with just you displayed against a competitor, otherwise, even with multiple colours, you will soon get a rather unintelligible "pigs breakfast."

The results are generally a lot more insightful and more objective than a basic SWOT analysis, as there is normally a lot more thought needed and judgement being tested.

Cost can not only be compared between players but also over time and in a dynamic way. Figure 1.7 shows how such comparisons can be made dynamically in order to target where you want to be in the future; you then work backwards to identify the strategic cost breakthroughs that might get you there.

To introduce more dynamics you can indicate through arrows where you think the direction of movement is, or has been, so that it is now more than a snapshot. Typically companies do shift quite a lot over time. I have always found it fun to track this for retailers. Besides the Tesco example, that I would probably have given a score of about 4.2 on average by 2012, this would have been probably around 2.2 by 2002! Likewise, I tracked Mark's and Spencer's, which I would have given a score of 4 in 1995 but which fell by 2000 to 2.1 in just five years. In both cases it's a hard slog back to parity and to real competitive advantage. *Once again a static framework can be brought to life to have an astonishing dynamic.*

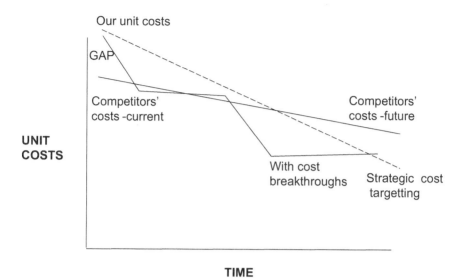

Figure 1.7 Strategic Cost Gap Analysis

Obviously this calls for an even more dynamic representation of the competitive advantage over time and from my earlier training in mathematics. In Chapter 5, I will introduce the "competitive advantage-over-time curve" and alongside that a number of other "over-time" curves that together are a part of a very real revolution in dynamic competitive strategy.

So we have now taken a look at five core tools of competitive strategy, namely:

- SWOT analysis;
- PEST analysis;
- Porter's Five Competitive Forces;
- "GE" (General Electric) Grid; and
- Competitive positioning.

We have begun to explore how they can be evolved beyond their originally static representations to something more powerful, and indeed, contemporary, by emphasising the dynamic dimension. But we have only scratched the surface.

I have taught now at six major business schools over the years, and it seems to me that MBA courses are stuffed to overflowing with tools and processes such that a huge amount of time gets involved in putting all that over as theory. But how much time, if any at all, is spent on actually interrelating these tools, in integrating them as a system, or even using combinations in any kind of a dynamic way at all?

When I help others to learn strategy I always focus a lot of time on showing how the techniques operate as a coordinated system. In particular, the PEST factors will

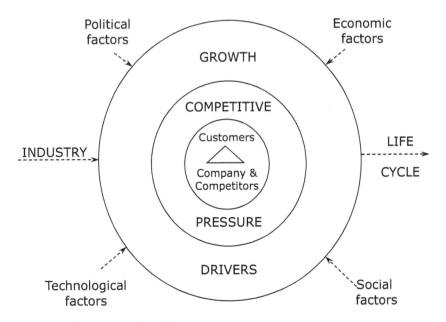

Figure 1.8 The "Strategic Onion"

have an impact on market growth (which we will learn later on in the book can be captured through a "Growth Driver" picture; see Chapter 5). Market Growth (or a lack of it) will have a major influence on the Competitive Forces. Also the Competitive Forces will determine which areas of competitive advantage are paramount.

So integrating the various Figures 1.4 to 1.5, let's imagine this as a simple onion model showing each of these as a layer with the PEST at the outer and company's position at the centre (Figure 1.8). With one integrated picture you can now think through the current strategic position of a company, and look at what may lie around the corner. This same picture gives you an overview of what we will learn later as being the first criteria of strategic decision-making: "strategic attractiveness." Not only that, but the "strategic onion" can act as an *aide-memoire* in constructing futures storytelling using scenarios.

It can be no mean task to visualise not just the present and the future using the same picture (although that's not impossible – I and many others have been doing this for years!). But in the very act of writing this book I experimented by splitting the two out so that we could get a more dynamic appreciation of present and future. The result was Figure 1.9, where I show a separate onion for the present, or "the now," and an onion for "the future."

This also helps the mind, now that it's more "hands free," to explore the events, the forces and the influences that will move and accelerate or slow that movement to the future. This is shown as a two-way line on Figure 1.9, not only elegant, but intuitive and practical. Indeed we will see throughout this

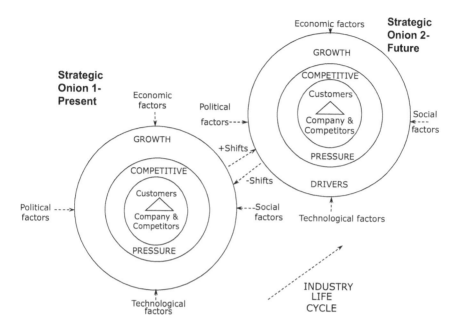

Figure 1.9 The "Double Strategic Onion"

book that what we are doing is using the tools as basic thought structures from which we then *do agile strategic thinking and create Dynamic Competitive Strategies.*

Whilst creating that picture probably took 25 minutes, the actual thought of doing it that way seemed to come in at a maximum of about one and a half seconds. I practise mindfulness, and it does seem that when I do get flashes of strategic insight where I recognise patterns and linkages it seems to happen around the speed of recognising a face as someone that I know. We will come back to that phenomenon of strategic thinking that I feel we should call "hyperagile thinking," which seems to be a very mindful and logically focused form of intuitive and instinctive thinking when we look at cognitive processes, later. It is also extremely quick! We will come back to that.

Introducing "Speed"

A new insight that emerged out of this chapter was that we need also to have some way of representing the non-linear dynamics of the forces for change that impact on and within the external and competitive environment. I had been reading an MBA final project report on an industry buffeted by change in Trinidad: the ice crème manufacturing and retail industry. The MBA student had done a pretty good conventional environmental review and had come up with, from the PEST and Porter, things like: weakening international comparative

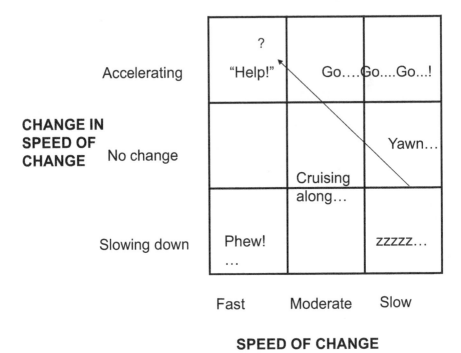

Figure 1.10 The "Speed Grid"

advantages, dumping of cheap ice crème, increased labour supply costs, export tariffs, government subsidies, lack of economies of scale, financing constraints etc.

I could see the external position for that industry not just being gloomy but that this was happening fast! I also imagined that some of these factors might not just have a fast impact, but that the speed of change might even accelerate! So I played with a matrix of the speed of change (the x axis) mapped against the acceleration (or slowing down) of that speed (y axis) – see Figure 1.10 for a new Matrix, called the "Speed Grid." The worst case scenario: the North-West box was clearly the scariest. I pictured the "The Runaway Mine Train" ride from Disney experiences.

Different organisations vary greatly in terms of their resilience to a high and accelerating speed of change! This also now brings us back to the theme that we began to explore in Figure 1.10 of *strategic movement*. In Figure 1.10 we saw movement from the Now to the Future, from one strategic onion picture to another and then accelerated or slowed in that progression.

Clearly we perceive these changes building up momentum in the actual commercial world, through real world observation, such as in the credit crash where in a matter of half an hour of panicked selling the secondary market for subprime mortgages went into free fall.

Any mathematician will recognise this clearly as being the land of the quadratic equation, where a value changes disproportionately over time. But I will spare you any more on that! Instead I plunge you on this journey into an everyday but graphic chain of events that will affect almost one in two of us over our lifetimes.

A very non-linear area of change occurs in the example of certain cases of precipitous marital breakdown. Sometimes a marriage crumbles slowly over a very long period and then it just comes apart, all at a fairly constant speed. But on my second marriage (which is my present wife's second one too) there was not only an increase of the speed of change but in the last few weeks, days and even hours before the "defining moment" this speed accelerated off the Richter scale, exponentially! The Speeding Grid captures that as a curve shooting up into the high-speed zone asymptotically (that's so, so steep!) – see the curve that I drew on Figure 1.10. I hope you are not in that mode!

Obviously, PEST and Porter's forces will not always behave like this. Indeed, some factors will start to decelerate and thus their speed of change will go down too, like perhaps the impact of price competition as the market gets tired of losing money and losing its appetite.

Dynamic competitive strategy from previous theory

Previous theory on dynamic competitive strategy is either oblique or scant. In terms of traditional competitive strategy there are hardly any theorists, except Tovstiga (2010), Stalk (1997), and Day, Reibstein and Gunther (1997).

Tovstiga suggests that where a company has an innovative strategic opportunity in an emerging market then there are some big choices in the timing and the speed to implement a strategy. He calls this "opportunity-response" analysis. Basically, his view is that typically a company's relative competitive position is often potentially stronger earlier on when the market attractiveness in the "here and now" is low. As time passes the good news is that the attractiveness of the market is rising on a steeper gradient, but the bad news is that over time its potential to have a very strong competitive position will fall. So finding the optimal window of opportunity is hard.

Tovstiga's third variable is response time. If an organisation can respond very rapidly then it can afford to wait longer (relative to the response rate of competitors and new entrants) to see what evolves.

Tovstiga also applies Kenichi Ohmae's "Three C's" – Customers, Competitors, Company (Ohmae 1992) – to chart competitive space to try to highlight where it might be expanding or shrinking. But for me that leaves many questions about how to detect market signals and mobilise ultra-quickly in practice.

Tovstiga's point, and it is a valid one, is that much of strategy in formative markets has to do with the relative dynamics, and that unique competing space changes over time. But these models were never supposed to do more than serve a limited role in any framework for dynamic strategy. So this and the other bits of existing theory *still leave us hungering for a lot more* in terms of capturing the dynamic.

Another limited input to theory is Stalk and Hout's (1990) work on time–based competitive advantage, which is a more general way of emphasising the dynamic. But this does seem to be more or less the same thing as saying that "speed matters," and stressing the obvious need to take advantage of "windows of opportunity."

By far, the richest source of inspiration was from the Wharton book (Day, Reibstein and Gunter 1997). This book provides some useful foundations for dynamic competitive strategy. It emphasises much more the need to game the various moves that competitors might make and their interplay and payoffs.

Some specific insights which are well worth taking with us are:

- the use of Game Theory and behavioural modelling to understand potential competitor moves and counter moves;
- micro-economic analyses of the likely financial effects these may have on the players, and on customers too;
- a dynamic understanding of the investment process to build a distinctive competitive position and to harness that as a strategic investment decision;
- strategic assets get imitated or decay over time and there are then lags and slowness is felt in the effects;
- the use of signalling of intent, and of concrete commitment, to deter offensive competitor moves, and to stake a claim over competitive space;
- the need to understand the mediating role of perception and bias which influences strategy-making.

Like my own book, this is an eclectic account of strategic, economic, behavioural and cognitive forces that shape dynamic competitive strategy.

Besides these more "content-related" theories that deal with the content of strategy, there are also some frameworks from a more process-oriented perspective to strategy. These include:

- Mintzberg's "deliberate and emergent strategy" (see my Chapter 2);
- theories of stakeholder analyses (Piercey 1989, Grundy 2014) which we pick up in my Chapter 10;
- Quinn's "logical incrementalism" (1980) (which suggests that strategic decision making is rarely purely "rational" in the conventional sense. It is a mixture of the rational and the irrational. I address this through discussions of *intuition, bias and cognitive flow* (Chapters 2, 11 and 12).

How is the book different?

Most books on strategy usually divide into two kinds. First, there are the ones that are primarily academic, dealing with theory and concepts with a sprinkle of case illustrations. Their format is either designed around a course curriculum to convey a learning system, or it is an even more academic one which seeks to create a theory. What I do like in them is their structured, logical and grounded nature.

Second, there is another kind which has a much more practical slant and quite often the message argues that you "should be doing it this way," i.e. the writer's way, and if you do "everything will turn out well" as in children's books. Frequently things don't turn out well, and many pitfalls are simply ignored.

In this book I seek to transcend this divide by having theoretical discussions followed by looking at the pros and cons of different perspectives, which for the most part turn out to be complementary, or just useful in different contexts. There are huge differences in the latter (e.g. in the evolution of organisational life cycle, size, complexity and styles), and also in its strategy processes. Having spent over 30 years of my life as a strategy consultant "out there" in the commercial world, I approach this from a practical standpoint.

There is a large variety of more practical books on strategy, and many suffer from promotion of a particular way of thinking about strategy and its process and the order in which things should be thought about – *and the way in which that is done too*. For instance, there are many books that operate according to the model order of vision (or mission): strategic goals, strategy-plans-implementation (sometimes labelled "mobilisation") and monitoring and control. But where is competitive positioning in that scheme? And what happens if the vision or mission is flawed? Or what if the strategic objectives that you start with then turn out to be unrealistic given what you find to be the competitive position, the environment, and the strategic options available? Don't you need to reiterate and go back a stage? Such books are often the antithesis of "dynamic."

Often such books over-emphasise some "guiding light" shining ahead that is supposed to make strategy coherent, but they fail to deal with underlying competitive realities.

So I will take what is good and solid from theory, particularly which is more empirically grounded in behavioural research, and then relate that to practice via a lens offered by over 30 years of experience as a strategy consultant, senior executive developer and coach.

My account will also be much helped by the fact that over that period I have developed my approaches considerably, based on what seems to work in many contexts. This is now an interesting system of tools that has been used by many, many organisations of different sizes, kinds and industries, and also in different countries. So we will truly get the best of both worlds.

The evolution of my thinking

The whole process has indeed evolved in a number of previous books (Grundy 1994, Grundy and Brown 2002, 2012 and now in this one). Indeed, the steps that it has gone through have gone through many generations (actually now, in its fifth generation), namely:

Model 1 – Strategic Analysis and Planning (1989–1993):

This was about analysing strategic positioning, and evaluating strategic options – informed by my MBA, plus from my experiences of strategy consulting both with two big firms and independently, and also from my PhD research.

Model 2 – Strategic Planning and Implementation (1994–1999):

This applied techniques of change management to implementation and is then integrated into a unified strategic planning and implementation process. I emphasised "Helicopter" vision and focusing on helping managers to do the shift from operational to strategic thinking. I taught this as "breakthrough strategic thinking" and over the next fourteen years trained (until 2009) around 1,200 senior executives in that process at Cranfield School of Management.

Model 3 – Strategic Thinking and Influencing, and Implementation (2000–2002):

This expanded the tools for influencing stakeholders, making them a lot more dynamic. I also began to define strategy as the "Cunning Plan" to underline the relentless search for strategies that transcended the mere "average" and with my "55 ways of being cunning."

I then developed the process of scenario storytelling to not only tell a story of the future environment but also to develop both strategic vision and strategic options by working backwards from the future to develop present strategies. I also beefed up the sophistication of my Strategic Option Grid after it was tested out (and refined) in some household companies to become the engine that drove the core of their processes.

Model 4 – Strategic Thinking and Influencing, Implementation and Behaviour 2002–2016.

This became the mature process covering the behaviour associated with the strategy process based on my empirical research at BT (Grundy 1997b). I also extended the applications of techniques like the Strategic Option Grid to specific decisions like: acquisitions and mergers (Grundy 2002), strategic projects (Grundy and Brown 2003) and HR strategy (Grundy and Brown 2004) I also incorporated insights from studying the strategic thinking process of six leading CEO's and the work of Kahneman on cognitive bias (Kahneman 2013).

Model 5 – Dynamic Competitive Strategy (which is Phase 4) as above, plus the Dynamic dimension 2017 and before.

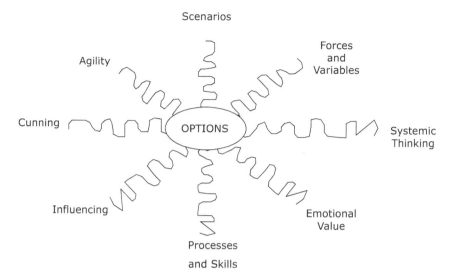

Figure 1.11 The "Dynopus" – Eight Dimensions of Dynamic Competitive Strategy

I also developed a number of techniques that plotted some strategic variables over time, which had been somewhat piecemeal. I now evolved a new set of ways of generating strategic options for different things such as costs, careers, brands and threats. There were also systemic models for value creation and for competitive advantage and also for economic value creation, too. I also increased the emphasis on using ideas from Game Theory, which looks at competitor interactions and also from the art and insights of cognitive psychology.

So in this Fifth Generation model we now have something not only more sophisticated but also capable of taking on the challenges thrown up by the environment as we accelerate fast through to 2020 and well beyond.

In that model I now embrace a number of dimensions of "Dynamic" including (see Figure 1.11, the "Dynopus"):

- Agility
- Scenarios
- Forces and variables
- Systemic thinking
- Emotional value
- Cunning
- Influencing processes and skills.

Here's what you will get out of this book

Looking back makes me realise just how truly limited the conventional application of planning techniques is. Existing, traditional planning techniques can have an added and far more dynamic expression than most organisations appear to have realised. Throughout the book I will uncover how new techniques allow you to think in a much more sophisticated way so that you can model your business and deal with competitive challenges and opportunities in non-linear ways. In particular you will learn:

- Some new tools that you can use in making your own strategic decisions;
- How these can be applied through real case examples;
- The theoretical basis of the tools and how you can take the best from a range of different ways of looking at strategy;
- How to think about strategic (and more tactical) issues much more in non-linear ways;
- About the process issues involved.

These teachings will make you more knowledgeable, higher-skilled, self-confident *and marketable.*

On my last point, so many of the more senior and higher paid jobs in management insist on "strategic skills," but many managers have to bluff their way (if not "fake it") in that department. Yet how many managers have the time to attend even a short, intensive course like a mini-MBA in strategy, let alone a full blown one? So they rely on sound-bite substitutes. Watching a couple of videos by strategy gurus on the internet may give you a superficial understanding of some issues, but to really become a strategic thinker requires a much fuller immersion; my book helps fill that gap.

If, for example, you already have an MBA you will still learn a lot about strategy and strategic thinking from this book. Typically, most MBA's will only teach a fairly small range of techniques, and these will be almost exclusively made up of the static models. Purely static models are like when you stop the picture on your SKY television and you ask someone to tell the story that will follow from that for the next 30 minutes or more. That's really hard!

For the majority of my readers who won't be blessed in all probability with an MBA, don't let this daunt you – you will be in safe hands. I will take care to break things down to their simplest elements and promise not to "blind you with science."

In terms of how best to digest this book, obviously this isn't a read-all-in-one without a break! But don't go to the other end of the spectrum by reading just a few pages at a time – try to digest a chapter in one sitting, then allow for some digestion to occur. Learning about strategy occurs more through a kind of osmotic process.

Who is it aimed at?

This book is for those who are involved in or interested in the strategies of their organisations and who either wish to improve how they do strategic thinking and implementation. That should greatly interest CEO's, Functional Directors, Entrepreneurs, Investors, Consultants and Professional Advisers, and also Strategic, Marketing and Financial Planners, Change Managers etc.

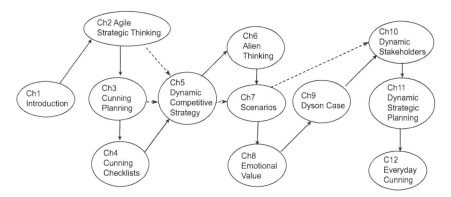

Figure 1.12 The Structure of the Book

It will also be invaluable to MBA students who want to be exposed to the very latest thinking on strategy, and who want to learn how to do strategic planning in practice. Finally, there are MBA's who graduated years ago who want a refresher on strategic thinking.

Outline of the book

Figure 1.12 gives you the visual logic of the book. After this Introduction, there are three interrelated chapters which cover the themes of cunning plans/planning.

Chapter 2 **From Strategic Planning to Agile Strategic Thinking**, suggests that some of the philosophy of "agile" might usefully become more central in strategy. I look at different forms of strategy (e.g. deliberate strategy, contingent strategy, emergent), and at issue- and insight-driven planning. I show how one can tap into the brain's creativity through much more intuitive thinking, and conversely, how cognitive and other forms of bias can send strategy off the road.

Chapter 3 **From Average to "Cunning" to "Stunning"** challenges plans and planning to be more creative.

Chapter 4 deals with the 101 ways of being "cunning" with the **Cunning Checklists**.

Chapter 5 **From Static to Dynamic Competitive Strategy** then takes a very fresh way at looking at strategies using the time dimension and also systems thinking.

Chapter 6 **The Art of Alien Thinking** then explores how adopting a deliberately "strange" mind-set can generate strategic insights and ideas.

Chapter 7 **From Projections to Scenario Storytelling** looks at scenario storytelling as one way of looking over the horizon.

Chapter 8 **Emotional Value: The Key to Competitive Advantage** examines another rich source of "lines of enquiry" – the extent to which bringing emotional satisfaction to customers, for example, can build switching costs, deter entrants etc.

Chapter 9 contains a substantive case study of **Dyson Appliances** which illustrates how Dyson evolved over nearly 25 years, from its market entry to its dominance phase, then from the company's challenges and changes. I round off with its international expansion and related product diversification in recent years.

Chapter 10 **Dynamic Stakeholder Analysis** examines the importance of finding novel ways of persuading stakeholders to do a strategy.

Chapter 11 **Dynamic Strategic Planning and Implementation** runs through a large number of rich ways of making planning processes a lot more productive and efficient, looking at dynamic inputs, planning processes and outputs.

In Chapter 12, **Lessons and Conclusions**, I summarise the book, with some humorous and practical everyday examples.

Key insights and learning lessons from Chapter 1

- Conventional strategy tools are typically extremely static and give a very limited picture.
- Today's typical pattern of competition is typically very dynamic, vulnerable to disruption and disrupters and non-linear.
- We need to think in a completely fresh way about competitive strategy and strategic thinking and planning.
- Even SWOT can be made much more dynamic through looking at the interdependencies between each of its four elements.
- PEST and the Competitive Forces can be looked at as causal chains that link changes rather than being purely pictures at a particular time.
- Environmental changes not only have a variable speed of impact but that speed in itself may be accelerating or slowing down – this can prove crucial where an organisation has a complacent mind-set: as we see in the "Speed Grid."
- The "GE Grid" or "General Electric Grid" of market attractiveness against relative competitive advantage can not only be used to map the present position of a portfolio of business areas, but their directional shifts can also be shown, *both in the past and even more importantly in the future.*
- The Competitor Profiling tool can focus in on that second element of the GE Grid shift – "relative competitive advantage" – and help us to think around not just one's own relative shift in competitive position, but also in terms of its relative movement (same, better, worse) against other competitors
- We can also draw the whole picture of dynamic, interdependent systems impacting with each other through the "Strategic Onion," which has interdependent factors in the environment impacting on the company's internal

position. I found it useful to incorporate further dynamic through the shift of the present onion to the future onion.
- In this chapter we have hopefully learnt to think strategically, not merely in terms of a singular "where we are" or "where we want to be," *but each and every time* in terms of *interdependent interaction and change over time*.

Reader exercise:

- Consider carefully how all factors might be changing over time and maybe in non-linear ways, and where one emerging change can have an impact on another.

2 From strategic planning to agile strategic thinking

The human mind is the dynamic mediator between the environment and the strategy.
When it purrs sweetly, strategic decisions are good, when it misfires they it be horrendous.

– Tony G

Introduction

In this chapter we contrast the paradigm of planning as a cognitive style with that of a much more agile style that characterises true, strategic thinking. I am going to use the "agile" notion here to inform our thinking on strategy so that it can become more dynamic, so I will first talk about "agile."

"Agile" may have the feel of being just another management fad that may soon be passé (just like Total Quality Management ["TQM"] in the early 1990s, but where is it now?). In both cases that is or would be a pity.

In this chapter, I will be looking at why "agile" has not become more central in strategy. I will also take a look at how some different forms of strategy incorporate agility within themselves. We will examine the deliberate strategy–contingent strategy–emergent strategy continuum: where do these three forms of strategy come in to both the creation of strategy and its implementation?

We also look at the challenges of not just being agile in strategy but in their fine tuning – maintaining a high degree of fluidity and flexibility without freaking out from anxiety. We also look at how to cope with strategic plans that may actually need to be held in a "contingent form" as the conditions for firm commitment are not yet aligned.

We then turn to how the strategic thinking and learning should not be switched off just because we started to actually implement it and to invest in it; even where a strategy is committed there can still be the mindfulness, flexibility and reflection to adjust it. And I am not just talking about some form of conventional control system here. I have in mind that for strategies undergoing implementation their assumptions are continually reviewed to see what appears to be working well or not working well and why. During implementation you can still be on the hunt for that better plan, the "Cunning Plan" or even the "Stunning Plan."

We then look at how to transform the thought process from a more bureaucratic and traditional process to one that is far more issue-driven with insight-hungry planning.

Finally, we look at the creative workings of the brain. We examine the opportunities and threats of intuitive thinking, particularly looking at Kahneman on cognitive (and other forms of) bias. It is so incredibly easy to be fooled by situations where the setting and the way in which information is received, together with one's natural cognitive habits, can lead to profound deception and mistakes, particularly on Strategic Issues. We need to avoid inflexibility of thought as that will lead us to errors and mistakes.

Defining "Dynamic"

But before we get fully into what Agile might have to offer, let's now define "dynamic" specifically in the context of competitive strategy. This has a number of central ingredients:

1   It is about the **time**, not only the future, but the past, too.
2   It is about **change** – which isn't constant, it is variable.
3   It is about change in **direction**.
4   It is within **competitive space**.
5   It is **systemic**, involving complexity and interdependency.
6   It is a particularly flowing and agile style of thought, or **dynamic cognition**.

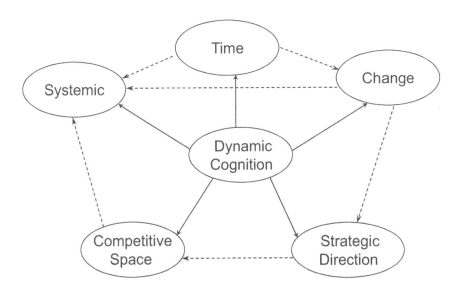

Figure 2.1 The "Dynamic" Mix in Dynamic Competitive Strategy

In Figure 2.1, I show arrows radiating out from "dynamic cognition" at the centre, as this is the focus and the hub of our attention. Also, the dotted lines show some interrelationships between the variables including:

- From *time* to *change*, as it is only through time's existence that we can have change
- From *change* to *strategic direction*, as it is change that causes adjustments in Strategic Direction
- From *strategic direction* to *competitive space*, as change in strategic direction moves one into different Competitive Space
- From *competitive space* to *systemic*, as changes in the competitive landscape cause shifts in systems within the macro and the competitive environment and in the business model
- From *time* to *systemic*, as that shifts systems within the macro and the competitive environment, etc.
- From *change to systemic*, as systems will always change and evolve.

I define "competitive space" as a way of carving up zones of competitive areas either in terms of markets, segments, regions, styles of competition, and clusters of players with like strategies and mind-sets as a kind of a landscape. I also define "dynamic cognition" as a flexible way of making sense of competitive reality, which is only part linear and frequently based on insight and hypothesising, modelling what one thinks is really going on and why. Such thinking often requires at least a partial debunking of mind-sets.

"Dynamic cognition" is at the very hub, and it is the key to *agility of strategic thought, behaviour and action.*

So what can "Agile" bring to strategic thinking and planning?

"Agile" is an idea that was born in the domain of projects, and out of software projects in particular. Whilst Agile management has increasingly been a hot "buzz" idea over the last five to ten years, its origins can be traced back to the 1970s. It began as a reaction to project planning that tried to grasp the scope of a project, all of its deliverables, all of its options, all activities and timescales, milestones and resources needed for the entire project upfront. Software projects are particularly vulnerable to chronic uncertainty, caused by many variables that are individually very volatile, but when brought together they can cause havoc.

In Agile, any notion of definitive stages that were once reached can then enable the next stage to be more easily reached. This is a dream according to Agile. (The latter is sometimes called the "waterfall" approach to planning. In the world of strategic management we might recognise that as "Logical Incrementalism" (Quinn 1980) – where we add new strategies or change them as time passes and as the results of previous decisions are absorbed and learnt from).

Agile has many ingredients, some of which seem to be "nice to have too." It seems to me that some are included to make the whole practice more substantial, attractive and maybe cynically speaking, something that is certifiable, and therefore requires some formal training, and thus is a product which you can charge money for. This appears very analogous to how Six Sigma (second generation TQM) has been packaged. But let's not throw all management fashions out with the bathwater, as not only has TQM reborn at its core got a lot that makes sense (just as had TQM)) but it also has some good things that we can learn from in the realm of strategic planning.

Agile suggests that the following:

- All – singing, set-piece planning processes for complex and uncertain and interdependent issues (especially strategic ones) are very likely to be too ineffective and too rigid to deliver much real added value.
- Where the end product (e.g.. strategic decisions, plans, etc.) has to be innovative, a more comprehensive and rational process is at best going to produce banal outputs that aren't particularly robust and resilient when exposed to stress testing.
- Once these plans are in their final form then they are likely to be set in stone, and not able to be adapted or reshaped, or steered around emergent obstacles.

Instead Agile, by contrast, prescribes that we should design planning processes that are:

- *Iterative*: instead of a linear process of development we take ideas and are willing to rework them;
- *Tentative*: the first form a plan takes is merely a "prototype," a working model that we can then refine and re-engineer, perhaps by doing "thought experiments";
- *Fluid*: the organisational context needs to be less formal and more flexible so that we are able to flesh out more issues and are able to explore ideas in unexpected directions, in very creative ways;
- *Exploratory*: instead of doing an end-to-end plan of the entire process, we plan in detail the quite short phase and after that, the next, to progress happily through incremental steps

These ideas are all ones that are attractive to any contemporary strategic planner in a fast changing and uncertain environment, and one exposed to potentially accelerating change (see again our Figure 1.10 in Chapter 1, the "Speed" Grid).

The potential of applying Agile style processes to strategic planning has been spotted by a few astute commentators, but these comments come more from project management theorists. *Mainstream strategists do not appear to have shown interest.*

Reflecting on this philosophy and principles, I recognise a number of elements in what I have used in the consulting and facilitation process over recent decades. For instance, I have found it generally better to break down the facilitation process from being an incredibly intensive and totally immersive experience of two or three days to a series of one day events. Whist the intended process is still planned out for later stages, this will be revisited depending on for example:

- What has come out of Day One (and subsequently out of the Day Two) in terms of insights, new questions, hypotheses, options and their evaluation?
- And even new data needs – plus how responsive and engaged, quick or slow, have the participants proved?
- What now seems to be most important, valuable and do-able?

A more incremental, iterative and fluid process thus enables the participants to digest what is coming out of the process cognitively (for instance in adjusting their assumptions). It will also allow time and space emotionally (e.g. for letting go of attachments and commitment to strategies and ideas that are proving to be unattractive). It can also ease political adjustments (shifting what one might support or not support, and revising one's own personal and political agendas).

But caution is needed; stories of Agile group working where there is very loose brainstorming and freedom from any preconceived process may not prove that productive. (This is actually called "scrums" in Agile practice – like rugby where you throw the ball in and everyone piles in all at once in the hope that something comes out of it.) In order to have effective innovation through strategic thinking, my general view is that one needs to have some structure and process in people's heads.

My other caveat on applying the Agile philosophy in an untailored way to strategic thinking and planning is that it runs the risk of resulting in too tactical a process and in overly incremental thinking. Regardless of the fact that in strategic planning one needs to work in incremental steps (like diagnosis, option creation, option evaluation, cunning revisions of the options), one must still have one's sights on the big picture – to find a robust and cunning strategy.

Consider the challenge of climbing a mountain. You might start off with what you think is the easier slope but then find your progress frustrated by obstacles and difficulties. This results in you going around it at the same level and then attacking a different part. You might do this a number of times until you get to the very top. But whilst you might have mastered on the way up a number of incremental steps from which you can just see tidbits of the whole thing, when you do reach the very top (always your goal) *only then* do you see and grasp the whole thing.

But Agile might also extend to other things beyond the strategic planning process too, for example to the actual forms of strategy which I have described elsewhere (Grundy 2014).

The six forms of strategy

> "When I walk, I always walk with purpose; but sometimes my purpose is just to wander."
>
> Dr Carolina Yepes, at the very top of Prague Castle, 6 September 2017

My six forms of strategy (Grundy 1997a) grew out of just two which go back to Henry Mintzberg (1994):

- Deliberate strategy
- Emergent strategy.

"Deliberate strategy" can be defined as being one "that has a clear logic, that is based on the position (internal and external), and the opportunity–set of a company and is crystallised in a number of strategic decisions."

"Emergent strategy" can be defined as being "a pattern in a stream of decisions or actions. It can typically be observed or discerned only after the event."

Mintzberg's ideal (1994) is for these two forms to be in balance; just like someone walking will first move one leg forward and then the other, then a company might experiment with some developments, find a combination that seems to work (emergent strategy), then review, refine and fine tune it, make a plan for it and formalise the strategy. At that point, it becomes a deliberate one.

Unfortunately there is often a tendency for the "emergent" form of strategy to be dominant. Continuing the analogy further, if one were to be walking with just one leg being active then you would be walking around in a circle!

Figure 2.1 depicts the ideal world of emergent strategies with them neatly aligned. In my experience, they are rarely like that without vision, leadership and a good deal of strategic thought. In most organisations reliance primarily on the emergent model results in a lot of frustration, disappointment and wasted effort and resources. It is also even more vulnerable to personalities and politics.

Strategies can be deliberate at one level but emergent at another. Thinking now about how these strategies are reflected in the political environment, the obvious example was Brexit, where by a very small margin the British electorate desired to get out of the EU. But the "how" of getting out of it was left emergent, and so was *the where you wanted to be instead*. In reality, we, the electorate, should have been asked three questions – whether, how and why!

As an armchair political strategist, it was amusing to see the virtual chaos that a new UK government in late 2016 struggled to manage (an unexpected) "detergent", and then an "emergent" strategy in order to deal with that mess. It was unexpected to almost all, including the Brexit campaigners, who then found themselves having to extract an advantage with across-the-table negotiations with not just the EU power blocks, but also with the U.S. (and Mr Trump another "emergent strategy") without an apparent game plan.

I even offered my help to Theresa May, our PM, but was sent a polite "No" by 10 Downing Street (see my letters in Chapter 12!).

After deliberate and emergent strategy, my next three forms of strategy (Grundy 1997a) are:

- *Submergent strategy*: the strategy isn't working but is still committed to.
- *Emergency strategy*: the strategy isn't working and commitment is low, but no-one knows what to do about it strategically.
- *Detergent strategy*: a strategy to sort out the mess is under way.

These strategies seem to move around in a cycle like in Figure 2.2. Deliberate strategies begin to lose their form, and over time it becomes clear that they

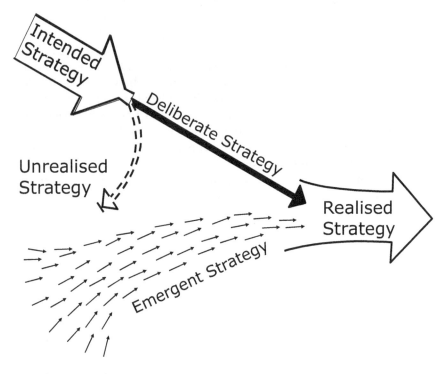

Figure 2.2 Forms of Strategy

aren't working; then commitment corrodes, the strategy is abandoned or dismantled and a new strategy to sort out the mess (the "detergent strategy") is formulated.

At any point in time a strategy might be something of a mix between two or more forms – hence we sometimes call this framework the "strategy mix" (see Figure 2.3). For instance, it might be mainly emergent with some deliberate elements, and also some things that don't seem to be going well – or "submergent."

In Figure 2.3 we are also able to visualise the dynamic of the forms of strategy. A strategy that starts off as "deliberate "might be overtaken by new elements – the "emergent" – and then start to become enmeshed with the "submergent." Then it really begins to fall apart in the "emergency "phase. A new leader is brought in and tries to sort the mess out by stopping or changing the strategy ("detergent strategy"). This then becomes the" strategy cycle." So this picture can be used not only to anticipate ahead, dynamically, but also to assess whether the strategy is on target or drifting. This dynamic has to be stratified at different levels: the form of strategy can vary at the same time between corporate, business, functional, team and project levels.

Besides there being a "pure" deliberate and a "pure" emergent strategy, there are also cases where you can have a "deliberate/emergent" strategy. That is one that's not embarked on through pure chance but where it is recognised that the

Figure 2.3 The Strategy Mix (1)

environment is so inherently uncertain that rather than to "design" a strategy it is better to try some things out whilst seeing if they coalesce into a pattern, then align into a coherent system. So, we cultivate a naturally evolutionary strategy.

A combined "deliberate/emergent" strategy is one where, whilst you may not be sure what will happen with an emergent strategy, its pattern has an overwhelming logic and attractive strength that you fine tune.

Up to this point you have probably been picturing more externally focused strategies in your minds than internal ones aiming at change. In the latter case, surprisingly, I have seen even more twists and turns through the various strategy forms, and in shorter periods of time! Especially where there has been some sort of organisational intervention – like a leadership development programme, team-building and culture change; these transitions seem to happen really quite quickly – over months or even weeks, instead of quarters and years. Often a second intervention needs to be brought in to rework one that has already been partially tried. This may be because the strategy was under-scoped in the first place, or it wasn't done very well or there was a lot of resistance or inertia.

Finally, let us add in our last of the six forms – contingent strategy – which combines the two related properties of being dynamic and Agile (Figure 2.4).

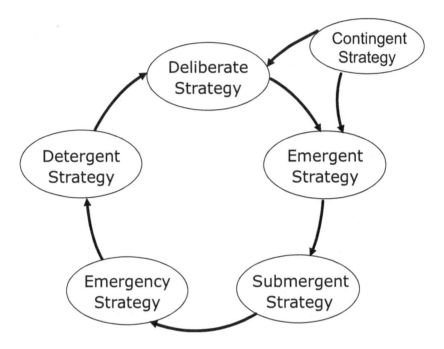

Figure 2.4 The Strategy Mix (2)

We start in the military domain:

In the 2003 Iraqi war, on Day 4 U.S. troops got bogged down in the south of Iraq at Uum Nasr. As reported by Sky News:

> Their strategic intention is to take Umm Qasr, to clear it and to use the port. But they haven't been able to use this yet.
>
> Now General Tommy Franks will say this is "No problem… in other words it is a reactive plan, a multi-faceted, multi-levelled plan, a very complicated plan and it is rather like going into a fish mongers to buy fish – they [the US troops elsewhere] are waiting – they will pick up that [particular] fish [i.e. launch their big attack] when they want to have that fish, and not only are they thinking of letting it [as it were] run [i.e. when they are operationally ready for that]. In other words, you might have intent to buy a fish of a certain kind, but this is partly dependent upon the catch of the day.
>
> At a higher level, between the tactical, low level stuff and the strategic stuff, the generals are planning what 'happens next.' They will have a whole range of options to select from. They will have other options to get back to what they do want to do without using these people [at Umm Qasr].

Inflexible is not the word, which you would use. A principle of war is flex-ibility; flexibility is the key to planning. Plans don't last, plans are just there, plans are something in the future, and once you start you adapt as necessary.

Source: ITV News Channel, March 2nd, 09.43. 2003

I love the metaphor of going to the fish market that General Tommy Franks reputably used to emphasise the fluidity of strategic intent; one may have a contingent agenda to buy, but one keeps one's options open. In military strategy, a "contingent approach" is thus essential, given the interacting effect of many uncertainties. So why can't managers use a similar model for strategy in an environment which is choosing to rival that?

Strategy is about managing the future – a future which is frequently uncertain. All of strategy is thus a bet about the future, and the conventional response is to try to absorb this uncertainty through some form of business or strategic plan. But any entrepreneurial approach to strategy recognises that all strategies and business plans are bets. But how can we improve the odds of success? And how do we manage strategies which are essentially contingent on aligned future states of the world? Maybe we need a working label to legitimise strategies that are just "might do's."

With a contingent strategy, instead of making a single relatively irrevoca-ble commitment to a course of action, the commitment is held in as fluid a form as possible, reducing exposure to the bet. This should, other things being equal, both increase its return and reduce its risk, as you would see in Financial Option theory where the value of the portfolio is greater if one defers com-mitment to a strategy until the point where the indicators are more promising.

Indeed, in a relatively uncertain world (as we find today), "contingent strat-egy" might even be a more frequent form of/appropriate model of strategy than "deliberate" or emergent strategy.

A "contingent strategy" (Grundy 2014) is:

> "A strategy which will be committed to only when certain external and inter-nal conditions are in sufficient alignment and which is then communicated."

A contingent strategy is a strategy that is:

a) Fluid and extremely flexible
b) Holds commitment in suspense
c) Requires fluidity and flexibility within the organisation.

Whilst "deliberate" strategy makes it easier and more comfortable to deal with the emotional aspects of making a strategic decision, it can come at a cost. More open-ended, or "contingent," approaches may prolong the ambiguity as to what we are actually going to be doing, and this might heighten anxiety. However, this could give us better results, as learning would be optimised and one would have less of being dragged endlessly around the cycle depicted in Figure 2.3 of deliberate-emergent-submergent-emergency-detergent.

What "contingent strategy" can hopefully allow us to do is keep the strategy grounded in at least some deliberate strategy with agility preserved through not just emergent strategy but also with quite a lot of strategic thinking done around strategic options that you might do, giving the best possible balance between structure and fluidity.

In that context, "deliberate strategy" can be at least partially substituted in many contexts by "contingent strategy." Whilst there may be a small core of business strategies which may be a "must-do," in any situation (deliberate strategies), around that core there might be an important set of existing contingent strategies which one will pursue, given certain alignment conditions being in place. And surrounding this set of initial contingent strategies may be a second set of contingent strategies which are presently future and latent (see Figure 2.5). That is, they are strategies, which will be triggered only if future conditions are met, effectively focussing on future "strategic fit."

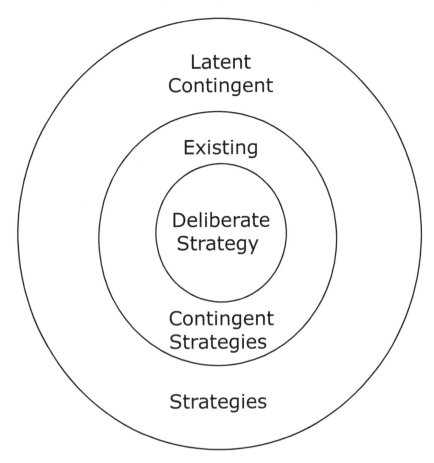

Figure 2.5   Deliberate, Existing Contingent, and Latent Contingent Strategies

"Contingent strategy" is not the same thing as having a "contingency strategy," which has to do with counter measures if something actually goes wrong.

As an "alien strategy theorist," (we will learn more about that perspective later in Chapter 6) that makes me think that "deliberate" strategy might have been labelled a "design" strategy, an "emergent" strategy as a "fluid" strategy and a "contingent" strategy – if you were to like the word – an "agile" strategy.

"Contingent strategy" is thus an essential ingredient within Dynamic Competitive Strategies as it deals with multi-futures rather than the snap-shot, present position, or just that projected into a singular future. It also embodies the concept of agility through preserving maximum flexibility of commitment and deployment of resources. It is open to adjustments of the strategy in light of emerging conditions, indicators and signals. It is absolutely essential for dealing with unpredictable responses by competitors, customers, suppliers, staff and other stakeholders.

The consequence of having a contingent strategy are that:

- Resources earmarked in plans and budgets are allocated and subsequently managed in a *contingent* and flexible way. Resource availability may thus be contingent on both a) achievement of key success indicators within the strategy itself, and also on other alignment conditions surrounding the strategy (i.e. in the environment); and b) satisfactory alignment of other strategies (and continual achievement of good results) in the company generally. (So, besides contingent strategies we may also need "contingent budgets" too. This has radical implications for everyday management of the business).
- Processes for communicating, monitoring and adapting specific contingent strategies need to be put in place. This is not pretending that it will be easy. But it probably isn't that far from where some businesses, with more advanced, digital systems now are especially in the digital space, already
- Interestingly my invention of "contingent strategy" was, I remember, in 2002. I was coming back from organising my second wedding with my then fiancé from a registry office in High Wycombe and we were stuck at some traffic lights. Using one of my Cunning Checklists, I asked my unconscious mind to give me the "one big thing in strategy" that I had missed and could be very useful in the future. The lights went amber, then green, and the thought flashed in my head:

"Contingent strategy," Well there you have it. (It's a shame I only applied that principle of "what's the one big thing I forgot" to that second marriage after the wedding, rather than before!)

Steering implementation

Besides strategy content being fluid, this fluidity needs to be continued into implementation where things can get even more dynamic! So how might one see or judge whether a strategy's implementation path is on target or not? Well before my idea of contingent strategy was born I came up with "wishbone analysis," which helps to keep track of a strategy during implementation.

One of my three main definitions of strategy was:

"What is it that you really, really, really want?"

This goes back to a famous song by the British girl band, the Spice Girls.

This vision was the start, or the "wishbone" on the left. (Some readers may be thinking of another and related tool, the "fishbone analysis" that is applied when things go wrong. Wishbone analysis is the opposite of that; it explores the conditions under which things are positively aligned, which is a perfect fit to the model of the "contingent strategy."

My first ever example of a "wishbone strategy" was that of Dyson Appliances in Figure 2.6 of "Dyson Beats Hoover" (Grundy 2002). This was drawn with that form in 1996 when Dyson had just burst onto the scene by taking market leadership from Hoover in just over two years, truly a phenomenon. To the right of the wishbone are all the things that need to align in order to create success, including things like: a bag-less product, its superior design, the product wasn't imitated (as yet), etc. These "wishbone" elements were thus "the necessary and the sufficient conditions of success."

So, in order to track the dynamic of implementation we thus now have not only a methodology for detecting whether a strategy is likely to work, but also one for way of tracking it. In Chapter 5 we will look at other ways of doing this, including the "Difficult-Over-Time Curve."

A second tool that is timely to bring in here is one normally associated with scenario storytelling called the "Uncertainty Grid" (Mitroff and Linstone, 1993). This tracks the assumptions that you are making about the future.

The grid works equally well with mapping the alignment factors on the wishbone. So for instance we might position the alignment factor that the Dyson model would be imitated as being very important and very uncertain.

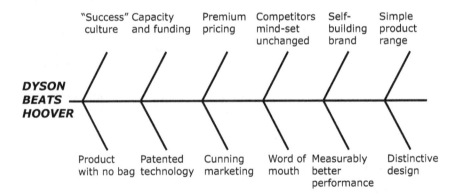

Figure 2.6 Wishbone Analysis

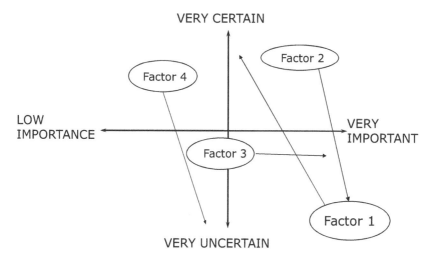

Figure 2.7 The Uncertainty–Importance Grid (Illustrated)

These qualities place this alignment factor right in the "Danger-Zone" southeast quadrant of the grid (see Figure 2.7).

One of the most important things to remember about the grid is that you must frame the assumptions as such that they are supportive of things going right (and not in their going wrong). So you not only get consistency of assumption definitions and evaluations, but also, you capture and test some things that at first sight don't seem that sensitive and thus would have got omitted from a regular uncertainty and risk analysis. These might now get tested and prove to be volatile using the Uncertainty Grid.

The Uncertainty Grid, even though it is mainly just a picture, is a valuable, initial way of not just picking up emergent change and thus more than hint at a dynamic, but also as it can then allow one to speculate where these alignment factors may be headed over time. Figure 2.7 illustrates that only a little movement with four alignment factors is likely to result in a shift – but in quite different ways. Here we see alignment factors 2 and 4 looking worse, as maybe on reflection these both appear to have deteriorated in uncertainty but gained in importance, too, which is not unknown when these are more deeply probed. Only alignment factor 1 shifts to a safer area.

Again, when some of these alignment factors/assumptions have been plotted, then it is now much easier to recognize more dynamic scenarios for the future.

One useful way of preparing for that is to do what I call an "overlay" of the tools. Taking the "wishbone" as our basis we can do some mini Uncertainty Grids to evaluate each of the "wishbone" elements. (see Figure 2.8).

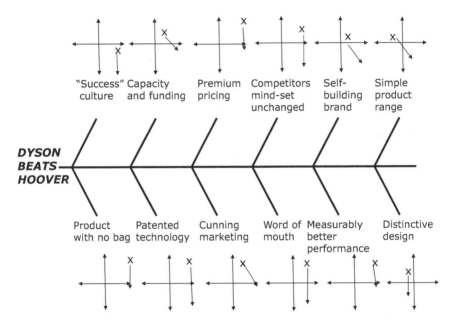

Figure 2.8 Wishbone Analysis – with Uncertainty Grid Overlay

In Figure 2.8 the wishbone plus Uncertainty Grid overlay highlights that Dyson's fantastic set of alignment factors were actually very vulnerable to the competitive dynamics. Indeed, the directional arrows were drawn in this way over the period 2008 to 2009. These were quite scary and highlighted:

- *Success culture*: could rapidly be overtaken over by some complacency (signs of that by 2000)
- *Capacity and funding*: whilst Dyson's margins were so strong expansion was self-funding in 2002 Dyson decided to take all manufacturing out to Malaysia
- *Premium pricing*: by 2002 there was much increased price pressure putting a big squeeze on Dyson profits
- *Competitors mind-set would be unchanged*: they recovered from the shock and Hoover and others launched bag-less machines with single cyclones
- *Simple product range*: by around 2000 the product range was already proliferating with greater complexity
- *Product with no bag*: sustained but novelty wearing off
- *Patented technology*: I picked up that Dyson's major patent was due to expire in 2002!
- *Word of mouth*: this effect became diluted as not all loved the Dyson – for instance the upright was heavy and sometimes disliked by smaller, older or weaker people

- *Measurably better performance*: again this became bitterly disputed and wars of words have raged over the years between Dyson and its competitors
- *Distinctive design*: this was probably one of the easiest to imitate advantages that Dyson had

Not only do the two techniques give us a very rich insight into Dyson's competitive dynamics over the earlier years, but they also illustrate really well how, even initially, static looking techniques can be brought more to life with arrows showing the directional movement over time.

Briefly commenting on the Dyson analysis, remarkably Dyson bounced back from its earlier set-backs to get back to its previous levels of super-profits and to grow internationally, although it has not been without its challenges (see Chapter 9).

Strategic planning: from a set piece to issues–driven planning process

We now look at the style of planning process that is in keeping with fast, external, competitive dynamics. Traditional planning feasts off a set piece series of tasks which tend to focus around delivery of the PLAN, with far less emphasis on exploring what the really important strategic issues are anyway. *In each cycle of strategic planning you are very likely indeed to be facing a different set of strategic issues.*

The "current position" is seen as more or less taken as read, and the main challenge being to determine one's strategic objectives (or "strategic goals") and then to allocate sufficient resources to deliver the assumed growth and in the areas where you think that is going to happen.

An "issues-driven" strategic planning process ought to be far more concerned initially about defining the really big challenges and understanding these deeper, and one's current strategic position, inviting strategic diagnosis.

The point of defining these issues is three-fold:

1   To determine where to spend most/least of our time;
2   To determine current strategic position and also define the initial Strategic Gap (the gap between where you think you will be in future on present plans and position, and where you really want to be);
3   To help identify whether "there is one big thing that we have missed."

For instance, following a family argument over whether it was misleading to attach the word "chicken" to "Quorn," the vegetarian food, I recently contacted its CEO to share perceptions of its strategic issues. In the earlier family argument, I was making the point that seventeen years earlier I had successfully persuaded Quorn management to challenge the mind-set that "we must never associate it with actual meat." I actually suggested to them that they put 15% real meat in to enhance the real meat flavour and texture. This would have become a high vegetarian/low meat product for meat eaters who just wanted to be healthier yet still wanted some real meat taste! Funnily, I spotted (*Daily Mail* April 29, 2017) a new label for precisely such consumers, called "flexitarians." Maybe I was ahead of my time!

Then Shock, Horror! After rejecting the idea initially as almost blasphemous, a year later Quorn called me back to look at the options again with them.

The next morning, I looked at Google and in about 15 minutes I had a pretty good list of strategic issues for them and duly sent a nice email to their CEO detailing some and suggesting we have coffee. The strategic issues I came up with from Google and also of course from the dynamic competitive strategy tools in this book included:

- *Prioritisation of strategies*: especially internationally, but also in terms of the product.
- *The future of food consumption*: globally and what is the upside market potential in 10, 15 or 20 years.
- *Brand*: "Quorn" is a name that if we forgot it we might wish not to have used: what more can be done with it/create new brands?
- *Intensifying product and price competition and pressure*: e.g. from the supermarkets in the UK.
- *Product development*: so far the product remained as a stand-alone part of a meal rather than a whole.
- *Leadership and management skills, processes and style*: to cope with international growth.
- *Product localisation*: e.g. in China and India there might be different products, some of which might come back to the UK.
- *Driving down costs with even more efficient manufacturing organisation*: in terms of scale and unit costs. (Like a TV police detective, I smelt something here!).

This initial list of strategic issues derived from general knowledge and observation and Google searches and analysis of industry and market life cycle effects was sufficient to give a pretty good initial shopping list.

In our final take on agile strategic thinking processes, let's now take a look at the role of cognition. We look at this in this book as it never stays still. Each day you wake up you do a reconstruction of your model of your competitive world and how it is developing and changing. Sometimes that cognition can whiz so much faster than external change, and sometimes it can seem like a Netflix movie with a poor Wi-Fi connection – freezing and breaking up, lagging and out of synch with external events. With more agile strategic thinking there is, if anything, even greater exposure to cognitive bias and an even greater need for mindfulness of that.

The dynamic role of cognition, bias and deception in strategy

So, as per my initial quotation, the human mind is the dynamic mediator between the environment and the strategy. This sophisticated processor and its workings need to be understood. When it purrs sweetly, strategic decisions are good; when it misfires or when it seizes up, they can be horrendous.

My interest in cognition goes back to my studies of the Philosophy of Mind at University (Davidson 1967) and the way that meaning is constructed by the mind. I also became equally fascinated by the theories in Social Psychology of the Social Construction of Reality (Berger and Luckmann 1966), and Husserl's "Phenomenology" (1980, 1982, 1989 – republished). Fast forward fifteen years through my corporate career and once again I found the fascinating way in which the mind studies the world. In 1989, as soon as I had finished my MBA I started my PhD at Cranfield into "Managers' Perspectives on the Links between Strategic Analysis and Shareholder (or 'Economic') Value."

My focus was on strategic decisions where there was a major investment involved. I decided to look at *managers' cognitive perspectives of those linkages: how did they currently model them, and how could they model them more effectively?* That took me into the cognitive processes within strategic thinking. I was also interested in how those perspectives might be changed, which then led me into the domain of strategic learning (Grundy 1993).

From this I was always sensitised to the influence of cognition in strategic thinking and planning. Indeed, at that time when I became an academic strategist, we all knew of the Nobel Prize winning work of the two psychologists Tversky and Kahneman (1974) on the influence of cognitive bias on human (and thus management) decision making – see their paper "Judgment Under Uncertainty: Heuristics and Biases" (originally published in 1974).

In his more popular book, called *Thinking, Fast and Slow*, Kahneman (2013), he details in over 400 pages innumerable experimental studies of a whole myriad of biases that infect human decision making. Because human decision making is highly reliant on intuition, and even more so is strategic decision making, *this really matters*. This is not just true of emergent strategies but also of deliberate ones too, where not all assumptions are validated facts, as we saw with the Uncertainty Grid.

Also, Tversky and Kahneman highlighted the "good and bad news about intuition":

- *The good news*: it is very quick and low effort, and often reliable.
- *The bad news*: it can also be profoundly dangerous as it may omit important data, and is highly vulnerable to bias.

In Kahneman's book, he characterises different styles of thinking of the human mind as "Thinking Fast" (intuitive thinking) or "System 1," and "Thinking Slow" (logical and deductive) or "System 2" as polar opposites. He suggests that most humans facing every day and fluid tasks will tend to default to intuitive, quick thinking, as opposed to much more ponderous, logical and deductive styles. That would tend to explain the preponderance of emergent strategy in many companies even though their official plan model is one of "deliberate strategy."

One might object to this idea that we are either in System 1 thinking or System 2, and for the vast majority of the time we are in System 1 (Thinking Fast), that we shouldn't generalise across the population. There are of course people who have different cognitive styles, for example there are alleged "nerds," or those who allegedly enjoy very deliberate and rational steps in thinking, so it is conceivable that these two very different styles of thinking that Tversky posits are not quite as mutually exclusive as the model suggests.

The other caveat is that the two styles may not be the only modes of thinking that are possible and that others might be conceivable too. For instance, in Chapter 1 I hypothesised that a mode might be that of "hyperagile thinking" where one makes an intuitive jump, but not a haphazard one in the thought process. Here, the normal process of sorting out all the chain of thoughts – like ducks in a row – just seems to happen in a few blinks. But could it be that there already lies in the brain an almost complete thought chain and then suddenly everything just hooks up? So whilst the sudden "Ah Ha" linkage is like lightening that obscures the fact that previously there has been a lot of deduction that is now "in storage" at an unconscious level. Suddenly, looking at it from a very slightly distant angle or in a more detached way yields a flash of genius? I do think that plausible. Maybe there is a "System 3" here?

To make more practical use of these ideas it might be good to be more mindful of which mode you are in by visualizing these modes in colour as:

- *Red*: System 1–"Fast"
- *Blue*: System 2–"Slow"
- *Purple*: System 3–"Hyperagile."

Kahneman's theory highlights some major perils of cognition, especially with System 1. Some of the worrying biases that appeared to be strongly supported by psychological experiments are found (and there are more) in a telling table (page 105) in that it:

- links a sense of cognitive ease (i.e. "I find this easy") to illusions of truth, pleasant feelings, and reduced vigilance;
- infers and invents causes and intentions;
- neglects ambiguity and suppresses doubt;
- is biased to believe and confirm;
- exaggerates emotional consistency (the "halo effect");
- focuses on existing evidence and ignores absent evidence (WYSIATI – "what you see is all that is");
- responds more sensitivly to losses than gains (loss aversion);
- frames decisions narrowly, in isolation from one another.

All of these are pretty scary as all of these are so characteristic of what are the worst features of tactical, operational management and are precisely the kinds of things that strategic thinking is trying to combat.

On top of this are other sources of bias too. For instance, there's "group think" (Janis 1972) where outlying opinions in a group become narrowed towards a consensus with the core of the group so that sound challenges to a particular strategy get shouted down.

There is also "commitment bias", which was graphically described by Straw (1981) who researched the way in which commitment escalated as a non-linear curve: as you start to put effort into exploring a possible strategy then you are already halfway to commitment as no one wants to see wasted effort. This was later underlined by Ghemawat (1991) who noted that commitment typically built up much faster than the rate of learning (the "learn to burn rate).

I have found the scariest manifestations of bias to be in the strategic decision to form a longer term relationship where, try as one might, it seems impossible to avoid bias, and even the whole idea of popular, romantic love seems intent on encouraging that! Some decisions I made even I am embarrassed at!

Others too have also added to that picture of Strategic Decision Making being impacted by bias from many directions. For instance, there was the social psychologist, Argyris, who studied the social and cognitive processes that kick in when there is a major (strategic) error (1980). He uncovered a tendency to effectively cover up the errors which he named "self-sealing errors."

To add colour to this, in a BBC Horizon TV programme, Kahneman took viewers through a vivid series of reconstructed articles that graphically illustrated bias. We see city traders, taxi drivers and everyday passers-by exhibiting forms of non-logical thinking, and we finally arrive at the powerful and true case of police detective who were convicted of manslaughter. He was at the scene of a murder where a man from an ethnic minority was killed, and he appeared to have stood by and watched it all happen.

He claimed that he really didn't hear or see anything at all, which didn't seem to be a credible defence. Psychologists then conducted an experiment where joggers were asked to follow a runner in front of them and to watch the back of the person in front of them. A short distance away to the right a simulated mugging was staged whilst the stream of runners ran past the brawl.

Apparently, the vast majority just ran past and could not remember any fight going on later at all! This, being outside the runners' attention, was not seen (or heard) at all – as if it really didn't exist. But the worrying thing was the narrowing of attention; the switching off of mindfulness seemed to render incoming sensory data non-existent – like deleting incoming emails.

A key danger of cognitive bias is that it is this quick, instinctive and purely intuitive thinking that leads us to be very vulnerable to deception. Over the last 10 or more years of my personal life I have been offered some rich opportunities to observe the processes operating in deception, and this has made me not just a lot more mindful of the risks of' little list but also of if only I had been more vigilant and less trusting.

Over recent years, the media has given us some illuminating investigations into this phenomenon of cognitive bias relating to that deception. For instance, in another TV documentary there was the story of how in the First World War German U Boats started to sink British vessels at will, and at that time there was really not a lot of defence. So the British hit on a most ingenious plan! They took a merchant ship and camouflaged a large gun on it. They then put a crew of sailors on it dressed in women's clothes with the plan of getting a U Boat to surface, which it did! They then sunk the boat!

It does seem remarkable that they seemed so easily taken in by the trick, but they did seem as if they saw what they wanted to see, which is my personal experience of deception (again-"WYSIATI "-"what you see is all that is").

Another story was that of the only ever escape from the "inescapable" U.S. prison Alcatraz. Some prisoners fooled their guards night after night with mannequins made of papier mache night after night as they dug a secret tunnel out, somehow got over the outer walls and swam off the island. Their bodies were never found!

But my *piece de resistance* comes curiously from a film with Will Smith called *Focus*. I was tipped off by a friend to watch it whilst I was writing this book. The film is about how a con man demonstrates his tricks of deceiving his victims by directing their focus of attention. However bright the victim is in the film, they fall prey to deceptively presented information.

In the film, there is an expert thief named "Nicky" (Will Smith). A rather nice-looking blond called "Jess" becomes Nicky's "intern." Nicky controls his victims' attention and leads them to where he wants them to go.

Nicky   "*At the end of the day this is a game of focus. Now, attention is like a spotlight and our job (of deception) is to dance in the darkness*" (*passing her watch that he has taken from her back to her*).

Nicky: "*Hey I didn't feel you take that.*"

Nicky: "*The human brain is very slow, and it can't multi-task*" (*passing back to her one of her rings*).

Jess: "*Jesus! What?*"

Nicky: "*What we are talking about here is much more complex*" (*giving her wallet back to her.*)

Jess: "*When did you take my wallet?*"

Nicky: "*You take Zoomba????*" (*showing her a Zoomba card*).

Nicky: "*You have got to get inside the victim's mind, see things from that perspective. Human behaviour is very predictable. When I look at that with my hands obscuring your eyes, it pulls your gaze. But when I look up at you, you look directly at me*" (*giving her sun glasses back to her*).

Nicky: "*If I touch you here, I steal from here. If I step to here then you would slap my face if you knew where my hand was*" (*passing back her bag to her which she left on the ground*).

Jess: "*Oh I get it, I get it.*"

Nicky: "*If you get their focus you can take whatever you want*" (*and then walks off*).

To relate back the concept of deception to strategy even more let's look at a fascinating case study from the Second World War and some remarkable trickery – the battle for El Alamein. The purpose of this is to emphasise how the mind is channelled to think along certain lines conditioned be a network of assumptions, beliefs, expectations, biases not to mention desires and agendas. How does that stack up in a very dynamic situation such as in a competitive combat or a war? Not so well without cunning and agility.

A magician in the sands – the battle for El Alamein: Operation Bertram

By 1942, the war in the West was not going well. Germany not only had control of Europe but had made major advances in North Africa such that they would soon threaten Suez. Rommel, the German commander, seemed invincible. Pitted against him was Montgomery for the British. The situation seemed so bleak that facing what seemed would be inevitable defeat, desperate and cunning measures were needed.

Some curious events then unfolded which were to turn that tide. According to a History Channel documentary called *Road Map to Pearl Harbor*, a man named Jasper Makelyne, who before the war was a magician and was conscripted to the Army corps, was musing that what they all needed was some of a magician's disappearing acts to protect their tanks! This chance remark was not forgotten and sparked a chain of creativity which was nothing short of remarkable. Truly, this was a "deliberate/emergent strategy."

Montgomery's Chief of Staff got Geoffrey Barkas and Tony Ayton together for some ideas to enable the British army to appear to be where it wasn't, and to be where it didn't appear at all. In effect, they were deploying stealth strategy decades before that technology existed.

Barkas and Ayton were reputed to have gone somewhere quiet to have a think and came up with the thought that what they needed to do was make tanks look like trucks, and trucks look like tanks. So they went back to Makelyne, who came up with an ingenious solution.

According to Wikipedia on Operation Bertram:

> The idea for the Sunshield came from Commander-in-Chief Middle East, General Wavell himself. He sketched a tank mimicking a truck in a handwritten note which reads
>
>> Is it a wild idea that a tank could be camouflaged to look like a lorry from air by light canvas screens over top [sketch]. It would be useful during approach march etc. Please have it considered.
>
> The note was passed to Barkas, in his words "not long after my arrival in Middle East…The whole idea was there. It was only a matter of design,

development, and arrangements for manufacture." The first heavy wooden prototype was made in 1941 by Jasper Maskelyne, who gave it the name Sunshield.

(https://en.wikipedia.org/
wiki/Operation_Bertram)

The "tanks" that were thus paraded were only three quarters the size of real ones. Here cognitive psychology came to the rescue as the team reasoned that the German pilots would not have much in the way of special reference points in the desert, and also they would not be able to gauge depth as it was the desert. So they would see what they expected to see, as in a magician's trick, then the mind would fill in the details.

They also built pretend pipeline and storage facilities where the dummy tanks were and also left the facilities deliberately unfinished to mimic the appearance of readiness. The Germans totally bought this: a German General who was captured in the subsequent battle told his capturers that he believed an attack was weeks away.

This preparation followed an elaborate plan with a large and very well thought through combination or skills and resources. In all nearly six hundred dummy tanks had to be fitted with Maksleyne's "Sunshields." So whilst the idea was part randomly generated it was crafted into a work of genius; it had all the initial hall-marks of an emergent strategy but in addition its whole organisation was agile. Its carefully thought through and executed implementation was very much a deliber-ate strategy.

In the eventual battle Rommel's army was totally fooled and the British were able to mount a totally surprise attack. Rommel lost 20,000 men and the course of the North African war was turned.

This case study is not only remarkable in itself but underlines the following lessons for dynamic competitive strategy:

- Strategic decisions are strongly influenced by the way we perceive things by default, through filters and biases.
- When we observe a competitive arena our attention is drawn most to what is moving or changing, and away from that which isn't – the magician's trick – so competing by seeing that you are actually still can be profoundly effective.
- Deception is perhaps the most powerful competitive weapon and – with the exception of the Chinese military strategist Sun Tzu (in *The Art of War*) gets minimalistic coverage in the world of strategy theory.
- Where the situation is horribly dire and difficult that is precisely the time to hunt for a "Cunning Plan."
- In its origins, a strategy can be emergent but can be made agile and eventu-ally deliberate – maybe even having some contingent elements.

In fact, deception on the battle field is something that continues as we speak. For instance, the Abrams M1 tank is now 80 tons as compared to 18 tons in the Second World War. A single tank also costs a fortune too! So the race is now on, to:

- halve its size and make it faster;
- put stealth triangle shields on the round barrels that are a radar magnet;
- use hybrid electric motors to reduce noise and heat what can be detected; and
- produce much better hard-to-see shapes.

These new shapes are now being tested in a kind of opticians' laboratory, where a tank spotter is asked to pick out where they think the tank is on a visually simulated battlefield (not quite "Specsavers," but more of a "Tanksavers!")

So where does all of this fascinating discussion of cognitive bias, deception both in terms of vulnerability to it, and also as a competitive opportunity, take us? Well, what is clear is that in unravelling the dynamic nature of competitive strategy, cognition plays a huge role. Cognition (and cognitive bias) will shape strategic decisions especially in an environment where there is data overload, where there are gaps in that data, and where managers can make "snap" decisions where they are, frankly, fooled (through Kahneman's "System 1"). Indeed, we ended Chapter 1 with the emphasis on "dynamic cognition" as the hub of the six dynamic aspects of strategy.

So to counteract this tendency to be sucked along by apparent competitive dynamics, we do need to slow things down and not only ease into System 2 thinking, but we need mechanisms to do that whilst preserving intuitive thought, creativity and inspiration – or "System 3." That is exactly what the tools and process in this book are all about, which is where we will be going in Chapter 3.

Also, we need to be able to control the attention so that it doesn't narrow too much (like Kahneman's joggers who missed the mugging in the shadows). That means that we need to cultivate the sort of "strategic mindfulness" – see my book based on empirical research: *Demystifying Strategic Thinking – Lessons from Leading CEOs* (Grundy 2014), based on what they told me about "when we do it well, *this is how*." In the hurly burly of a very dynamic world we need that inner peace, tranquillity and stillness that goes with the mindfulness that a Buddhist priest would practice.

This is not about jumping on a trendy bandwagon – indeed I have practised meditation for twenty years, and I can attest to the value of it in shifting my strategic sensing and thinking capability to another level! Those who know me well often wonder how on earth I have written sixteen books in that time. Well it's all about getting into a space of mental clarity, peace and effortless flow, then the mind is as smooth a Rolls Royce. We will be coming back to this property of "flow" later on in the book with a slightly obscure thinker, Mihaly Csikszentmihalyi (pronounced "Me-Hi Chick-Sent-Me-High"). Flow as a cognitive process to create faster thinking – like jumping on a fast-moving escalator at an airport.

Summary and conclusion

In this important chapter, which mainly deals with the dynamics of the strategic process, we looked at the value of the agile idea to the strategic thinking and planning process. Whilst not embracing agile as a fad, there is much we can draw from this philosophy of fluidity. Agile stresses the dynamic flexibility of the process.

I then took you through six key forms of strategy ranging from "deliberate" and "emergent," then on to the "submergent," the "emergency" and the "detergent." There is often a dynamic between these forms, and I described and explained what I saw as being a better dynamic and mix. This led to my final form, contingent strategy, which in a very Dynamic Competitive world has some large benefits, although there are challenges for a more arthritic organisation. "Contingent strategy" is certainly very close to the agile model.

I also highlighted that however deliberate a strategy seems to be when it's mobilised, fast implementation turns it "emergent" once again. This needs to be carefully realigned, and I suggested "wishbone" analysis to check for systemic alignment. I also showed how to test these using the Uncertainty Grid done as an overlay.

We then looked at how the process should avoid being a set piece but instead Issue-Driven, and I illustrated that with the example of Quorn showing that it is relatively easy to deduce the strategic issues of a business from the outside.

Then we uncovered a bed of worms – cognitive bias, strategic thinking styles, errors, deception – and how to turn this from a threat to a potential competitive weapon. In Operation Bertram, we also saw another fabulous example of the Cunning Plan. This suggests constant mindfulness of potential cognitive bias and building in checks and balances in strategic decision making.

Key insights and learning lessons from Chapter 2

- Dynamic competitive strategy has six key ingredients: *the time dimension, variable change, changes in direction and in competitive space, interdependency and systemic models and also dynamic cognitive dynamics.*
- Whilst structure is essential in strategy and strategic thinking it is insufficient and needs flexibility as found not only in the strategy mix but also in "contingent strategy."
- For contingent strategies to work out they need considerable alignment. They can be mapped out using wishbone analysis and tested with the Uncertainty Grid.
- In order to have a robust planning process, it is sensible to make it an issues-driven one.
- Whilst flexibility, agility and intuition are all essential in the strategic decision-making process, there is an ever-present danger of it being hijacked by many forms of cognitive bias. Decision-making needs process-checks, use of strategy tools and an evidence-based approach.

In the next chapter I acknowledge that conventional planning is horribly average in its inputs, its processes, its outputs and in what you then do with them. It is like a very leaky pipe. To take us up a level I look closer at the idea of cunning planning but also at a large number of ways – actually 100 – to create one.

I then look at using these prompts and a semi-structured brain-storming technique, the "Optopus," to widen our degrees of thinking. Turning then to the engine of the Dynamic process, the Strategic Option Grid, we learn more about how to explore, evaluate, re-craft and evaluate again, and how to test our possible strategies.

Reader exercises

- What could you apply the concept of "contingent strategy" to? What would it tell you if you did?
- What cognitive biases do you exhibit when making bigger decisions in your business and life?

3   From average to "cunning" to "stunning"

Strategic planning is so very often a rain dance to please the Gods so that a good harvest will come.

– Anon

Introduction

As I have said, so much conventional planning is average and adds so very little other than ornamental value to a business. It is very much caught up between the operational and financial world of conventional budgeting, and something that is truly strategic in its processes. It suffers from being almost totally linear and has little dynamism.

Most commonly, it is a stretched financial forecast with some talked-up aspirations for the business. To give it more of a feel of being genuinely "strategic," it also often has a little sprinkling of "strategic vision" on the top and sandwiched between the vision and the aspirations and the plans and budgets is a more detailed set of strategic

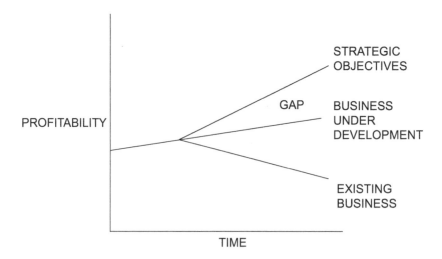

Figure 3.1 Strategic Gap Analysis

objectives. But where is the "how"? Quite often this is inadequate. Invariably there is a major gap between what the strategy is supposed to deliver and the strategic objectives that have been laid down. The "how" is necessary but isn't sufficient to achieve the goals. Strategic gap analysis (Figure 3.1) focuses attention on the space between strategic objectives and financial projections. The task of strategic planning is to close this gap with new strategic options. But we need the "Cunning Plan" to do that.

In this chapter we cover:

- Strategy as the "Cunning Plan"
- The "Optopus"
- Inside the engine room: the Strategic Option Grid
- Interdependencies and the "deep-dive" techniques for creative option generation
- Testing the scores and the "challenge and build" process
- On strategic thinking and cognitive flow.

Strategy as the Cunning Plan

I define the "Cunning Plan" as follows:

- It works backwards from the result.
- It is fundamentally simple.
- It achieves its goals by a combination of obvious, and less than obvious, ideas.
- It isn't particularly easy to imitate.

To become cunning invariably strategy needs to be dynamic.

In the television comedy series *Blackadder*, a comedy set in both Elizabethan times and the first World War there featured a character known as "Blackadder" renowned for getting into all kinds of scrapes. His companion, a most scruffy and disgusting character called "Baldrick," often used to help him try to get out of these scrapes, usually with disastrously funny results. But a constant theme of this immortal series was that they would usually come back to the Cunning Plan to rescue them.

As I have said already, I became frustrated over many years that managers seemed content with more or less any kind of strategic plan, even if it was an average one. The fact that it looked a little different, even though it might have been no better than average, and often they were just happy to have a plan. So I latched onto the idea that average plans, or even slightly above average plans, simply wouldn't do. What we really wanted was the "Cunning Plan." Instead I extolled them obsessively to search for a "Cunning Plan."

But perhaps as most managers typically don't see themselves as being innovative, let alone "cunning," they need a lot of help.

The very best example of this focus on the Cunning Plan comes not from *Blackadder* but actually the Millennium to celebrate its very start in an episode titled "Back and Forth."

In this, Blackadder and Baldrick invent a time machine so that they can go back into the past and steal things that can be sold as expensive items, like

Nelson's boot. Unfortunately, things soon go wrong in this exciting venture when Baldrick falls by accident on the time controls and they go back in time but then can't get back to the present because they didn't note down what setting "now" is on. (This is an example too of the need, when doing strategic thinking, to always ask oneself: "what is the one big thing we've forgotten?").

On their ventures up and down time they arrive in Roman times and find that they have been reincarnated as Roman soldiers standing on top of Hadrian's Wall in Scotland. Unfortunately, the wall is only three feet high, which is a metaphor in strategy for the importance of not spreading yourself too thin. In strategy terms, this illustrates how you must choose and this frequently means saying "no" to options. In strategy, never spread yourself too thin.

The Roman general arrives to boost morale by announcing a retreat back to Rome, just as Blackadder and Baldrick spot a movement on the distant horizon. The Roman General's assistant says:

"Is that an orange hedge moving toward us?"

And then seconds later his lieutenant says:

"No, it's the Scots!"

A hoard of crazed Scots with nasty looking weapons overwhelm the wall, and surround the time machine where Blackadder and Baldrick are cringing, hacking at its wooden sides with their blades. The obvious lesson here is the need in strategy to be continuously vigilant and to monitor signals in the environment.

There is another reminder here about "what's the one big thing that we have forgotten?", too. When the Roman General appears on the scene he is fully armoured on the top of his body but down below there is nothing other than his shorts, reminding us of the story of the emperor's clothes.

What might have the options been for our two anti-heroes to be able to find out the setting on the time controls? Working backwards from the result one might, for example, have gotten:

- Deep hypnosis
- Some kind of truth drug
- Torture
- Shocks.

But the really cunning one is yet to come in the story.

After many attempts at going up and down in time to try to get back to the present, Blackadder begins to show real frustration and reflects:

"So I am going to be cursed to spend the rest of my life being in a small wooden box with the most stupid man in the world."

Then Baldrick shows an unusual burst of creativity:

> My lord, I think that I have a Cunning Plan: well you know that if you are at the moment of death that your life flashes before your eyes? Well, if we were to drown you we could take you back to the moment in your life when I feel on the time controls and just at that moment of death you would see the controls on the time machine, and then we would bring you back to life and we would all get back to the present.

Whereupon Blackadder looks very thoughtful and says:

> "Well, Baldrick that is quite a Cunning Plan, but I think that I have got an even better one."

And with that word he then punches Baldrick unconscious and the next thing that we see is Baldrick's head being pushed down a loo to half drown him, held only by his legs. Each time he surfaces he gets closer to remembering and finally sees in his head the control settings saying:

> "I am back in junior school. No I am graduating junior school. No they sent me back to junior school," and then:

> "I've got it! I wish that we had flushed the loo!"
> Or, "what's the one big thing that we forgot?"

There are thus a number of most important ideas about strategy that come out of this story:

- However good a strategy is, it will fail if implementation is bad.
- Always ask yourself "what's the one big thing that you forgot?"
- Don't spread yourself too thin, and strategy is about saying "no."
- Sense and interpret signals from the environment.
- Strategy is about options.
- Strategy is about the "Cunning Plan."
- The Cunning Plan can be further refined to be the "stunning" plan.
- It entails mental time travel (into the future).

The Cunning Plan in the *Blackadder* case was most certainly arrived at by thinking about how one might remember something that one had forgotten: under what conditions might this actually happen?

It became easier for Baldrick and Blackadder to work out the Cunning Plan in terms of taking the near-death experience as a vehicle, and working out exactly how this could be done in a controlled way so it didn't turn into a real death. And whilst this plan had elegant simplicity, it wouldn't be that easy to imitate, so it satisfies all our criteria for being a "Cunning Plan."

We already saw in Chapter 2 a couple of examples of Cunning Plans from the art of deception. For instance, there was Operation Bertram in North Africa. Here the weak position of the British army was turned around by a surprise attack against the German army – manufactured through the idea of genius from an ex-magician and a couple of inventive fellow soldiers who created an entire dummy army that fooled Rommel about the location of his enemy and into thinking that it was totally unready for battle.

But perhaps it is a lot easier to begin to understand what a "Cunning Plan" looks like after the event than to be able to come up with one yourself. And it is here where the idea of "dynamic" – in the form of thinking – comes in again. For conventional, deductive and incremental thinking unsurprisingly fails to shift the frame of reference and to enable us to leap over obstacles and constraints. And typically, dealing with strategic issues requires a bigger leap and thus much more fundamental shift in how we see things.

To introduce this far more dynamic ingredient into our thought process we have to be able to curve the line of thought sometimes at tangents, to make a leap, then to go back and see how we got there. Clearly this is about non-linear and very quick thinking, not slow, ponderous, and snail's pace thinking. So we need to jolt ourselves out of that thought style so characteristic of the normal understanding of "work."

Thinking about something in a cunning way frequently involves taking a reverse perspective. For instance this might be:

- starting with your vision of a solution or being in the future, and then working backwards from that;
- reversing how you see an issue: e.g. seeing a problem or a threat as an opportunity;
- deconstructing the system that has caused the problem of constraint and recreating it;
- imagining you are really not where you are now but somewhere almost unrelated to that – *where you could be, or would love to be*;
- looking at something upside down in reverse: for example in a mature commodity market what could happen that would simply turn it on its head (or "upside down" thinking); that's where "Upside Down Thinking" comes in!

All of this has the hallmarks of the agile philosophy (Chapter 2).

So how can we think about options? Enter the Optopus.

The Optopus

Options can be generated creatively using the "Optopus." This greatly enriches the strategic thinking process by typically doubling or even tripling the range of strategic options that we can imagine (see Figure 3.2 to tease out new possibilities). The Optopus has eight generic dimensions of choice, or "degrees of freedom."

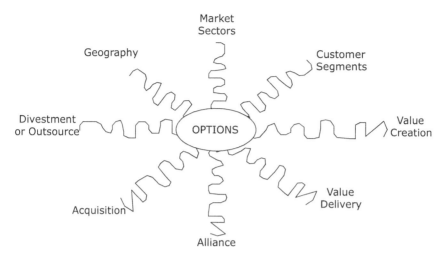

Figure 3.2 The "Optopus" – For Option Generation

These include:

- *Market segments*: the different types of market that one might serve: private/public.
- *Customer segments*: the different types of customer with different needs.
- *Value creation*: the different ways in which value is added to the customer.
- *Value delivery*: the technologies, media and distribution to take it to market.
- *Alliance*: different partners and different types of alliances, doing different things.
- *Acquisition*: different types, different targets, to do different things.
- *Divestment and outsourcing*: alternative ways of configuring value adding activities/scope.
- *Geography*: nationally, regionally, and globally.

  Each of the lines of enquiry that we have listed here contains many branches and sub-branches, so a well-developed "Optopus" could easily cover a white board. It is also possible to do a tailored Optopus. Take for example, generating options for holidays. Look at this extended example, which actually has nine dimensions:

- Where to go (country, region, place)?
- How to get there (car, bus, train, ship, aeroplane)?
- What to spend (premium, value for money, budget)?
- When to go (peak/off-peak, time of year)?
- What to do when you are there (activities/chill out)?
- How long for (fortnight, 10 days, a week, mini break)?

- Where to stay (hotel, all-inclusive/non-inclusive, rental)?
- How to buy it (package, internet)?
- Who to go with (solo, with partner, family, extended family, friends, group)?

The lines of enquiry of the Optopus can be explored either separately or perhaps through possible interdependencies. The Optopus can help to provide some prompts/structure to option generation at a macro level. For competitive strategy, partly de-skilling the creative process and extending the possibilities of strategic options is key.

Whilst these eight generic lines of enquiry are widely applicable, they can be refined, adjusted or added to. For example, others that I have used in the past are:

- Brand options
- Pricing options
- Competitive mind-set
- Resource base.

Pricing options are particularly interesting in the case study below on Virgin Galactic.

These can involve thought experiments of much greater or much lower pricing, or pricing on a more flexible basis. Suspending the normal assumptions about pricing is a major departure from the industry mind-set and is a classic example of strategic thinking by focusing on the customer's perspective.

So let's look at the interesting case study of Virgin Galactic. Essentially, the idea behind it was to develop a technology which was capable of delivering a number of independent passengers into space for a sub-orbital flight. Travelling at a height of around 50 miles, these passengers would then enjoy seeing the earth from a distance in its glory and in state of weightlessness. This was to be made available originally at a low budget cost of $200,000.

This was to be made possible by launching a small but light space vehicle from another launching craft to reach sub-orbital flight in two stages. This followed the idea of the re-useable Space Shuttle, but with one important difference: the craft would not have a heavy heat shield to avoid it burning up on re-entry to the earth's atmosphere. That meant that it wouldn't need as much fuel and a separate stage to get into space.

The "Cunning Plan" was to design a large fin that could be put up like a sail that would gently and gradually allow it to re-enter the atmosphere without burning up.

The concept only allowed for a relatively short journey of 90 minutes (the duration of a football match or a yoga class). Allowing for at least half an hour to get up there (as the launcher craft that carries the spaceship up into high altitude had to reach maximum height before the real launch) and back (the glide down would take a lot longer than a conventional re-entry), this didn't leave a lot of time to enjoy the view.

Around that time the business model was relatively simple, with the idea to charge a flat rate, to market it to wealthy people and to make provisions for passengers to float around the cabin for a few minutes of weightlessness.

I visited Virgin Galactic's offices in London some years ago and took with me a whole stack of ideas:

Market sectors:

- End-customer corporates – e.g. as city bonuses, corporate entertaining, acquisition deal meetings
- Governments – e.g. to promote ecological awareness, and promoting world peace

Customer segments:

- Business millionaires – by industry
- City dealers
- Celebrities/wives (e.g. footballers/pop-stars etc.)
- Footballers/sports people
- Not so rich – by sponsorship or via a lottery
- People who are economically unfortunate/disadvantaged
- Religious groups
- The larger person (charge by the weight? excess baggage?)
- The general public (lottery)
- Politicians
- Groups of individuals

Value-creating activities:

- Astronauts club/season ticket holders
- Present (a very big one!)
- Differential pricing (premiums seats/service)
- Differential pricing: for latecomers pay more (as airlines do) or a big premium
- Extras – e.g. for technology-based enhancements of the experience, such as advanced telescopes
- Space parties
- Two or three flights at once, like *Star Wars*!
- Corporate networking opportunities and deals in space!
- Space walks
- Simulated space wars (two or more crafts)
- DVDs etc.
- Remote conversations with earth friends

- Webcam links
- A 50-mile-high club!
- Experiments in space
- Enhancement of Virgin Brand generally
- Weddings/dating
- Funerals (again!)
- Easy payment terms
- Life insurance!

Value delivery:

- Media (TV Channel) – e.g. celebrity knock-out programme in space
- Alliances
- NASA
- Virgin Airlines
- Media company

Divestment/outsourcing:

- Different aeroplane manufacturer

Geography:

- By customer – e.g. US, European, Middle East, Japan, China etc.
- By flight – anywhere, subject to launch sites (world network)

It certainly has potential for being a global business.

In all, this yields over forty options, and there are more if we tried.

Another thing to consider is to look at both deliberate and relatively random combinations of options. For example:

Deliberate:

- China/India
- Lottery
- Not so financially well off

Random:

- The very rich
- IT business founders

- From California to China and back
- Ecologically aware
- Business networking/deal making

Each one of these options or bundles of options could then be evaluated using the Strategic Option Grid.

An interesting possibility is to charge a lot more than $200,000, which would come up if we had used "pricing" as an additional strand of the Optopus. What about charging $500,000 for the inaugural flight, for example? Or one might have one flight at $200,000 a seat for a more basic trip, say over the U.S., with an extended flight to the Caribbean for $300,000. Apparently, Richard Branson was very keen on keeping the price at $200,000 (now $250,000), but that did restrict one of the degrees of freedom of the venture: pricing. Why not set that as the base price and then have premium packages on top of that?

The main constraint on differential pricing is stakeholder agendas, so one needs a Cunning Plan to address that. For instance, what about giving Richard Branson two envelopes: one with the base plan where the price per flight gets eroded in value through inflation and revenues are restricted, and another where this isn't the case and there is plenty value innovation which gets paid for. The economic value of the value innovation option is 50% higher. So you say, "Richard, are you really sure that you don't want this, given that your core flight price is still $200,000?" A cunning, influential plan (see the Cunning Checklists in Chapter 4, especially on challenging constraints).

Interestingly, when I spoke to Virgin Galactic some years ago they had reported customers asking for customised things, but other than that they hadn't, in those early days, thought about the opportunities in a more holistic way, which is encouraged by the Optopus. Even when a business in its formative phase it is all too easy to settle for a model which meets original goals and works reasonably well. However this may inhibit thinking about optimising it (as opposed to "satisficing it"). So even early on strategic thinking can get switched off and limit the model.

The main "So what?" of this analysis of Virgin Galactic is the sheer richness of opportunities that the technique reveals. There is a big potential here to get most of the cash flow from sponsorship and media opportunities. This is a common experience.

In conclusion, the Optopus is a rich way of generating strategic ideas. It is far more effective than purely brain-storming. It is not unusual to be able to generate between 50 and a 100 possible options if there are a number of sub-groups working on the same business. *The structure of "lines of enquiry" greatly facilitates the cognitive and group dynamic.*

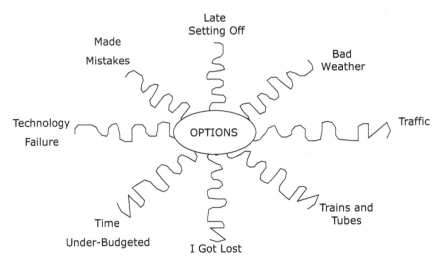

Figure 3.3 The "Excuse-Opus" – for Being Late

Before we leave the Optopus let's just take a quick look at an example of how one might use this process on something from everyday life: how to make up excuses for being late! I will call this version the "Excuse-Opus" (see Figure 3.3). Eight degrees of freedom here might be:

- Delay in setting out
- Weather
- Traffic
- Trains and Tubes delayed
- Got lost
- Under budgeted on time
- Technology didn't work (car, mobile etc.)
- Made mistakes (e.g. went wrong way, had to refuel, had to go back for something)

Of course there might be other ones, like "I couldn't be bothered" or "I actually wanted to be late," but I guess those might be rude.

Anyway, the point is that you can make up tailored Optopuses for different kinds of issues, such as:

- Cost management (see Figure 3.4) – the "Costapus"
- The "Customer Value Optopus" (which we see in Chapter 8)
- Strategic influencing (which we see in Chapter 10)
- The "Brand-opus"
- Business performance improvement
- Internal change
- The "Career Optopus" (for exploring career options)

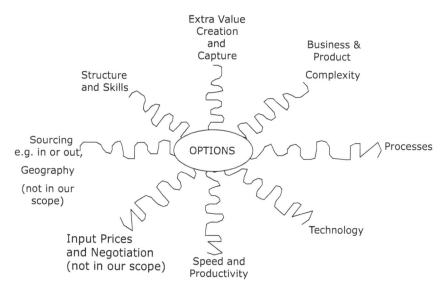

Figure 3.4 The "Costapus" – For Option Generation

Inside the engine room: the Strategic Option Grid

Once we have derived a set of options (and also preferably once we have done further work to optimise these, and maybe add some new ones (using the Cunning Checklists in Chapter 4), we are then set to do our evaluation using the Strategic Option Grid – see Figure 3.5

I created this technique 27 years ago when advising on strategies to privatise British Rail, and its use helped to save an organization: Britain's National Train. This was done in six hours' work with the CEO to flesh out scores on a matrix of five decision criteria and nine strategic options, a sub-set which saved the business from closure. That's 45 cells to be debated and evaluated, just over five minutes for each. That's focused and productive. Thousands of Strategic Option Grids have been done across hundreds of companies since.

The Strategic Option Grid can be used for a whole range of applications at the corporate, business, functional, project, team and individual level. It can be used for market development, product/service development and new technology development. Apart from the really big corporate strategic decisions, it really comes into its own with acquisitions, divestment, alliances, diversification and turnarounds. Then there's also organisational structuring options, all strategic projects, and cost breakthroughs right through to career strategies. There are also strategies in everyday life (even holidays and dating opportunities to apply it to).

The specific choice of the five criteria appeared to closely reflect the unconscious and informal decision-making heuristics which managers use, especially the criteria of "financial attractiveness," "uncertainty and risk" and "stakeholder acceptability."

Options Criteria	Option 1	Option 2	Option 3	Option 4
Strategic Attractiveness				
Financial Attractiveness*				
Implementation Difficulty				
Uncertainty and Risk				
Acceptability (to Stakeholders)				
Scores	X	X	X	X

Score: 3 = very attractive, 2 = medium attractive, 1 = low attractiveness.

* Benefits less costs, - net cash flows relative to investment

Figure 3.5 The Strategic Option Grid

To use the Strategic Option Grid, you need to:

- Explore what options might be available, especially using an Optopus.
- Look at options for "How" a strategic option might be done, and the timing options.
- For each option we then develop a "Cunning Plan."
- Then evaluate the scores, based on what is behind these criteria (Note that high implementation difficulty and "uncertainty and risk" are scores of 1, and not 3, ticks). *Half ticks are not just possible but are desirable to have.*
- After that it may be time to check out any facts, especially the cells on the grids which the Option Grid evaluation looks most sensitive to.
- Finally, we may need to revisit the Cunning Plan, and finally ask the question "what's the one big thing that you have missed?"

To minimize unnecessary bias, it is crucial to work down the columns and not from left to right. This also has advantages of greater cognitive flow as you are not in-and-out of options all the time. Try to save cross comparisons until later!

I define the criteria as follows:

- *Strategic attractiveness*: this is the external market attractiveness and the relative competitive position. "Market attractiveness" is based on things like the growth drivers, Porter's Five Forces (see Figure 1.4) and perhaps PEST analysis (Figure 1.3). Judgements on "strategic attractiveness" should always be checked against the "General Electric" (GE) Grid (see Figure 1.5 in Chapter 1).

*   *Financial attractiveness*: these are the long and short term returns from the option (or possibly its economic profit/net cash flow after a charge for capital).
*   *Implementation difficulty*: this is the sum of difficulty over time to achieve the strategic goals.
*   *Uncertainty and risk*: this is the volatility of the assumptions.
*   *Stakeholder acceptability*: this is the extent to which stakeholders favour, disfavour or are neutral regarding that option.

The time dimension needs to be set so that there is no confusion as to what the time scales are under consideration. Where there is a perceived big change in attractiveness over time, then this should be discriminated somehow. For example, one might split up some of the boxes into two to differentiate the shorter term from the longer term, to begin to capture the dynamic. This may be helpful, especially in looking at situations where, for example, there may not be a short term financial attractiveness, but there is one longer-term, or vice versa.

This again suggests that we have in our minds the model of the "attractiveness-over-time curve," at least for the aggregate of the Strategic Option Grid scores (See Figure 3.6).

This curve plots the total score out of 15 over time for the Strategic Option Grid. Here we see the overall attractiveness going up initially and then dropping back, then going up again, but then severely dropping to the end. Here the time scales could easily be five years.

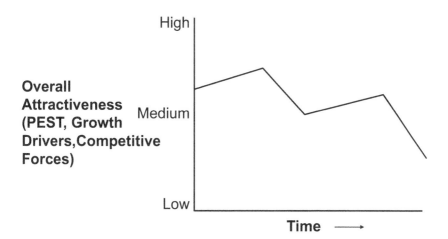

Figure 3.6 Overall Attractiveness-Over-Time Curve

Clearly, it is possible to do individual curves for each of our five criteria separately and build these up as a way of making the analysis more dynamic than snapshot.

To interpret the overall scores, my rule of thumb is that you would like to have at least a score of 12 and anything lower than a nine should be looked down upon (assuming you have tried already to be cunning). During the debate, the scores are likely to move up and down quite a lot as one goes through a "challenge and build" process and tries to improve their cunning.

The scores can, of course, be weighted mathematically, but personally I find that's a bit too quasi-scientific, unless one criterion stands head and shoulders above the others. Even then, it is usually sufficient to just bear that weight in mind qualitatively rather than indulge in furious work on a calculator or getting lost in a spread sheet.

The criteria might in exceptional circumstances be extended, but generally speaking, it is probably better to stay with the simpler number of five criteria. The only criterion which generically has competed in my mind on occasion is that of "timing," particularly where a market opportunity is fluid, embryonic or fast moving, or it is highly affected by the economic cycle. I can see a case for adding that into the other five.

Where an option criteria looks to be pretty terrible, then one is challenged to give it a half score, and maybe only a zero. The question in the latter case is whether one should still add the scores together or whether the option loses *all of its points* – or in footballing terms it gets "sent off" (I once rated one of my ex long term relationships as a zero on one criterion).

Should there be minimal threshold criteria scores? Well maybe, for example we may decide that for one criterion we really do need a score of, say, a two. This can be of a lot of help in dealing with any dilemmas.

Another possibility is to put the five generic criteria to one side and to do a totally bespoke set of criteria. The advantages of that are that it captures the nuances of exactly what you are looking to do or get out of it. The disadvantages are that we lose the glove fitting other tools (we call these "deep-dive "tools, like the GE Grid) that take us down to the underlying variables. But some things such as everyday strategic decisions can lend themselves more to this.

For example, after a long term relationship had "completed," I went on the search for a new partner. I decided that I should do this in way which wasn't just superficially based. I needed some solid criteria to make a decision. Figure 3.7 shows the five that I came up with after much deliberation:

- Attractiveness
- Personality and Intelligence
- Fun and Flexibility
- Stability and Family
- Financial Independence.

Options \\ Goals	Option 1	Option 2	Option 3	Option 4
Attractiveness				
Personality and Intelligence				
Fun and Flexibility				
Stability and Family				
Financial Independence				

Score: 3 = very attractive, 2 = medium attractive, 1 = low attractiveness. Half scores are possible.
* Benefits less costs, - net cash flows relative to investment

Figure 3.7 The Strategic Option Grid – with Tailored Criteria-Acquisition of Longer-Term Partner

Now it is interesting that however hard you try to break this down into rational criteria it is phenomenally difficult to be free of bias and to avoid missing some fundamental difficulties. But, having these criteria and rating them over time did enable me to track how this strategy in real time, just as one should do for any business strategy that you have embarked on.

In the case of one relationship that started off as a 12.5 score, it started a slow process of decline down to 10 and then more rapidly down to a seven (at which time help was sought) but then proceeded to worsen as I had caught myself in one of the most fundamental biases of all: the "cumulative escalation of commitment over time."

I tried to learn from this experience in my next attempt to find a congenial partner. Instead of five criteria I had twelve, and even these were broken down into five "indicators," so there were 60 things in all! After the relationship was twelve weeks old the relationship scored 89%. This time something big that had been hidden came out of the woodwork at Month Seven, and when I redid the score it was now a 48%! This time I had a real wake-up call, and within five weeks the relationship was over.

So I put most of the blame the first time around on my vulnerability to bias and the usual "rose-coloured glasses" of a new relationship. Of course the emotions here, not helped by the drug oxytocin, are much more powerful that those affecting most corporate decisions, but many of them do have some significant feelings around them, so that does need some management. The Strategic Option Grid, plus some evidence-based decision making and a challenge and build process within a team rather than a single person, helps to avoid the worst dangers and most terrible mistakes.

As all management tools are prone to the effects of bias (see Chapter 2), I highlight that an inexperienced user of the Strategic Option Grid might be caught out by:

- "Strategic attractiveness": may be scored without any real thought about really thinking through all the layers of the "Strategic Onion" e.g. external competitive pressure environment: also this may not capture the nuances of the "attractiveness-over-time curve."
- "Financial attractiveness": may not be looked at dynamically or be viewed as more about short and medium term, not the longer term.
- "Implementation difficulty": may be largely a subjective and emotional impression, rather than detailed thinking about how enablers and constraints might these will change over time.
- "Uncertainty and risk": may lack any granular thinking about what specific assumptions are and how volatile these are.
- "Stakeholder acceptability": may be done at a global level without thinking about the complex dynamics these have in their mutual interplay.

Besides the more obvious use of the Strategic Option Grid on more "deliberate" strategies, it can also be used for more emergent and detergent strategies within the strategy mix.

Another important feature is that Strategic Options can be broken down (through a "Strategic Option Tree," Figure 3.8) into options for:

- What the strategy actually is about?
- How it would be implemented?
- When it would be implemented?
- And maybe even, with whom?

So, potentially, each one of these could be split into separate grids. There are three main strategies to enter a market:

- Organic
- Acquisition
- Alliance.

There might then be four options of companies to acquire. And this might be done through investing internal funds, through bank borrowing or through raising equity and this might then be looked at as:

- Immediate effect
- Action after more detailed co-planning of six months
- After a delay of one year.

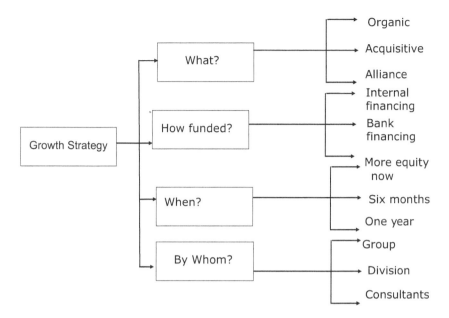

Figure 3.8 the "Strategic Option Tree" – Breakdown of Strategic Options into Separate Strategic Option Grids

So we could have further Option Grids here.

And finally, this might be done:

- On our own – either by group or by division
- Us with integration consultants – e.g. on the brand, the systems, organisational change, and development.

It is always important to try to make each option relatively specific. For example, something like an alliance is hopelessly general. You should define who it would be with and for what and through what kind of vehicle, e.g. through a dedicated legal joint venture of a looser collaboration agreement.

Not only is the definition of the option something far from trivial, but also one can look at different scenarios for the portfolio of options for a topic, for instance where:

- Options are mutually exclusive.
- They are complementary.
- They are combinations of different specific options where these are genuinely synergistic this will enhance the scores.
- Where an option is complex and composite it can be broken into sub-options and these can be displayed for a single overall strategy on a grid all on its own.

Where there is a lot of variation in our scores and they change over time as there are a lot of dynamics it is even possible to show these as a time series (see Figure 3.9)

Criteria \ Options	Prototype Development	First 2 Years Flights	Years 3–5 Two vehicles	Years 6–10 Multi routes
Strategic Attractiveness	★★	★★½	★★★	★★★
Financial Attractiveness*	★½	★★½	★★★	★★★
Implementation Difficulty	★½	★★½	★★★	★★½
Uncertainty and Risk	★½	★★	★★★	★★½
Acceptability (to Stakeholders)	★★	★★½	★★½	★★½
Scores	8 1/2	12	14 1/2	13 1/2

Score: 3 = very attractive, 2 = medium attractive, 1 = low attractiveness.

* Benefits less costs, - net cash flows relative to investment

Figure 3.9 The Strategic Option Grid – as a Time Series: Virgin Gallactic

Criteria \ Options	Option 1 "out"	Option 2 "in"	Option 3	Option 4
Strategic Attractiveness	★★½	★		
Financial Attractiveness*	★½	★		
Implementation Difficulty	★★★	★		
Uncertainty and Risk	★★	★		
Acceptability (to Stakeholders)	★★½	★		
Scores	11 1/2	5		

Score: 3 = very attractive, 2 = medium attractive, 1 = low attractiveness.

* Benefits less costs, - net cash flows relative to investment

Figure 3.10 The Strategic Option Grid with Scenarios – No Brexit *v.* with Brexit

Another possible exercise is to do a Strategic Option Grid for the very same option but then split the scores for two different states of the world. In Figure 3.10 we see the same strategy score in May 2016 before the British Referendum on EU membership with a particular market growth strategy in the scenario of staying within it (no Brexit) that is much better than that of being without it (with Brexit). So the Strategic Option Grid can cope with divergent realities, thus again being able to handle external and dynamic uncertainty.

Finally, the grid can be used not just on new options but to evaluate existing strategies.

Interdependencies and the "deep-dive" techniques for option evaluation

There are important interdependencies between the five key criteria of the Strategic Option Grid (see below). This partly explains why managers using the Strategic Option Grid for the first time may find that they sometimes confuse the criteria which lead to scores being biased and potentially to double counting them. The main things to watch for are:

- "Strategic attractiveness" being all about whether an opportunity has an appeal, or is desirable; this is actually more about stakeholder acceptability.
- Or is this attractiveness lower because of the uncertainties: No, again, as its rating is set by considering "the most likely" view of the world, whereas "uncertainty" is uncovered by looking at the more volatile states of the world.
- "Financial attractiveness" being considered lower because the option is financially risky; no, that is to confuse it with "uncertainty and risk." "Financially attractive" is set by the most likely economic outcome alone.
- "Implementation difficulty" being high because it is uncertain as to how easy it is to do; again, that has more to do with "uncertainty and risk."

A number of key interdependencies exist that can be depicted visually (see Figure 3.11 as follows), between:

- *Strategic attractiveness and financial attractiveness*: the assumptions on the environment and competitive advantage (these all drive the sales growth rate, the operating profit margin, and the investment levels and thus net cash flow.
- *Strategic attractiveness and uncertainty and risk*: which variables are key and most volatile under different scenarios.
- *Strategic attractiveness and stakeholder acceptability*: given stakeholders' views of the level of attractiveness including opportunities and threats.
- *Financial attractiveness and stakeholder acceptability*: in shaping stakeholder agendas through the prospects of high returns.
- *Uncertainty and risk and financial attractiveness*: in looking at the volatility of returns.

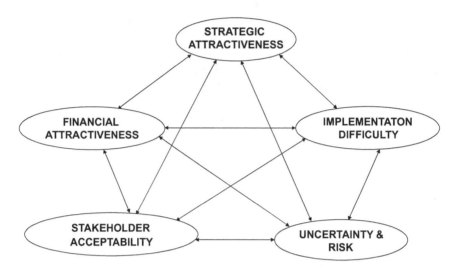

Figure 3.11 The Strategic Option Grid – Interdependencies Between Criteria

- *Implementation difficulty and uncertainty and risk*: implementation risks can be crucial.
- *Financial attractiveness and implementation difficulty*: through stretch targets and over-stretched resources making implementation harder
- *Implementation difficulty and stakeholder acceptability*: in deciding the level of acceptable implementation challenge.
- *Uncertainty and stakeholder acceptability*: in shaping the risk appetite and aversion of the stakeholders.

Each of the five decision criteria can now be tested out with a number of "deep-dive" techniques. For instance, "Strategic attractiveness" for an externally facing strategy should be checked out primarily with the GE Grid or the "General Electric Grid" (see Figure 1.3 in Chapter 1).

Managers have to be continually convinced and persuaded *not* to short-circuit their thinking on these first criteria of "strategic attractiveness," supporting it with the GE Grid and with its second-tier techniques, like Porter's five forces.

"Financial attractiveness" means those factors which (in combination) will deliver a return on investment, or perhaps the more sophisticated concept of "shareholder value creation" will add incremental economic value.

"Uncertainty and risk" is arrived at by using the uncertainty–importance grid (Mitroff and Linstone 1993) (see Chapter 2 Figure 2.3). Then, some of the most critical assumptions about the strategy actually working out alright are identified (perhaps using post-its). We then position them in terms of their relative importance, and also in terms of how certain/uncertain they are perceived to be. A cluster of several assumptions in the South-East part of the grid (the "Danger Zone") would suggest a highly uncertain strategy (or a one tick).

To summarise, for each criteria we might use:

- *Strategic attractiveness*: the PEST factors, growth drivers, Porter's five forces, competitive bench-marking, the GE Grid.
- *Financial attractiveness*: return on capital, net present value etc. – there's more to come later in the book.
- *Implementation difficulty*: coming in Chapter 5 through force field analysis and the difficulty-over-time curve.
- *Uncertainty and risk*: the "Uncertainty–Importance Grid, and scenarios (see Figure 2.3).
- *Stakeholder acceptability*: stakeholder analysis (see Chapter 9).

The Strategic Option Grid scores are only as good as your creative thinking and especially your Cunning Plan. Whilst the Optopus helps to generate more imaginative *original content*, the grid also helps with the process of being more imaginative in refining the options. In Chapter 4 I give some in-depth prompts for greater creativity through the 101 checklists for being cunning.

The "Challenge and Build" process

Whilst one might have hoped (from the last section) that the Strategic Option Grid now tells us the best possible thinking about each option, often this is not the case. Frequently there is further scope to outline the options to make them better – to make them "cunning" (or more highly innovative) or even (with further refinement) "stunning."

To achieve this, it is often useful to narrow the field of attention down to a small number of boxes on the Strategic Option Grid. Perhaps, for example, focus on:

For Option 1:   *implementation difficulty*
For Option 2:   *uncertainty and risk*
For Option 3:   *financial attractiveness*

Equally, it may be appropriate to "challenge" the scores, either through specific focus on the uncertainty and "risk" boxes (with the Uncertainty Grid), or by asking "what is the one big thing we have forgotten?" across any box. Or you might test for the resilience of particular strategic options against different possible states of the world (or "scenarios"). Here the *same* option is scored across the different columns, each one reflecting a different alternative future.

On strategic thinking and cognitive flow

All of these techniques need to be harnessed within a cognitive and behavioural flow (the latter I deal with in Chapter 11 in "Strategic Behaviour in Teams").

It is well worth it to look at some of the theory of Cognitive Flow, which is a key aspect of being able to think dynamically about strategy (e.g. in cunning planning).

Cognitive *flow* is a concept developed by the Czech psychologist Mihaly Csikszentmihalyi (pronounced "Me-Hi Chick-Sent-Me-Hi" – which sounds like a mix between women and drugs!).

Flow is a highly creative and natural flow of ideas that comes when facing a cognitive challenge that is complex but in a state of relative effortlessness at a conscious level (1975). Everything seems to be naturally in gear. To melt most effectively into that flow you need time, preparation and a clearing away of distractions not just externally but also internally by quieting the internal monkey-mind chatter; there has to be concentration, meditation and some mindfulness.

Not only does this state produce mankind's greatest scientific and artistic breakthroughs, but it is also manifest in things like Ronaldo scoring a superb free kick or a new song by Adele. And we can find that space in everyday moments, especially in business. In fact, during the writing of this book things came through to me without apparent effort, like the:

- Double strategic onion in Chapter 1
- Multiple Uncertainty Tunnel in Chapter 7
- Competitive landscape, competitive space, and the competitive mix in Chapter 9
- Stakeholder Map in Chapter 10.

Key insights and learning lessons from Chapter 3

In this chapter there are many insights about the dynamic nature of the process of analysing and evaluating competitive strategy.

- A strategy review process is often best kicked off by a "Strategic Gap analysis" a means of framing the challenge, as long as that doesn't lead to too many *excessive preconceptions of desired stretch*.
- You also need the "cunning" plan.
- To generate options it is better to use the "Optopus" rather than less structured brainstorming as you will get a much broader range of options.
- The dimensions of the Optopus can be adapted and added to; for example, with brand and pricing options.
- Further options can be developed by the "pick and mix" of different combinations of ideas.
- The Strategic Option Grid is applicable across a very wide range of decisions and existing strategies.
- To make strategic choices we need some criteria; for instance, strategic, financial attractiveness, implementation difficulty, uncertainty and risk and stakeholder acceptability.

- The scores on the "Option Grid" are only as good as the Cunning Plan.
- Scores can be weighted, but don't get carried away by artificial precision; better to deploy judgement.
- Scores are also susceptible to bias, which can be countered by a "challenge and build" process.
- Besides its use on more "deliberate" strategies, the grid can also be used for more emergent and detergent strategies within the strategy mix.
- The grid can be used to look at options of what to do and how to do that, and the latter can be broken down.
- The overall "attractiveness" of a Strategic Option will shift over time – in the aggregate and for each criterion, too.
- The option scores can be weighted and given thresholds and qualifying, target levels.
- The scores should be evidence based – in fact doing an initial evaluation can help you target data needed
- There are options not only for what you do, but also how you do them, and when you do them, and even who you do them with. Each of these can be analysed on the grid.
- The differential scores of the very same option can be assessed, but in different emergent worlds.
- The grid can be used not just for decision-making but for influencing and communication.

Reader exercises

- Using one of the Optopus pictures for one area of your business, what new ideas come up?
- For both a new strategy and for an existing strategy, what does the Strategic Option Grid tell you?

4 The Cunning Checklists

My goal in my everyday life is to have at least one Cunning Plan a day.

– Tony G

Introduction

In 2016 when the first thoughts for doing this book came into my head I decided that, one way or another, I was going to try to get more cunning into everyday strategic behaviour. A book title that I thought was cunning: *How to Have a Cunning Plan a Day*. Sadly, a significant number of publishers sniffed at this but it wasn't enough for them. Undaunted, I left it to my unconscious mind to come up with the solution (Cunning Checklist no. 79), and inspired by the "Joy of Constraints" – the principle that if someone tells you that you can't do something that you get even more excited and inspired to find a way of doing it (Cunning Checklist no. 31). It also led to these disparate ideas to come together to form the "stunning plan"! (Cunning Checklist no. 82).

In this chapter on Cunning Checklists I take you through a wealth of ideas for how to look at strategic (and other issues) in a far more innovative and creative way. This follows closely from Chapter 3, which looked at option generation and the Cunning Plan. Towards the end I also make some suggestions on how you can then use them in practice; for example, to remember and internalise more and more of them so that you are constantly on the lookout for *having at least one Cunning Plan a day!*

Origins of the Cunning Checklists

The Cunning Checklists first came into being around the turn of the millennium when I ran some workshops for senior executives from Marketing, Operations and HR at Dyson Appliances, the then UK market leader in carpet cleaners. At that time it was felt that whilst Dyson was highly innovative *it could be even more*. I already used a number of recipes for helping managers to think differently about problems and opportunities, but we needed a really good toolkit of ideas, so I synthesised ones from mine and ones that had worked for other people.

This became my list of "55 Ways of Being Cunning" that became central in the strategic thinking process of this book – as in Model 3 (Chapter 1). But I was always aware that there were other valuable prompts emerging over time. "Dynamic competitive strategy" gives an opportunity to catch up and further add to these. So now we have "101 Ways of Being Cunning."

I suggest that as you read them extract the ones that you like particularly by taking some notes, or mark those you like in the actual book. They are there to be used! You have my permission. You might choose to do that either in just a very general way or with some particular strategy issues in mind. Once you have gone through them – and that will take time – please spend twenty minutes of your time thinking about what options or sub-set of questions you find most valuable.

We then look at a couple of illustrations and how to use the checklists.

101 ways of being cunning

For each of these checklists I have added a few notes of expansion or explanation in italics:

1   Remember, never try to go directly from problem diagnosis to solution; always go through the land of options ("Winnie the Pooh").

> *Instinctive problem solving typically is in such a rush to get to a solution that only one or two options are usually explored with an almost certainly non-optimal solution.*

2   Work backwards from the future (time travelling).

> *Whilst finding your current position may make you more aware it may well anchor you too much in the problems and constraints of where you are and have been rather than what you can become and what I just over the horizon. Stretching that future even further away in time can also enable you to think a lot more creatively, and to take advantage of turning points in your environment.*

3   Work backwards from your desired result.

> *Separate from that just visualising your end goal and its alignment factors can make it easier to work through all the steps that are needed on the way. It is also helpful in visualising some of the later steps with clarity that would otherwise be fuzzy. (This has been called "backward induction").*

4   Imagine that you have never worked in the company before: what options can you see?

> *This is a classic example of mind-set agility which is a brilliant way of avoiding the stickiness of over-identifying with yourself in a potentially treacly situation.*

5   Imagine that you have never worked in the industry before: what options can you see?

> *One of my favourites: effectively you are an "industrial anthropologist" looking at things as if they were strange; this allows you to discard some of your*

assumptions, beliefs and expectations that are all a part of the "industry mind-set". More specifically it can also bring to bear specific industry perspectives from elsewhere that will fundamentally challenge "how we do things around here."

6   Imagine that you are actually an alien!

Another version of mind-set agility that is not only very incisive but a lot of fun: many industries have such peculiar and idiosyncratic ways of doing things that entering into an "alien mind-set" will inevitably generate radical ideas: e.g. I once went into a funeral shop in alien mode and they told me that "oh yes we are busy." It turned out they had one customer a week or so, so the alien's first thought was why did they need a shop? Why not use the internet and do site visits and have a storage facility?

7   Tell your story about how events in the future might unfold, including what different players decide to do why and when, and with what consequences (the "Uncertainty Tunnel").

Storytelling can be a great way of effectively putting your car headlights on "full beam" – then you can see twice as far ahead. It works not just for coping with change and uncertainty of a negative nature but also for seeing the fuller potential of an opportunity and also much more clearly what its timescale might be (just as important).

8   Imagine you are a competitor.

In imagining a competitor you really have to enter their mind-set and see the market as them with their resources and likely/possible intent. This might suggest strategies you haven't thought about and ones that you could do yourself.

9   Imagine you are a new entrant.

This mental experiment can be even more ferocious in waking you up from competitive complacency and almost certainly will show you that other market and competitive positioning are possible. For instance you might have a much simpler and direct service offering, greater pricing clarity, much simpler business model and cost base and combination of strategic assets and competences.

10 Work backwards from customers' needs to develop your strategy.

There is probably no better or high value added source of strategic data than your customers, who are the cheapest strategy consultants! You can ask them how you might add more value to them, cut out waste and value dilution, or find out from them what products and services you might supply to them now or in the future that you currently do not. You can enter a dialogue with them about their own future customers and market needs and how you could enable them to compete and grow in their future markets. Just by daring and asking such questions that significantly enhance your relationship with them.

Comments on checklists 1–10

In these initial checklists we see the power of doing mental experiments in terms of adopting different mind-sets from our own, and in the case of our customers, even going out and asking them where they are actually at. We also coupled that with agile thinking by shifting the reference point from the "here and now" to another space – time location: the future or the result. It is all about "mental elasticity."

11 Have the "out of body experience" of being a customer, an alliance partner, a supplier or a regulator.

> *This is about practising that mind-set agility in a wider domain, to anticipate their behaviour and how effective your existing and new strategies will be in dealing with them.*

12 Be a real customer of your own business.

> *What this means is that you actually "go undercover" as a customer of your own business – what is it actually like to experience the delights (hopefully!) but especially the frustrations of dealing with your own business? Are there things that really, really entice you to move swiftly and easily through the buying process or are there silly or stupid things that are full of friction and maybe even such a distraction that you might think of going elsewhere? Why do they exist and what can you do about them?*

13 Deeply understand customers' buying processes and criteria.

> *Knowing what your customers' buying criteria are intimately on a customer–by–customer basis (or on a segment-by-segment basis, if "business-consumer") gives one great agility in tailoring one's competitive strategy. "Competitive strategy" isn't identical regardless of the competitive landscape of course! Just in terms of HSBC's "Think Global – Act Local" slogan, there is flexibility and agility about competing at the micro levels. Also, customers' buying processes can be as variable if not more so than their actual buying criteria.*

14 Look at their value-over-time curves. Re-engineer them.

> *We will come onto value-over-time curves more fully a little later. Suffice it to say that these represent the perceived utility or value as experienced through obtaining, consuming and digesting a product or service: high, medium, low or even negative – as a curve over the whole consumption life cycle. Here, peaks can be strengthened and lengthened, dips and droops smoothed – but of course you have to think: "how?" The curve won't necessarily fix the problem just by itself. But it certainly helps focus the attention on phases of the experience over the time dimension where there are problems and opportunities.*

15 Understand the customer's business value system and think about how you can help make it more valuable, and how you can help them quantify the improvement.

> *A "business value system" is a mind-map of the key value creating activities of a business and their interdependencies both ways. Unlike a "value-chain" it is*

not constrained by being linear and is interactive. It can be redrawn to show new activities, new configurations and flows, and simplifications and deletions, thus generating new ideas for value creation. It can be drawn too for past, present and future. We will be exploring it in more depth later on (in Chapter 7*).*

16   Avoid all possible areas of inconvenience to buy.

Much value is lost in the process through which latent customer demand once attracted then gets lost through distractions and leakage caused in part by frictions that make it hard and inconvenient to buy. A classic is Boots the Chemist and WH Smith the newsagent in urban areas in the UK, when even before lunchtime there are long queues so people who only have three minutes to find what they want, buy it and get out or leave empty handed! It is perhaps no coincidence that these two retailers are market leaders and often market leaders are prone to complacency. Inconvenience, generally, can result in a high percentage of demand – sometimes 30–50% being lost.

17   Make things ultra-convenient to buy for the customer.

The mirror image of number 16, but here instead of taking out areas of most obvious friction and leakage we actually redesign and re-engineer the operational and service systems from scratch.

18   What technologies that are already available – and maybe in use in other industries, or coming available in the foreseeable future – would enable you to add value in new ways?

The advance of particularly digital technology is now happening so quickly that human reaction time that is already slow and is further dampened by sluggish corporate practices means that new opportunities are there for the taking and create new opportunities for your business model. For instance, international conferencing technology is already good enough to do some executive coaching, selling of executive development internationally without having to go there; the main constraint is the current lack of a "recognised best platform."

19   Avoid all value destruction and dilution.

There are many sources of value destruction (which leave the customer or your business worse off than before) and even more sources of value added for a lot of effort and cost – and where value added could be a lot more concentrated than it is. If you can cultivate a sense of true honesty (e.g. explicitly declare a "Strategic Amnesty") then having a review of these things is likely to be very productive.

20   Make it absolutely irresistible to buy for the customer.

This is a separate aspect of customer value from sheer convenience: it works on the "bait" effect – something that is truly special that makes you feel some sort of "customer bliss" – that consumption of the product or service leaves you with a "glow" that lasts for some time afterwards. We can break these things into "turn-on's" that can be pictorially mapped so that you can see just how strong and impelling these are, and how these vary across different customers.

Comments on checklists 11 to 20

These checklists begin with the possibility of being more mind-set agile and then focus on the richness of evolving Cunning Plans largely with just the customer in your sights, including the value-over-time curve, the "business value system" and looking at things like irresistibility versus value destruction, making the service totally convenient as opposed to inconvenient. In the next tranche we turn to the wider competitive context. Notably, much of this analysis has a very dynamic element as customer needs and values change over time.

21   Study your competitors and do things even better.

> *Competitor intelligence is not just to ascertain broad relative positioning but to also gain deeper insights into the art of the possible. What is truly distinctive about how a competitor does things really well is the dynamic combination of these various capabilities and strategic assets – not just in their relative strength individually. And if we have identified that in some respects one of them does things in a cunning way, how can we go one step further with a "stunning plan?"*

22   Learn from how other industries do things even better and ask: if I were from another industry what options for adding more value/reducing costs might I come up with?

> *Insights from other industries can be even more interesting than from competitors.* This is because of the fact that *whilst the* competitor *will be more accessible and imitable, where we are learning from further afield there can be* even *more powerful insights.* Moreover, *these may be ones that are less transparent to competitors if you implement them* as competitors will be less likely to understand what is going on. *This is sometimes formally called "benchmarking."*

23   Build barriers to imitation.

> *When we define a "Cunning Plan" there is always the proviso that we are able to build in some difficulties that make it harder to copy, otherwise the competitive advantage is not going to be sustainable. Besides the obvious element of trying to keep some of the "how we do things" as low visibility as possible – ideally in a kind of "black box" (like the secret formula of coke syrup). Often these barriers come from doing things in a unique combination, or through implementing the strategy more easily. Or it may just be about being faster – thus gaining dynamic advantages. The competition can imitate, but by the time they have got to where you were a year ago you have now got a two year lead on them.*

24   And also barriers to substitutes.

> *A similar type of reasoning applies to substitutes (that is where value is delivered to meet a target customer need but it is delivered through other ways such as different distribution channels, technology, or through doing it yourself). This might involve trying to tie in customers with longer term contracts, through much stronger branding. Through strengthening the "value proposition" i.e. the message to the customer of what superior value they will get and how, and at what price?*

25   Make customer switching more difficult.

> *We return here to the customer, but in a competitive context: how can we make him or her dependent economically, and capability-wise, habit-wise, and emotionally-wise on what we do for them and how we do that? Obviously if we over do this – e.g. by making the customer over-dependent on our systems – then we run the risk of appearing to be competitively manipulative, which is more than a little dangerous. So this carries some health warnings.*

26   Use timing in negotiation to maximise your relative bargaining position.

> *Getting deeper into Porter's Competitive Forces, we now look at how bargaining position can be shifted Vis a Vis customers, suppliers, alliance partners, the vendor or buyer of a business, and other stakeholders. Where you have sussed that a rapid deal isn't coming and their perceived or real pressure to make a deal is then much greater, then you can play time to your advantage and take your time, nice and slow… tantrically…*

27   Manage your own perceived and real urgency to do a deal really well.

> *This is the reverse of the situation we met above in number 26. Be very mindful of the perceived psychological pressure on your side to do a deal, and just try to put that into total suspense – be patient until you see the signs of the other side beginning to sweat.*

28   Always try to maximise the number and quality of your options.

> *Before negotiation, already have researched the array of options that you have available. During negotiation avoid seeing "doing this deal" as the only option and have it very clear in your mind what that gives you in terms of being able to just put any negotiations into suspense – and also have a very clear idea of your "walk-away" conditions. Doing a deal is thus seen very much as a "contingent strategy."*

29   Keep your rivals guessing as long as possible.

> *This is all about the strategic management of time: keep your options open until as late as possible in order to avoid doing something whose wisdom is now a bit tarnished, and also make that decision on the basis of the latest information.*

30 When you move, move with surprise, speed, deception, and with shock and awe.

> *This is straight out of Sun Tzu's* The Art of War: *it is as important often to have a very quick and agile dynamic as having an appropriate strategy in the very first place (as in military strategy).*

Comments on checklists 21 to 30

Much can be done to leverage the competitive context through managing the impact of Porter's Competitive Forces, and in particular bargaining plus timings to maximise value in a cunning way. Above all, decisiveness and being dynamic and determined are often the keys to competitive success.

31 When someone says you can't do something, get even more determined and excited to get around the constraints (the "Joy of Constraints").

> *One of my all-time favourites! Literally, if someone says in a strategy discussion: "oh, we can't do that," or even worse, "we are prohibited from doing that," then I get very excited. I will stop at nothing to get around, go underneath or over the top of a constraint.*

32 If there is some kind of constraint, why does this exist, and how can we get around that?

> *This is the "Deep Dive" behind why something is difficult – maybe inviting a "fishbone analysis" of diagnosing the symptom and the root causes?*

33 Take out the most difficult constraint first.

> *This is taken from "Goal Theory," where to solve a problem you take out the most severe barrier or thing that is stopping you out first. This makes the others progressively easier to loosen.*

34 If we had a "strategic amnesty" would that enable greater creativity?

> *A "Strategic Amnesty" is where you collectively agree to come out with some of the strategic decisions or strategic projects that have been a mixed success or that failed and put them up to learn from. In the process it is useful to have a little bit of fun, too. The proviso is that this is not an opportunity for blame and punishment. This process can really unblock strategic reflection and learning, and may also come up with some Cunning Plans and insights.*

35   What options allow us to achieve a desired result in less time, with lesser cost and difficulty?

>   *This is a sub-set of the idea of the Cunning Plan itself. How do you reconfigure your strategy to be truly especially clever?*

36   What are the options for how to do the strategy? Practise the *Kama Sutra* (once you have decided to do something there can be 100 ways of doing it).

>   *This is an absolutely key checklist to bear continually in mind as it is ever so easy to default to the most obvious way of doing a strategy, particularly when there can be many in the first place to keep in mind!*

37   What are the options for **when** to do the strategy?

>   *There are equally many options regarding timing: a strategy might fail at Time A that might succeed at Time B.*

38   What are the options for **with whom** to do the strategy?

>   *As I have preached to you previously, always look for a range of options rather than one or two, and the same applies to who you do that with, whether that's someone internally, externally, short term or longer term.*

39   What degrees of freedom do we actually have? (i.e. what variables can we play with)?

>   *This is the question behind the "Optopus." "Degrees of freedom" are the dimensions of choice that you have – like which markets, customer segments, and ways of adding value to customer value, different means of adding value. Typically each one of these can give five or more options and even more in combination.*

40   Imagine it is a new business and you have most (but not all) of your Strategic Assets: what strategic options can you come up with?

>   *This is a great way of deconstructing your business. If you take away some of the things you rely and lean upon then this may also give you less baggage to constrain your thinking. For example, if I had no business in the UK, what would my purely global business look like and how would I do more international strategy consulting (i.e. not just executive development)?*

Comments on checklists 31 to 40

This is a very rich sub-set that takes you through the ideas at the core of the Cunning Plan, including the fact that there can be strategic options for what you do, how you do it, when you do it and even with whom you do it. I also showed how to generate some more specific ideas through exploring their degrees of strategic freedom, and through reconfiguring or adding to your base of strategic assets.

41   If you could have just one new strategic asset what would that be, and what could you do with that?

> *This is a most interesting one: where you visualise something that you haven't got, but you can imagine how exciting it would be to bring into your business value system and be a real catalyst.*
>
> *For example this very book itself is one of my Strategic Assets. Also there may be some most interesting spin-offs: e.g. a year before publication I have already floated it with five global executive development companies. When it's out there will be applications for doing conferences, business school courses, international consulting and strategic coaching opportunities.*

42   What move would throw your competitors most off-balance?

> *We are now entering the realms of "Game Theory" where you need to think through the interactive moves of others when formulating your strategy. You can throw off balance both by making an unexpected move, or a bigger move, or a move that they thought you would have done if you were going to by now.*

43   Where, and how, could we hurt our competitors disproportionately relative to any cost to us?

> *Ideally it would also be a move where what you have done, and how you have done it actually damages them more than it does you – financially, anxiety-wise, or both.*

44   How, generally, could you change the rules of the game and, if the rules of the game are changing, how could you bring that forward?

> *This is Game Theory again: it is particularly disturbing to a settled and comfortable competitor to suddenly wake up to find that someone is moving the goal-posts and is acting in contradiction to the prevalent "industry mind-set" (the assumptions, beliefs and expectations shared in the industry). This can give real leverage. And if you have done some scenario storytelling work of the future and if you can see change coming then even though it might be generally disturbing to bring to forward then that option might still be to your advantage if you have a lead.*

45   Where there is politics around something, imagine that doesn't exist: create a "politics-free zone."

> *This is something that you can actually announce explicitly. It comes in especially useful where a strategic issue is particularly sensitive or likely to be contentious.*

46   When you are trying to influence stakeholders, imagine you are telepathic – what's in their attention and greatest concern now?

> *This is a fabulously rich source of insights into the "parallel world" within "strategy" of stakeholder agendas. With practice you become much more aware of these agendas and their interplay generally – and outside the strategic arena. It requires a process of conjecture, inquiry and mental and emotional agility that improves over time and with learning.*

47   Study the ways in which particular stakeholders think and make decisions, and look for the "tipping points" (for making or rejecting a decision).

> *This is more about the decision-making style and process of key stakeholders and complements number 46 above.*

48   What is the optimal time to approach stakeholders or to try to "close the sale?"

> *Timing of influencing can be as important as the influencing strategy itself: try to avoid times when your target is feeling overwhelmed or frustrated or simply in a bad mood. Ask "is it a good or not so good time to talk about X."*

49   If you have low influence over something how can you create more influence?

> *This may seem counterintuitive, just as it might be to challenge the worst and most limiting constraints first. But quite often when you examine the reasons why you feel impotent there are usually a number of clues for getting around these. Some stakeholder analysis here might show you the way.*

50   Forget that anyone might be against the idea, at least during its initial formulation.

> *This one too might seem counterintuitive as stakeholder acceptability is such a fundamental part of the process of evaluating strategic options. But there is a case for setting entrenched resistance to one side. To even think about that would exclude more radical and more effective options for dealing with a strategic issue.*

Comments on checklists 41–50

These fall into two main areas. The first is how you can you use Game Theory to deal with competition. Secondly, how you can be cunning in the way of stakeholder influencing through understanding them better than they understand themselves – their agendas, styles and decision-making processes.

51   Where there is a threat, how can you turn it into an opportunity?

> *This is not an obvious thing to think of at all but it can produce the most astonishing breakthrough ideas: for instance just think if you happened to take the problem that you have a very influential negative stakeholder. There may be just something on their agenda to turn them around to your cause – maybe float that with them and just see what happens?*

52   Where there is a problem, why does it exist and how?

> *Again, when there is any kind of problem by doing some "deep-dive" causal analysis invariably surfaces the need to take a more challenging and fundamental approach to dealing with this, thus inviting what we will call later, "fishbone analysis."*

53 Can you reframe what the problem is really about?

> *An example of this is to look at a problem as an opportunity: but there are many other ways of doing this: looking at it for example as a problem not about one thing, but as another, as a bigger or deeper problem, as a "softer" issue problem rather than as a "harder" issue etc.*

54 Is it actually more than one problem, and by focusing on each sub-problem at a time can we dissolve it away?

> *Quite often a problem isn't a singular one but a multiplicity that each needs a "deep-dive" into – and an exploration of – the interrelationships between them.*

55 Why is any difficult problem actually difficult?

> *Where the problem is particularly intractable then you might just choose to hover over it and ask: "why is this such a difficult problem? ("meta-problem" analysis.)*

56 Can you create "white space": exclusive time to think about the issue so that you get a sufficient and undistracted look at it?

> *Sometimes you just need to take some very quiet meditative space out of all other things so that your attention can achieve singularity and your mind can enter the "flow." I have seen people take cigarette breaks in order to solve a problem at the same time (although personally I wouldn't recommend that – I actually prefer to do a head stand which clears the mind and is not harmful to health!)*

57 If you were to do an "end of the world" workshop – i.e. structured yet creative group work under time pressure as if you were needing to save the world – would that help?

> *This is a most effective ploy to use with a group where you have a lot to do and there are likely to be cognitive, emotional and political resistances to thinking differently and to gaining insights and making judgements. The "end of the world scenario" can create a real sense of urgency.*

58 Alternatively, maybe try some low pressure "play" to arrive at a solution.

> *Sometimes people need something safe, fun and non-threatening to warm themselves up, like a game where there's a prize for "How differently can you think?" (e.g. what uses could you find for a coconut?)*

59 If you can't think of a creative idea, who might?

> *You don't have to be your own exclusive network of creativity – surround yourself with other creative people. Why have a dog and then always be barking yourself? Don't be precious about gathering ideas from others!*

60 Can you find a solution from other walks of life?

> *You may arrive at a solution just through looking at how others have solved that kind of problem in either similar or different places elsewhere.*

Comments on checklists 51 to 60

In these checklists we looked at the importance of reframing the problem, on distancing yourself psychologically from it or, alternatively, blitzing it.

61   Instead of trying to solve the problem head-on, think *what alternative processes are there for actually solving the problem?*

> *I take this (generic) idea from modern physics theory, where breakthroughs have been made by simply devising an alternative way of thinking about the problem. For example doing scenarios and working backwards from the future might be one approach, as would benchmarking outside of the industry, too.*

62   Does going to "what do we really-really want" help to solve the problem? ("Spice Girls")

> *It is a refreshing and immediate way of gaining clarity of purpose and vison.*

63   What's the one Big Option that you have missed?

> *This is the opposite of "what's the one Big Thing that you have missed," and just like the latter often evokes a new idea.*

64   If you write down the problem, do a fishbone of it. Draw a picture. Does this help you get clearer about its structure?

> *This involves simply representing the root causes in the shape of fish bones. Just by doing that picture it allows you to detach and distance yourself from it, to see the interdependencies and to gain some view of what is most/least important.*

65   If you were to imagine yourself hovering high up above the issue in a helicopter, does that help you get clearer?

> *Possibly coupled with a fishbone or similar tool, Helicopter Thinking is an interesting way of making your thinking more agile just through visualizing yourself flying.*

66   If you saw a particularly difficult problem or person through the reverse lens of a telescope what might come out of that?

> *This is another creative visualization. It is really helpful when dealing with a very difficult person indeed by reducing them in size in your visualization it just seems to shrink them in reality. I did that very successfully in court when I was being cross-examined by my ex — very funny, looking back!*

67   How can you take out a competitor(s) by leap-frogging over it/them into the future?

> *This is a classical move in dynamic competitive strategy. Instead of just trying to close the gap with them, why not stretch your thinking to being as far ahead of them as you are now behind?*

68 How can you tap into the emotional value of something, even when it may appear to be a commodity on the surface?

> *We will be expanding on this later: even in fiercely competitive markets there can still be leverage in appealing emotionally to a customer/client – how can you make their experience, particularly how they feel, so much better than others do?*

69 If we had no business or strategy at all, what strategic options might we come up with?

> *This is sometimes called "zero–based thinking": through decluttering your outward facing strategies as they now exist and working from your current strategic assets (plus, maybe some new ones). It is a very refreshing thought experiment.*

70 Where do they do what we would love to do at an amazing level somewhere else in the world?

> *Besides the outside of industry benchmarking, looking at more evolved markets elsewhere in the world and how these operate can give you ideas two to three years ahead.*

Comments on checklists 61 to 70

These were mainly a mixture of two things; first, there were different ways of structuring or looking at problems. Second, there were some interesting and dynamic ways of competing through leap frog strategies, emotional value and zero-based strategies.

71 How can we exploit imperfections within a market?

> *Besides Porter's Five Competitive Forces, it is good, generally, to consider how market imperfections can evolve and be managed to create opportunities for spotting and capturing premium, economic value through industry structure of behavioural factors. These could be, for instance, actual or latent emotional value, intense concentration of a small number of competitors, or through imperfect knowledge. Or it might be identifying a "natural" positioning in the market that simply hasn't yet been occupied.*

72 When should we get out of a business when others still want to get in when it's actually best to exit?

> *Here we are in the land of M&A (Mergers and Acquisitions) – especially divestment: it is often a Cunning Plan when you see a market about to mature to seize the opportunity of others entering, wanting to expand to sell up.*

73 Before you start to be creative, give yourself the Formal Permission to think differently.

> *It may seem a bit odd to incentivise your thinking this way, but as soon as you start to think about something the assumed natural limits to thought will inevitably kick in: give yourself a Strategic Holiday!*

74   When an issue is complex, continually be on the look-out for promising "lines of enquiry" – imagine you are a police detective.

> *This is a great metaphor to use. For instance when I am facilitating on strategic cost issues I feel that I am constantly sniffing for hopeful leads that will bring us to a prize. I have been even known to role-play the famous U.S. television detective, Lieutenant Colombo (younger people please Google!)*

75   Imagine that the problem isn't yours, but someone else's, especially when it is very important to you.

> *Much stickiness of problem solving is around the fact that you own the problem. If you let go of emotional attachment to it this can double your Strategic IQ.*

76   Leave the problem for a while and come back to it, maybe from a slightly different angle.

> *If you have time, back off the problem and reconstruct it again sometime later. Not only will you get the benefits of the working on it by your unconscious mind, but you will for sure see it slightly differently a second or third time. Maybe try to collect some fresh data in the meantime to test and stimulate your thinking.*

77   Imagine you are a consultant advising yourself.

> *This is cheap strategy consultancy at its best! Not only is this perspective-altering, but it can lead you to much more radical options.*

78   Ask your customers to think about what your strategic options might be.

> *Customers are a very rich source of input, but we are naturally shy to ask them what they think we can do. Don't worry, they will feel flattered as long as you tell them why you are doing it.*

79   If you are really, really stuck, send the problem to your unconscious mind and ask it to come up with a solution in the next day.

> *It works! When I suggest this people usually smile. Inside I think, "they are feigning interest," but they won't try it because they are not sure it will do any-thing, or because it's too spooky. It takes a few seconds only to "send" it to your unconscious mental processing machine – what's the cost of trying this? Well, technically nothing.*

80   What value would you get if you spent, say, half the money if you were to deploy that or, say, double the money so that the extra is used for doing things differently?

> *This is similar to zero–based strategic thinking, except here we are simply stratifying our resource base to wrest out the effects of diminishing or increasing returns to scale.*

Comments on checklists 71 to 80

These were some eclectic ways of dislodging old thinking patterns – e.g. by getting customer input, imagining you are a consultant, looking for lines of enquiry, stratifying your resources, and even asking your unconscious mind to "take the strain."

81 Simplify the process.

> *From Business Process Engineering – or "BPR" – simplification can come up with very interesting, alternative business models.*

82 If you have reached a "Cunning Plan," what last thing would make this a "stunning plan?"

> *As we covered in the* Blackadder *story, you can even go higher up the creativity spiral with the "stunning plan" – where there's just one last ingredient added to reach "strategic bliss."*

83 If you were to visually sketch some matrices of variables, like products, markets, channels, geography, customer types, and different customer needs (in different combinations), what new opportunities (in the blank squares) would you come up with?

> *This is an extension of mapping what businesses we are in/might be in, but with six different variables.*

84 What is the bait that might turn on stakeholder support as the strategy is now irresistible?

> *Focusing on the turn-ons, can we introduce some factors that will be a positive tipping point?*

85 What are the turn-offs which are preventing stakeholder buy in, and how can you take these out?

> *Focusing on the turn-offs here, can we neutralise some of the negative factors that will thus act as positive tipping points?*

86 What are the options for influencing strategies that might be cunning – e.g. deciding who to influence, when and through what communication media etc.? (Use the Influencing Optopus in Chapter 10, which is a diagrammatic representation of the various, eight, different angles that influencing can take.)

> *Invariably there are a myriad of potential influencing strategies that you may not realise unless these are explored through all their dimensions of freedom in a systematic way.*

87 Working the analysis back from the minimum stakeholder positioning needed to move forward, how could you modify the strategy so that the existing stakeholder positions shift to that space?

> *This is in effect a clever version of "break–even" analysis.*

88   What happens if you blend different options from the "Optopus" in both complementary and (separately) not so obvious combinations?

   This is a similar point to the one of the "Influencing Optopus," except that this deals with dimensions such as market sectors, customer segments, target customer value added and the means of adding that value, etc.

89   Try to see what happens when you take an option that initially seems unattractive on the Strategic Option Grid: how can you re-engineer it to be e.g. more financially attractive, less difficult and uncertain and more acceptable?

90   For any plan that you are about to embark upon, what is the plausible pre-mortem story? How did it fail and fail badly, and what can you learn from this?

   You may well laugh at this one but it is seriously worth doing; not only can strategies be formulated by working backwards from a future of delight but also from a future of failure – so we can avoid that!

Comments on checklists 81–90

In the above section we mainly re-engineered how something is done even where *prima facie* the option may have not looked that good initially.

91   Write down all the features of your mind-set (beliefs, expectations and assumptions) and throw them away (maybe burn them?); ask what the issue really is and explore options as if you have had strategic amnesia.

   This is the most generic and extreme version of managing your mind-set.

92   Allow yourself to have ideas, even ones that may seem initially silly, stupid or simplistic.

   This is a classic brainstorming formula.

93   Allow yourself to think out loud (after gaining permission).

   This is possibly a way of venting an idea stream in such a way that through talking out loud it allows a better flow. But also, this may be used through a dialogue with someone whose opinion you trust. Or, it may have applications where you are trying to influence others and would like to surface some potentially unpleasant thoughts for them to consider, so by getting permission ahead of that you gain attention.

94   Never criticise without being constructive at the early ideas generation and formulation stage – "Build as well as Challenge" (Diageo).

   This is a great process rule: being overly critical or evaluative too early on can kill valuable ideas.

95 Agree to the "P" behaviours you don't want to have: e.g. "political," "personal," "picky," "prickly," "pedantic," "procrastinating" etc.

> *This one truly saves lives! On the rare occasions that I have not put this in place early on I wished I had!*

96 Research things similar to the type of strategy that you are looking at and consider why they might have failed in the past: how could they be done differently?

> *There are rich bodies of knowledge around pretty well every type of strategic management issue that you can and should dip into particularly if as a team you are new and inexperienced in an area e.g. acquisitions, alliances, franchises, implementing the Balanced Score Card, BPR, Lean, culture change, international business development strategies (and by country) etc., etc. Use them!*

97 Where you need more data to evaluate options, what is the cunning way of collecting that data in the least amount time, with the least amount of cost and uncertainty?

> *"Cunning" doesn't just apply to the actual formulation of options but also to data collection. For instance just ask: "what are the options for doing it in 20% of the time?"*

98 Where something appears very difficult to do, look for the natural enablers in the situation.

> *A not-so-obvious one: as soon as we have labelled something as "difficult" that will bias our thinking. But if we can just park that mind-set and then look for things that are there in the situation but they are latent, unused, not activated – it is pretty unusual not to find anything. For instance this could be things like possible positive staff motivation for "better change", the fear of losing even more jobs – to be averted, or natural leaders in the ranks that can be brought forward to help lead forward.*

99 Imagine you are some famous and charismatic figure who could read inside a situation immediately and cut through the ambiguity: how would you see it and what options might you as that person come up with?

> *You might try, for example, imagining you are a Buddhist Monk or the Dalai Lama, Genghis Khan, Nelson Mandala, Barack Obama, Warren Buffet, Jack Welch, or Sir Alan Sugar.*

100 Remember that getting cunning ideas requires space, time, freedom from distractions, play and fun (find "White Space"). For example go for a strategic drive. Jump in your car and drive around randomly until you have at least one really good cunning idea!

> *This is, again, a plea to set the tone and the climate for playful thinking – this will be helped for sure by going offsite or at least somewhere that's a bit different.*

Comments on checklists 91–100

These mainly surround the creativity process of, for example, jettisoning mind-sets, allowing the flow of ideas – even "stupid" ones – without premature criticism, cunning data collection and simply giving yourself creative space and time.

Now for the final one:

101 I was emptying the water from our Hot Tub and it wasn't quite finished when it started going dark, so I let it go until the next day. It was rather windy too, so I thought it would be nicer to finish the next day. To let the water out I unscrewed the cap at the bottom of the tank and placed it nearby.

The next day I finished mopping up the remaining water – a mistake as it was now icy and my fingers and feet were numb. I got the hose pipe ready, but... where is that little cap? – GONE! Nowhere on the decking anywhere and not in the shed where all the tub chemicals are kept.

I really didn't want to be spending at least £15 on a new one including postage and waiting a week to use the tub, so I went around the house looking for caps that looked similar. I found one from a chemical jar and, although it had a child security feature, tried to use it and it seemed to go on nicely.

Unfortunately I left the tub filling up for nearly an hour to find it was leaking at the cap a bit. Oh dear, my tactical solution needed replacing with a more strategic plan – swallow the loss and get a proper new cap. But now, of course the cap wasn't coming off!

I was deeply regretting my tactical move. I got my entire toolkit on the job and managed to eventually get it off without damaging the pipe it was secured to, but it was very tricky with just a small hack saw, pliers and a chisel!

I decided to get into my more "helicopter" mind-set and detach myself from the issue before going back into it again. Our cleaner was in the kitchen, and giving myself a "strategic amnesty" I confessed to her what I had done.

She said: "Well it must be there." I said: "Yes, I haven't asked the fairies to get on the job yet – that usually works. I don't understand it. I know it has been windy but it could be anywhere now."

She replied: "Of course, when you have ordered a new one you will find it, as it was there on the grass all the time!"

I then walked off in the direction of the Hot Tub and this time trained my eyes on the grass – and look! – a small black cap that was six feet from the decking!

The Cunning Checklist – number 101 – is thus:

> *"When a problem is very difficult and complex don't always mirror that in your solution; look for the simple and easy option!"*

An overarching theme: abandoning or shifting mind-sets

Looking back over the 101 ways of being cunning I reflect that quite a lot of them involved abandoning or shifting your mind-set as a preliminary activity. For instance, in number 4 you forget you ever worked for your company and in 5 in your industry, too. In number 6 you imagine you are an alien. In number 8 you are a competitor and in number 9 you are a new entrant. Finally, in number 77 you become a STRATEGY Consultant advising yourself.

Letting go of mind-sets is a crucial strategic skill. It mirrors the process of cognitive behavioural therapy where individuals let go of beliefs about themselves and their worlds. Recent examples in my own business of instances where I have found shedding of mind-sets to be incredibly helpful were:

- *Mind-Set 1*: to get strategy consulting work you need to be invited in as a result of someone who already knows you: **False** – in a pilot of four approaches to CEOs only one didn't want to meet me.
- *Mind-Set 2:* you can't get the attention of CEO's since you have to go through their PA's, who act as their gatekeepers: **False** – create a pleasant and warm relationship with their PA's, then you can bring them on board and they can guide you in.
- *Mind-Set 3:* it is now virtually impossible to create Visiting Teaching relationships with business schools as they are all in-sourcing with Full Timers: **False** – I now have relationships with several different business schools!
- *Mind-Set 4*: it is easier to get Executive Development via training intermediaries than going direct: **False** – many of these intermediaries are not really viable given the lack of overseas market demand, their high fixed and variable costs and profit margins, and their client influencing and proposal formulation skills. Also, if I forage in a cunning way I can get some really interesting opportunities – e.g. by re-contacting old clients that have moved around now and are in senior positions!
- *Mind-Set 5*: I am really not going to find a better brand than the one I have had for 27 years "Cambridge Corporate Development" (I moved from Cambridge over twenty years ago!): **False** – in the 45 seconds between thinking about that and parking in Lidl a very plausible candidate popped up from my subconscious mind: "Strategy and Corporate Development" (Remember number 79: "If you are really, really stuck, send the problem to your unconscious mind and ask it to come up with a solution").

Nowhere in the world is the influence of mind-sets more marked than in sport. Consider the following contrasting mind-sets:

A tale of two teams: Arsenal and Barcelona

1)   *Arsenal v Bayern Munich*

In March 2017, Arsenal, who I support, played their Bogey team for the third time in about seven years in the European Football Champions League – Bayern Munich – who is an awesome team. Each time Arsenal has lost.

There are two "legs" to play – one away and one at home. Game 1: Arsenal loses their Captain, Laurent Koscielny, a pivotal player in defence through injury. Arsenal loses much belief. Bayern run rings around them. Arsenal scores just one goal against Bayern Munich's 5-1 to Bayern.

They then needed four goals to match Bayern in the second leg. And mustn't let in one: if they let one in they need to score six due to a quaint rule about how away goals count more.

Game 2: the home game at the Emirates Stadium in London: Arsenal plays very well and is controlling the game for 58 minutes and scores one goal! It is 2–5 on aggregate for both the two games (the scores away and at home are combined). They just need three more!

Arsenal's mind-set was "we can get back our goal deficit." But then their Captain Koscielny commits a foul. A penalty is given. Bayern scores, but in a bizarre decision Koscielny gets sent off! A mortal wound!

Arsenal's mind-set now shifts to: "We are never going to win it now as we lost one of our very few players of mental strength" (and simultaneously) "we must still attack rather than minimise the damage."

Bayern Munich then scored another four goals, making it another 2–5 score, or 2–10 on aggregate for both games (Arsenal, 2): *this was the worst score ever by a British team in the Champions League.*(See Chapter 10 for more on the stakeholder fall-out at Arsenal afterwards.)

2) *Barcelona v. PSG (Paris St Germain) – "Taste the Difference"!*

Game 1 in Paris: PSV dominates with Barcelona's star players not seemingly having turned up to play a challenging game, and the score is an embarrassing home defeat for Barcelona. The score is 4–0 to PSV.

In the second game Barcelona has to score four to match and five to win.

Game 2: Barcelona is now wide awake and dominant and scores two goals in the first half. Their mind-set is "we can win – indeed WILL Win. We are just too strong."

Second half: Barcelona scores another to make it 4–3 on aggregate. Then disaster strikes for Barcelona: PSV scores so Barcelona now has to score with hardly any time left at all! Barcelona's mind-set is now, **"We can still win! It's not over until the fat lady sings!"**

Barcelona scores another two! We are in the last few minutes of injury time; their goalkeeper joins the strikers up front; Barcelona's mind-set is "**they are crumbling – we can still nick it.**" They have built up such a dynamic pressure of play and such a dynamic mind-set that they are going to score. Seconds remain – Barcelona scores! All their fans go crazy, the TV commenters jump out of their chairs and one former England striker, Michael Owen, runs round the studio like a madman! The final score is 6–1 or 6–5 on aggregate.

You will probably not see a Champions league game like that for another 30 years. Make that 50!

But contrast the mind-sets of Arsenal and Barcelona: Arsenal exited in part due to their brittle beliefs about themselves and imploded under pressure.

Barcelona faced a similar chasm against PSV after conceding four away goals. I don't think it is just about raw skill but about their combined mental and physical strength: **especially their** mind-set.

At Barcelona, all of their top players stepped up; their three-pronged strike force of Messi, Suarez and Neymar showed up with Roberto, who nicked the winner.

What this case study shows is just how important mind-sets are in strategy, and how insidious they can be aligned with underlying beliefs.

Using the Cunning Checklists

One thing to do is to write up the main checklists that are likely to apply to a particular strategic issue on a flipchart or white board. This can then be used to stimulate thinking about the strategic options alongside the "Optopus." Or you can look at a number of ideas that are interrelated so that you get a more focused, creative take on a general "line of enquiry." For example, "alien thinking" is related to:

- Make things ultra-convenient to buy for the customer.
- Work backwards from the future (time travelling).
- How, generally, could you change the rules of the game and, if the rules of the game are changing, how could you bring that forward?
- If you were to imagine yourself hovering high up above the issue in a Helicopter, does that help you get clearer?

The more you apply these checklists, the more you are programming your mind to think in a lateral way rather than a strictly linear way. Truly, with regular practice these will lift up your ability to be innovative and creative by two orders of magnitude.

Summary and conclusion

Cunning Thinking (and Planning) has a very different dynamic to the more deductive steps that are characteristic of conventional strategic planning. The human mind needs to be freed to think about not just what is immediately in front of it, but what can also be created, changed and deleted from that field of attention. If the mind isn't naturally gifted is such skills or systematically trained in them then the planning process does seem predestined to limit itself to producing average plans.

Key insights and learning lessons from Chapter 4

I felt that the best way of distilling the key insights of this chapter was for me to simply list my favourite 20 items – not an easy thing to decide!

1   Remember, never try to go direct from problem diagnosis to solution; always go through the land of options ("Winnie the Pooh").
3   Work backwards from your desired result.
6   Imagine that you are actually an alien!
11 Have the "out of body experience" of being a customer, an alliance partner, a supplier or regulator.
13 Deeply understand customers' buying processes and criteria.
28 Always try to maximise the number and quality of your options.
31 When someone says you can't do something, get even more determined and excited to get round the constraint (the "Joy of Constraints").
36 What are the options for how to do the strategy? Practise the *Kama Sutra* (once you have decided to do something there can be 100 ways of doing it).
55 Why is any difficult problem actually difficult?
61 Instead of trying to solve the problem head-on, think *what alternative processes there are for solving the problem?*
62 Does going to "what do we really-really want" help to solve the problem? ("Spice Girls")
64 If you write down the problem, do a fishbone of it. Draw a picture. Does this help you get a lot clearer about its structure?
65 If you were to imagine yourself hovering high up above the issue in a helicopter, does that help you get clearer?
69 It we had no business or strategy at all, what strategic options might we come up with?
77 Imagine you are a consultant advising yourself.
82 If you have reached a "Cunning Plan," what last thing would make this a "stunning plan?"
84 What is the bait that might turn on stakeholder support as the strategy is now irresistible?

86 What are the options for influencing strategies that might be cunning – e.g. deciding who to influence, when and through what communication media etc.? (Use the Influencing Optopus in Chapter 10, which is a diagrammatic representation of the various, eight, different angles that influencing can take.)

91 Write down all the features of your mind-set (beliefs, expectations and assumptions) and throw them away (maybe burn them?); ask what the issue really is and explore options as if you have had strategic amnesia on that.

Reader exercise

• For one issue, using the Cunning Checklists, what is your *Cunning Plan*?

5 From static to dynamic competitive strategy

Life is a myriad of curves that shape experience, powered by the fuel of time.

–Tony G

Introduction

In *Demystifying Strategy* (2012), I distinguished between six key perspectives on strategy:

- conceptual
- cognitive
- emotional
- political and influencing
- processual
- implementation aspects.

But what was missing that is added by this book is **the Dynamic**, *which is another dimension of all of these.*

Within this chapter, ***which is the heart of this book***, we now look at some of the key dynamic tools which we can draw on to develop dynamic competitive strategy. I begin with what is called in science and mathematics, "vector analysis," which enables us to do a "deep-dive" into the outer layers of the "strategic onion" (PEST, growth drivers, Porter's, to give overall environmental attractiveness). I then take you on a journey through a variety of dynamic curves of different variables over time; for instance the market attractiveness over time, and the competitive advantage over time. There are also some further models that are drawn from systems thinking, such as interdependency models – e.g. for Porter's Five Competitive Forces and for competences.

Game theory is then introduced to the mix so that we never forget that it is arguably as important, or maybe even more important, to explore the possible and likely moves of competitors as it is to develop our own strategies. At this juncture we draw in some key and timely lessons from Sun Tzu's *The Art of War*.

Our next port of call is the phenomenon of the disrupters, which has become more topical in management circles through the use of new technologies. But it is not confined just to that – for example, Lidl, in grocery supermarkets, is not particularly high tech, but it is a disruptor, and likewise Metrobank in the UK. Such new players reduce the barriers to entry that have traditionally protected many markets. I also deal with the dynamics of recognition and adaptation lags.

Finally I return to systemic bases of competitive advantage in an evolutionary context with a most unusual case study of a strange but awesome animal called the "honey badger."

Core tools of dynamic competitive strategy: dynamic vector analysis – force field analysis

One of the things we were taught when I was doing my MBA was that one could represent any change as a series of forces and depict the enabling forces and the constraining forces as arrows. These were drawn in proportion to their importance and strength pro rata as vectors, as in mathematics and science.

When as an independent consultant I started to do change management many, many moons ago, I found that this technique (see Figure 5.1 for a change management version of it) was found extremely helpful by managers. In its original formulation by Kurt Lewin (1936), (over 70 years ago) it was often shown at 90 degrees to the picture, which is on Figure 7.1. I found that whilst this fitted well on flipchart paper, to get a good view of the balance of forces you had to almost lie down on the ground to appreciate it, so it's best the other way around as in Figure 5.1.

Figure 5.1 shows a generic picture of a change management initiative where there are 50% more enablers numerically than constraining forces, and these on

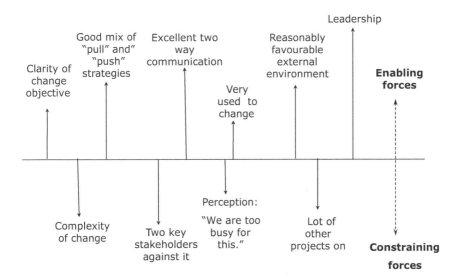

Figure 5.1 Force Field Analysis for Change Management

average are around 30% more influential. That all makes for what I would call a "medium difficult" challenge as ideally you need around twice the weight of all the enabling force relative to the constraining force to make it less than challenging.

The balance of these forces is a predictor of the speed of the change and its likely success.

Although Force Field proved invaluable during change facilitation, I also found that one had to be extremely disciplined about its use. Managers would tend to throw in all kinds of things – both those that were supposed to go in, such as the things in the change process and context which made it easier or harder to do, but also the benefits and costs of the change: oh dear that's wrong. You can have a very attractive change that is virtually impossible to implement!

So my golden rule is:

- You are only allowed to put the (net) benefits once and if and only if they are both perceived by key stakeholders then this motivation is a true enabling force. So, on the day, people are actively saying to each other: "we are really wanting this a lot so we must carry on."

So in the Barcelona v. PSG football case in Chapter 4, the attractiveness of avoiding getting knocked out is an enabling force at 86 minutes *because all the players are thinking about that and visualizing the crowd going mental if they can get three goals in seven minutes* (which is what actually happened). The fact that it would be beneficial to win needs translating into actual motivation to be an enabling force!

In my book *Implementing Strategic Change* (1993), I showed how this technique could be applied to all strategy implementation too, and not just to change management.

But a further leap forward was to create a more complete and integrated strategic thinking and implementation process. So I simply put change management tools into the strategy implementation process (see Figure 5.2 to create Model 2 in Chapter 1, which shows tools we have or are about to cover).

You will see that in the external analysis that I include not just PEST analysis and Porter's five forces (from Chapter 1), but also a further tool, "Growth Drivers"(Grundy 1994). This was a missing link for me, and I found its invention to be a crucial step to fill in the gaps in previous systems. For not only do we need to get our heads around the really big picture of the macro environment – things like the economy, technology etc. – but we also need something that helps us with market growth dynamics, before we ever get to the competitive structure and dynamics a la Michael Porter.

Just as with force field analysis there are a couple of rules for doing growth driver analysis:

- You need to clearly define over what time period this analysis is covering.
- The length of the line (positive or negative) is a function of how big a role that factor plays in either generating more sales volumes or higher prices (as a growth driver), or as reducing sales volumes or prices.

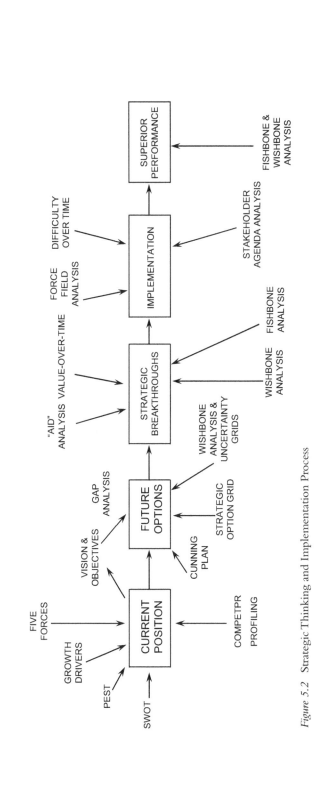

Figure 5.2 Strategic Thinking and Implementation Process

- Where there is a force that ensures that a market of this kind exists, but it is not currently either increasing or decreasing sales volumes or prices, then it would be misleading to show it as either a growth driver or brake. Whilst it may have played that role in the past it is not active at the present time.
- Where the length of any force is in dispute this calls for some empirical data gathering or estimation.
- Where something is a potential growth driver or brake this can be shown as a dotted arrow.

In Figure 5.3 we look at the UK funerals market. Whilst over the fifteen years from 2000 to 2015 market volumes had been shrinking, in 2016 the bigger UK players reported increases in volumes; a suggested cause is the increase in deaths through Alzheimer's. The industry is soft on price, the explanation for this being that there are no substitutes and demand is inelastic and if anything there is an increased preparedness to invest in respect for deceased relatives. Statistics suggest that industry inflation has been running at 6% per annum, although I am not sure that this may be exaggerated in order to underpin demand for pre-need planned funerals.

According to general industry sources, there is a growth in the sale of extras including memorials, and I have added the fact that estates almost certainly would have increased over the last five years due to house prices and over the last year due to the stock market. Balancing this, I am suggesting that increasingly the way that nursing home costs work is that many old people are forced by government to use up their equity to fund it; this growth brake may not as yet have fully kicked in.

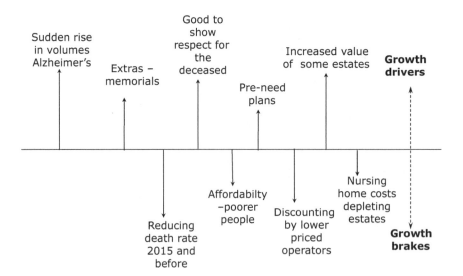

Figure 5.3 Growth Drivers: the Funeral Market

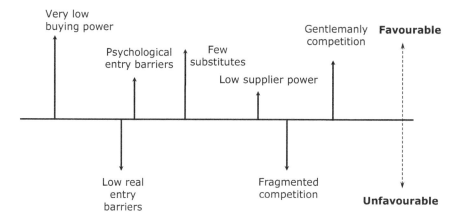

Figure 5.4 Competitive Force Field Analysis: Funerals

So overall Figure 5.3 shows a robust and healthy industry, and moreover one that seems very stable.

There are some sources of concern in the form of lower priced competition, actually to combat discounting at the lower end. Whilst this hasn't had a big effect yet, this is a worrying sign. Indeed, my take on the industry is that there is competitive space for a disruptive discounter, especially one with a web-based service: watch this space.

This analysis only took about fifteen minutes to research and to sketch out and another 10 minutes to do a PowerPoint picture for, once again demonstrating the speed of strategic analysis given these tools.

Besides using the vector analysis format to depict growth drivers, it can also be used to prioritise and evaluate Porter's Competitive Forces, too. For instance, take a look at Figure 5.4 drawn again for the funerals industry.

The starting point is to decide whether on balance the force is more positive or more negative. Next these lines are drawn in proportion to their perceived positivity or negativity multiplied by their perceived relative importance. To decide the relative length of the lines demands debate and judgment – plus asking the question "why do you think that?" – ideally done in a small group. If you want to be even more scientific, or gain an even deeper understanding, each individual force can be broken down on a separate picture into sub-forces.

In Figure 5.4 we see entry barriers broken down into two sub-forces; this can be helpful where a competitive force is going in two directions at the same time.

We can also apply the same thinking to the "PEST" factors – the political, economic, social and technological factors driving the macro environment. As these have relatively limited impact in funerals, I show these in Figure 5.5 relative to the UK supermarket industry in 2017. Here it impacts negatively on costs and

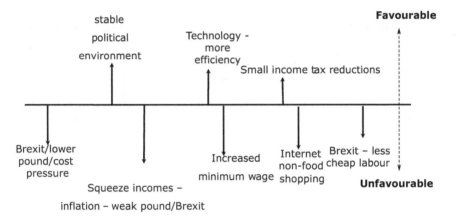

Figure 5.5 PEST Factors: UK Supermarkets 2017

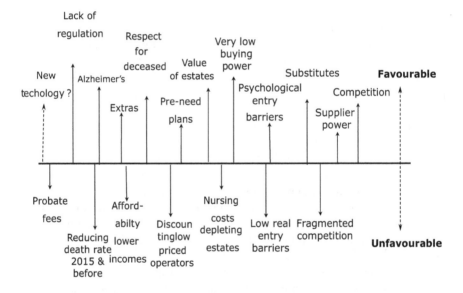

Figure 5.6 External Forces – Attractiveness: Funerals

on consumer incomes through the fall in the pound. Interestingly, before I did this picture I hadn't really appreciated that the PEST factors were on balance so relatively unfavourable – even though I am currently consulting in that industry!

Finally we can bring it all together by presenting all three outer parts of the "strategic onion" – the PEST, the growth drivers and the Five Competitive Forces on a grand external attractiveness forces picture. The first time this was done was with Goodrich Aerospace which repairs and reconditioned jet engines and is a global leader in the field. We start off at the left with the PEST, then the growth drivers in the middle and the Five Competitive Forces to the right. I revert to the example of funerals for that (see Figure 5.6).

In Figure 5.6 we have added the positive force that less regulation plays in the funerals business. Offsetting that are the changes in probate fees from April 2017, which increase the other costs of dealing with a death and also because of likely difficulties and delays of processing payments, for these are likely to complicate funerals administration and management.

I have also included a dotted line for possible new technologies in the form of greener ways of disposing of the body that might increase prices and margins, although the effect of the internet might go the other way: watch this space!

Overall, however, the balance of forces is positive, making this a rather attractive industry.

Indeed, one can imagine doing this for some even higher order economic model: for instance for the economy. In fact I originally did this for the UK economy as long back as 1988 when I was contemplating setting up my business. The economy had been booming for a number of years, and I was mindful of setting myself up as an independent consultant only to sail into the teeth of a recession. I drew the shifting vectors for things like industry and consumer confidence, the dynamics of the political cycle, the government sector borrowing requirement, the potential for the overheating of the economy and the possible impact on exports through a world downturn. I felt that a recession was no more than three to four years away.

In fact the first signs of the recession were in the autumn of 1990 – two and three quarter years later – it was to be a very deep recession and the recovery only really gained momentum around three years later. It was interesting to be up with, if not ahead of, economic forecasters by using my brain and a piece of paper: I wondered how big the department of economic forecasting was in the British Treasury?

It is time now to shift our focus to another way of specially representing dynamic shifts in strategic variables that takes me back to the mathematics that I once overdosed on at school: through looking effectively at graphs with "X" and "Y" axes.

Dynamic strategy curves "Amazon's responsiveness – what a little miracle in my life"

With a dynamic strategy curve, the variable that you wish to represent is depicted on the Y axis and the time dimension is shown on the X axis. Let's begin with the very first one that I came across when doing some teaching at Henley Business School in 1992, the "difficulty-over-time curve." Figure 5.7 shows this with a graphic which typifies a lot of strategic change projects.

The difficulty starts off medium and then climbs. Then it gets a bit easier, which is comforting but in a dangerously, illusive way. It then takes a turn for the worse and gets even more difficult. If one were to draw our stamina-over-time curve, this is likely to actually decline through the cumulative expenditure of effort.

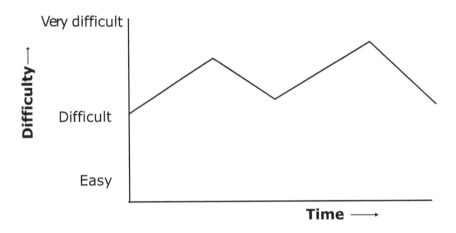

Figure 5.7 Difficulty-Over-Time Curve

Theme park case study: a "double dipper" curve

An amusing illustration of similar dynamics comes from a holiday that I had many years ago when my son, James, was about 10. We went to California for a two week holiday and the first few days we stayed in Los Angeles and went to some theme park rides. I recall that the parks were really quiet as it was during the week and the US kids had just gone back to school. We had a free run with zero queues early that day and straight away made a bee-line to a modest sized roller-coaster.

We eagerly boarded the roller-coaster – the little one and there was no one else on it. The one that was next door to it, and I remember thinking *"I am so glad we aren't going on that one"* – as when I was seven I went on a giant roller coaster at a theme park in Manchester called "Belle View" and hadn't realized that I had got on a giant one – I was white when I came off. I was petrified.

We came around the first bend and went up and down a bit, relaxing and a bit of fun. Then to my horror we started going up an apparently endless hill; it was at that moment I realised that there weren't just two roller-coasters: there was a little one and a big one and one Giant One!

I desperately tried to put myself into a state of mindfulness and tracked my "fear-over-time curve" which was now rising asymptotically (i.e. in a progressively steeper and steeper curve). I urged James to cling on as we dropped like a fighter bomber at an air show from a lofty height down and down and down, twisting and turning; then up and up and up…my fear-over-time curve had peaked – I was incapable of more. I remember thinking that if we did get thrown out then there was no one around so we might only get discovered the next day and they would pass our deaths off as an L.A. mugging!

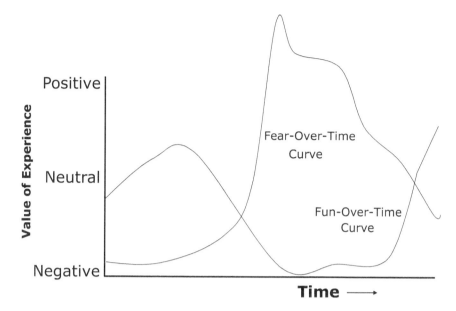

Figure 5.8 Fear-Over-Time and Enjoyment-Over-Time Curves on a Los Angeles Roller Coaster Ride

Then I detected a second curve kicking in: a "fun-over-time curve." About twenty seconds later as I knew we had survived this crossed with my fear-over-time curve (see Figure 5.8).

There are several morals to this story:

- First, any unexpected worsening of a variable-over-time curve that occurs after you had felt things were improving can really throw you, as in the double peaking curve in Figure 5.8.
- Second, there may be more than one variable at work; for example invariably within every strategy there is invariably both a difficulty-over-time curve, and also a value-over-time curve.
- Third, to manage these variables effectively it is really helpful to practice "strategic mindfulness."

Following on from these initial curves – which are at the heart of the thinking of dynamic competitive strategy – I would like to share with you a number of interesting dynamic external strategic tools. First of all we have the "Attractiveness-Over-Time Curve," which relates to a particular market. This can be cut either just for one of its three main segments – the PEST, the growth drivers, the Competitive Forces – or for all three. In Figure 5.9 I have opted to do this just for the market attractiveness due to the Competitive Forces alone.

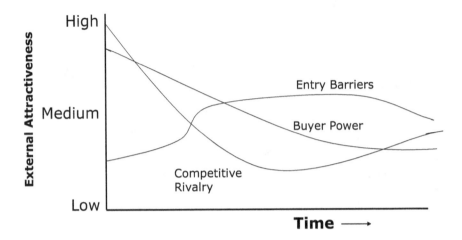

Figure 5.9 Competitive Forces: Attractiveness-Over-Time Curve: Breakdown

This shows how over a number of years this can alter quite significantly, due to industry life cycle effects, to changes in competitive structures, and due to learning effects of rivals, buyers, suppliers and entrants. It will also be impacted by the natural erosion of imperfect market characteristics by competition, less the moves by innovative players to generate new and more powerful value propositions through radical technology, brand appeal, product rejuvenation and channel, supply chain, and operational improvements.

In Figure 5.10 I now go down a level further to plot the micro level of the individual forces on an X-Y graph. I only show the most important three:

- Buyer power
- Competitive rivalry
- Entry barriers.

Notice that over a period of say five to ten years they will not always move in tandem, and over time, *ceteris paribus* will tend to show a decline in overall external attractiveness. *Notice that we are not at this juncture considering the very specific attractiveness to us – e.g. on the basis that we can meet those market needs, really, really well, or due to their fit otherwise.* That comes in separately in considering our relative competitive position and related things.

In these three curves, which probably mirror the evolution of some, but not all, markets they suggest:

- Entry barriers are typically low at first and thus not affording much protection (and thus "low" external attractiveness), rising as the barriers build but then being eroded in maturity as vulnerabilities to disruptive entrants might increase.

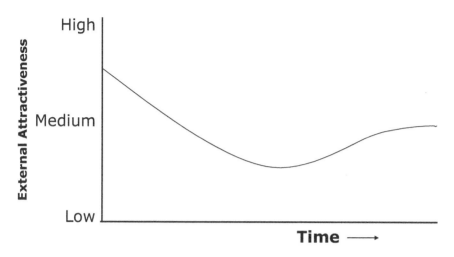

Figure 5.10   Competitive Forces: Attractiveness-Over-Time Curve

- Buyer power starts at a low level (so reversing that from an incumbent's perspective is "good news", "attractive"). Buyer power then strengthening over time thus eroding this attractiveness.
- Competitive rivalry low at first (so that's "very attractive"), then rapidly increasing (lower attractiveness), then reversing as there is some consolidation and as players mutually limit the intensity of competition by tacit understanding or just expectations.

Whilst these curves are not new to me (I published those many years ago) they may seem very novel to my readers, even with MBAs. Business schools for the most part preach the gospel of competitive analysis to Porter's five forces and then it stops. But Porter's diagram is very static! We need a lot more, particularly in the far more turbulent world that we now find ourselves in.

Another concern might be: "so how would I draw these curves with any degree of meaningfulness?" Well for one thing it is always best to do this in small groups or at least in twos. Following that, have a go and then show it afterwards to someone else who is well-informed about the market. Surf features and reports on Google. Ask people for their opinion who are "in the know."

The other way at getting better and better at it is to practise monitoring changes in variables in real time, and after the event compare and contrast the outturn with what you expected; learn from differences and from there causality.

Besides the purely dynamic dimension of these "over-time" curves another dimension is that of where you are within the "competitive landscape." For things like Porter's, growth Drivers and PEST analysis are highly variable depending on where you are on the continuum of the high versus the low end of the market. In Figure 5.11 I look at a sample of UK retailers from the very

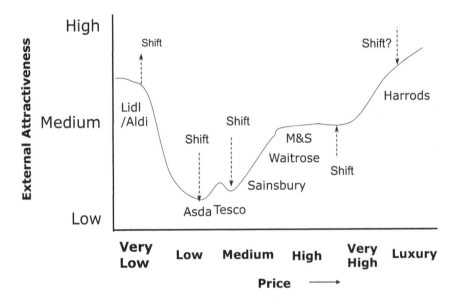

Figure 5.11 The Competitive Landscape: External Attractiveness – UK Retailers

"low" end to the highest. In this particular curve I heavily weight the competitive forces as the UK is (of 2017) experiencing relatively homogenous rates of market growth – with the exception of the discounters at the "very low" end as they are seizing relative market share.

The idea behind the "competitive landscape" is that to ask "is industry X or Y relatively more or less competitively attractive?" as Porter did in his seminal work *Competitive Advantage* in 1980 is a rather foggy question. For all industries have considerable variation, like for example the management training market which can attract per diem rates of anything between £300 and £10000 or more depending on who it is for, who it is delivered by and where and who delivers it!

I have often likened that to the question of "Is England an attractive country?" Well, we have some incredibly beautiful spots, like the Cotswolds, the Lake District, Kent, parts of London, Bath, Cambridge, Tunbridge Wells, and then you have less gorgeous spots like Slough and of course Swindon, with its incredible obstacle course of multiple mini roundabouts which sometimes go clockwise and sometimes counter–clockwise (the "eighth wonder of the world!").

Look now at Figure 5.11. Notice how Harrods occupies a nice competitive space protected by enormous entry barriers and because of its sheer exclusivity and its very low bargaining power with the customers. But sitting at that high end it is obviously a candidate for competitive erosion. I show this possible shift as a dotted line downward arrow and similar ones going up and down in different regions of the picture, adding a dynamic element.

At the medium to higher end are two retailers – Waitrose and M&S (Marks and Spencer's) foods – who have premium quality products but who are pricier and also offer a better feel of customer service. I was attracted into M&S on a "25% wine offer" for example recently to find that only a few wines were in my everyday wine budget of £6 a bottle, and thus even with the 25% off I was paying the same as similar quality wine from Sainsbury and Tesco, on my judgement. M&S food is very luxurious and good quality but still maybe too pricey.

But around this hilly part of the landscape there are good earnings for the players. But at the lower medium to medium end and just below it gets a lot worse, with Tesco and ASDA really struggling through 2015 to 2016. My map plainly shows the overconcentration of players in this zone just as customers have migrated either upwards for their luxury shop to Waitrose and M&S and to the discounters Lidl and Aldi for their more basic shopping. These stores who also sell a lot of non-food items are also pressed hard by online shopping and on top of that by their own home shopping grocery services. Equally, they have high fixed cost bases which are very expensive to exit, to reduce or to redeploy. So the result is competitive pain and squeezed margins.

Every time I shop in UK supermarkets it is a strategic experience. For instance my wife wanted a tiny lithium battery for some scales she had. In Sainsbury West Wickham there were two for £5. I thought that's so incredibly expensive. But we were just wanting to go home so I threw them into the trolley. But as my wife was looking through some products I told her I was going onto the net and found four batteries for £1.70 with postage included; that's six times cheaper than the Sainsbury product! I did go to Customer Service to give feedback and the lady told me "I can't do anything" to which I said "but you do work here? Maybe pass it on to the manager."

My strategic thought was that so desperate are supermarkets to crème higher margin to prop up their sagging profits that they will push customers to forego "convenience" for price. The downward pressure on the lower to medium positioned players will inexorably increase.

Another important cut of dynamic competitive strategy is the competitive advantage-over-time curve (see Figure 5.12), which shows the climb, the climb and the climb of Amazon so that at least until now it has very successfully sustained its competitive advantage. When I buy something in under two minutes from Amazon, which is often, it gives me a legal high! *A little miracle in my life!*

In comparison we see the changes in Tesco over time from its humbler beginnings in the mid-1990s as marginally less than average, to its dominance by the turn of the millennium, through to its cataclysmic fall and more recent recovery.

Finally, we see Lidl as a new entrant climb but then plateau for a number of years and then make a second dramatic push upwards. The assumption we are making here is that Lidl is very strong relative to the average supermarket company rather than it is necessarily far stronger than the other discounters.

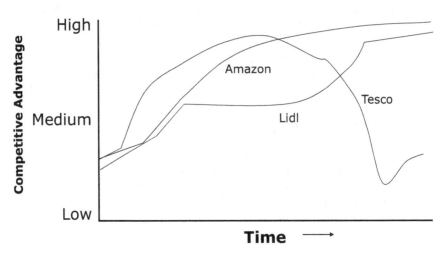

Figure 5.12 Competitive Advantage-Over-Time Curve: A Tale of Three Retailers

Notice that you can easily track up to three competitors over time. Of course, the "relative competitive advantage" is something that is not just gut feeling. It requires in-depth comparison of competitor profiles, as we saw in Figure 1.6, Chapter 1.

We see a lot of Tesco over 20 years in Chapter 7.

Other dynamic curves over time

Clearly there are many, many possible dynamic curves over time that you can draw. For instance, each one of the five criteria on the Strategic Option Grid can be supported/tested out by a variable-over-time curve, viz the:

- Strategic attractiveness-over-time curve – already covered through the External attractiveness and the competitive advantage curves – combined together of course.
- Financial attractiveness-over-time curve (or the value-over-time curve);
- The difficulty-over-time curve (Figure 5.7);
- The uncertainty-over-time curve;
- The stakeholder support-over-time curve.

Also, there are other variables that you might want to track for different needs and purposes, for instance:

- Energy-over-time curve
- Commitment-over-time curve

- Learning-over-time curve
- Strengths, weaknesses, opportunities and threats curves (preferably by each individual item of significance (e.g. brand strength-over-time curve, new product opportunity-over-time curve)
- Frustration-over-time curve,
- Enjoyment-over-time curve, and finally
- Trust-over-time curve.

I sum this up as:

"Life is a myriad of experience curves, powered by the fuel of time."

So having ridden the time variable almost to death, we now turn to another dynamic dimension: "Game Theory."

"How "Game Theory" fits in

"Game Theory" is one of those things like quantum mechanics that rolls off the tongues of intellectual managers easily when they probably only know very little about it. Wikipedia defines it as, "the study of mathematical models of conflict and co-operation between intelligent rational decision makers" and says, "Originally it addressed zero-games where one person's gain results in losses for other participants." (https://en.wikipedia.org/wiki/Game_theory). This was later extended into multi-person and co-operative games. John von Neumann was its founder, but later ideas were developed with Oskar Morgenstern in *Theory of Games and Economic Behaviour* (1944), which provided an axiomatic theory of expected utility, which allowed economists to treat decision-making under uncertainty.

Game theory is quite mathematical. Wikipedia comments: "Von Neumann's original proof used Brouwer fixed-point theorem on continuous mappings into compact convex sets." It is heavily focused on "relatively structured problems," which competitive strategy problems are not, so it has limitations. But the idea of exchange of utility and modelling the uncertainty of the "what if's" of different competitors has appeal.

My take on applying it is that you should do the following:

- Identify the key stakeholders on an issue.
- Understand their agendas through entering deep into their heads through the "out-of-body experience": what do they want at a calculative, rational level", and also what do they want/not want because of mind-sets, biases, or whether they are more "attack" or more risk averse-minded?
- Look at the potential end games and their likely pay offs (rational and non-rational).

- Consider the overall options that are available to the different players and also whether they are likely to have thought of them and would have the actual intent to do them.
- Think of some possible patterns or sequences of play: who might kick off a particular move and what reaction or countermoves that would spark?
- Role-play.

For example, in February 2017 the U.S. giant Kraft Foods launched a surprise, giant bid for the multinational FMCG Group, Unilever for £115 Billion: Unilever refused the bid and announced that it would be "aggressively looking at its options." Soon afterwards Unilever revised its profit expectations upwards, thus making the bid look less generous to the existing shareholders. It also launched a strategic review with the aim of already doing the things that Kraft would – such as selected disposals and cutting cost – making a change in ownership seem to add less and less value to shareholders. After only two days, Kraft withdrew from discussions with them saying that "talks ended amicably."

Now behind the scenes lurks a predatory stakeholder in the form of Warren Buffet, whose investment group Berkshire Hathaway, which together with the buyout house 3G own 51% of Kraft, was clearly pulling some strings! The refusal to do a deal was however painful to existing shareholders who lost 8% of their hiked value on news of the withdrawal of the bid.

The actual bid was mainly in cash that would have been funded by debt, so that was likely to have impaired Unilever's credit rating and thus the deal was curiously funded by the shareholders' own money, which Unilever was able to use as a counter-attack.

Now this curious and surprising turn of events is at odds with the fairly basic, soft gaming that I prescribe in my process. It is hard to believe that Kraft and its backers really thought through the severity of the defensive reaction that they would get from their victim. But Unilever has a very proud culture and whilst they probably never saw this coming – that's another story – they should, and they would inevitably draw in the ranks.

I imagine that even that very day they would have had hot shot investment bankers on the job and in their boardroom, and it wouldn't take the brightest Harvard MBA student to fathom that accelerating disposals of fringe businesses and cost cutting would significantly close the "Value Gap" (Grundy 2003), which is the difference between the value that the stock market puts on the company and the (discounted) economic value of its cash stream.

Indeed, there are a number of precedents for this. For example, in the early 1990s when the conglomerate acquirer Hanson pounced on the sluggish multinational ICI with the result of the total demerger of their Pharmaceutical business and Agrochemicals into Zeneca magically releasing £5 billion of value over 25 years ago! This then went on to become AstraZeneca through another merger. In the course of a bloody bid battle, ICI attacked the ethics and the personal integrity of its two top Directors – Lord Hanson and Lord White – so that was very damaging for their reputation.

Another case was that of the leisure and entertainment Group Granada, which made a hostile bid for the conglomerate Forte plc. who had a portfolio of luxury hotels, the Travelodge Chain, and two roadside café chains: Little Chef and Happy Eater.

After the shock of the bid was digested, according to close sources, the Group FD summoned its defence team and said to them orally:

> "Even if we do go down we will make sure that as we sink our biggest guns will still be pounding away raining shells down on them – so I won't be fun for them at all."

Much reputational damage was done to Granada, whose ability to add economic value to even its existing portfolio and to its previous acquisitions was severely scrutinised.

Had these predators gone through the basics of the process that I have advocated above then that would have been of huge benefit to them, and likewise to Kraft foods that seemed not to have one any real "out of body experiences" let alone role-plays and "what if" gaming.

Dynamic strategy according to the wisdom of Sun Tzu

Sun Tzu was an ancient Chinese writer on military strategy, and his book *The Art of War* percolates right through military thinking about strategy and this has spilled over into competitive strategy too. I have read Sun Tzu very closely and not just for my consulting role, but also as I had the dubious pleasure of waging a legal war which lasted a rather long time, so it seemed only natural to deploy its tenets.

So hang onto this wisdom which I have distilled:

1   *"You are not fit to lead an army unless you are familiar with the country, its mountain and forests, its pitfalls and its and precipices, its marshes and its swamps."*
    – This is all about diligent and detailed, analysis of the external environment.
2   *"Attack him where he is unprepared, appear where you are unexpected."*
3   *"Doing many calculations leads to victory, doing few calculations leads to defeat"*
4   *"A clever fighter is one that not only wins but excels in winning with ease."*
    – This emphasises the need for superior firepower, skill, agility and foresight.
5   *"Carefully compare the opposing army with your own so that you may know where strength is superabundant and where it is deficient."*
    – This is a plea for both competitor analysis and also for understanding competitor strategic options, stakeholder agendas, strategic intent resources and staying power.
6   *"Do not repeat tactics that have gained you victory, but let your methods vary by the infinity of circumstances."*
    – Obviously this is referring to the need to have a wealth of contingent strategies, and also to avoid being predictable.

7   *"When able to attack we must seem unable to; when we are near, must make the enemy believe we are far, when we are far we must make him believe we are near – warfare is all about deception."*
     – Dynamic competitive strategy should contain an element of deception.
8   *"Let your plans be as dark and as impenetrable as the night, and when you move, fall like a thunderbolt."*
     – This is emphasising the importance of stealth, speed, surprise and of sheer competitive power.
9   *"Ponder and deliberate before you make a move."*
     – This not only suggests having sufficient options to choose from but also to conduct a thorough feasibility analysis and evaluation of these.
10   *"The skilled tactician is like the Shuai snake: strike at its head and its tail will attack you, strike its tail and its head will attack you, strike at its middle and both its head and its tail will attack you."*
     Sun Tzu has a wonderful way with words, and this gem reminds me of the one about concentrating one's forces and prioritising so that you are not spread too thin. In this case, he calls for built-in flexibility in the strategy and also to have at ones disposal multiple points of possible attack. You would hate to be up against a Shuai snake. **I once fought a Shuai snake and won because I followed Sun Tzu!**

I especially used number 11:

11   *"If you know the enemy and know yourself, your victory will be complete."*
     – This is the ultimate challenge: to balance one's self-knowledge with competitor knowledge: this means knowing very clearly one's weaknesses.
12   *"Estimating the adversary, shrewdly calculating difficulties, dangers and distances, constitutes the test of a great General."*

All of the above twelve key principles are relevant to the disrupters that we look at in the last section of this chapter, but points 2, 3 6, 7 and 11 are especially applicable.

Strategic analysis needs to be thorough and also equally capture the implementation challenges, uncertainties and risks.

Number 1 above is quite an interesting one not only in that, like myself, it cautions not to get just wound up with the attractiveness of making a strategy a success but also the importance of dealing with the obstacles and the constraints. Sun Tzu subsumes both uncertainties and risks as "dangers" and he also, again like me, emphasises implementation difficulty. But he also brings in the idea of "Distance" which, outside its use in Strategic Group Theory, doesn't gain a mention in mainstream strategy literature.

I think that "Strategic Distance "does have some mileage, especially in being a notion of the length of the journey that the strategy is taking you on.

These "distances" could potentially be measured in terms of changes in:

•   Relative market share
•   Broader, relative competitive position

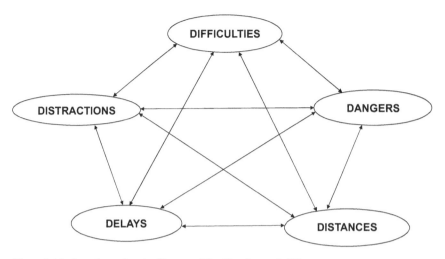

Figure 5.13 Interdependencies Between The Five Strategic D's

- Capability
- Financial position and performance
- Unit costs
- Cultural attributes.

Another point is that the three "D's" – *difficulties, dangers* and *distances* – also suggest two other D's: *delays* and *distractions*. So we might now have a five cornered star model (see Figure 5.13 where each one of the variables can make each other worse). It is the opposite of the alignment model, like the "S's" of strategy, systems, structure, style and skills.

Talking about "D" words leads me to talk about the dynamics of disruption, which is our ultimate topic in this chapter. But first, let me ease into it by telling you about a very special animal, the honey badger, who exemplifies not only an important concept – the "System of Competitive Advantage" – but is also a disrupter himself.

The system of competitive advantage and disrupter of the animal world – the honey badger

One of my earliest models of strategy was the "onion of competitive advantage" (Grundy and Brown 2002), which represented different aspects of competitive advantage in terms of the inner layers (e.g. culture) were the most difficult to imitate and the outer ones the easiest. The assumption of the model was that truly sustainable competitive advantage was likely only with "mutually reinforcing layers." My *system of competitive advantage* is a more sophisticated and evolved version of this.

This model came into being curiously through learning about an animal. The honey badger first came to my attention through my stepdaughter Fran, who was captivated by its awesomeness. She had seen a number of amazing videos of the honey badger on YouTube, and after just seeing a couple I was hooked too.

I include this as a case as it not only generated a new dynamic model of strategy but also because I feel that the more analytical and mechanistic side of strategy could be balanced more by evolutionary and organic models. The former model is predominant in most MBA courses, which gives too much of a "painting by numbers" feel to strategy formulation.

The model is dynamic in two ways: first, the elements are interdependent, and second it is evolutionary; they have developed over time, and through learning to compete in a tough environment over and over again. It also maps strategic assets that are skills-based and thus dove-tail into the Resource Based Theory of Competitive Advantage, which emphasises the importance of capability in achieving superior performance (Grant 1991), (Barney and Clark 2007).

I knew a bit about the honey badger, but then I saw a full documentary on BBC2. It was set in a game reserve in South Africa and had some fascinating hilarious footage of the honey badger in action. Readers wanting to get a flavour of the honey badger should look it up on YouTube.

The game reserve manager introduces the honey badger thus:

> I've had in my house hippos, rhinos, spotted hyenas, leopards, cheetahs, lions, but I have never had anything like a honey badger.
>
> The first I took in was Stoffel and his girl-friend Hammy: he caused chaos in the house, he damaged everything, and he would come and break in at the window, go to the kitchen, knock the dog biscuits over, go to the fridge, lie on his back and kick the door open with his feet. He would go and smell what's in the menu, get the frozen bacon and chew and eat it on the floor. And you didn't dare stop him!

The honey badger is awesome, not just because of its physical attributes but because of a whole system of competences. Watching this video as well as studying innovative businesses inspires me to draw a systemic picture of the honey badger that we see in Figure 5.14, which I will go into after giving more of a flavour of its tricks.

Not only are the ingredients of Figure 5.14 highly interdependent and thus dynamic, but these are all evolutionary and thus dynamic in a second sense, too. The honey badger learnt to do these or developed the skills, which are its strategic assets. Thus, the System of Competitive Advantage dovetails into the Resource Based Theory of competitive advantage (Grant 1991; Barney and Clark 2007).

Whilst Figure 5.14 shows a whole variety of mutually reinforcing competitive advantages, I want to hone in on its sheer cunning.

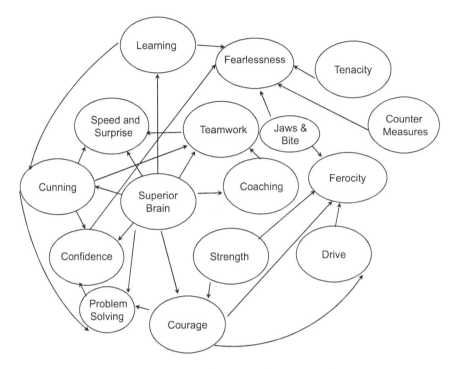

Figure 5.14 A System of Competitive Advantage – The Honey Badger

So let's fast forward first to the close encounter that Stoffel had with two hyenas:

Commentator: "With jaws twice as powerful as a lion a hyena can easily crush a honey badger with a single bite. But the hyena rapidly broke off (trying to get the honey badger's food). The cause of the hyenas retreat suddenly becomes apparent – what a terrible smell... One of the honey badgers seems to have deployed a concealed weapon. They use it in the same way that a skunk would as part of their defence to deter other animals. Fluid ejected from an anal pouch can be smelt at a range of forty metres."

It seems that the honey badger has cunning defensive measures to rival an F22 Fighter Bomber!

In order to contain Stoffel's deviant activities, the game manager decides to take counter measures. How is this for cunning and teamwork between the honey badgers?

Commentator: "They set up a high fence to keep Stoffel and Hammy in. Stoffel seems to have devised a way out. Stoffel would get the female to go up the fence and

> open the first gate. He would hold the first gate open and say "woman – go up – I am pulling you go up. She goes up to the top and pulls the second one out, he pulls it open. He waits for her to get down and they both go through the door together. The escape is no fluke: considering their small size, honey badgers have a remarkably big brain."

This also highlights the way in which the honey badgers show a uniquely strong ability to work as a team.

Commentator: "Whatever Brian did to keep him in, Stoffel was hell bent at getting out. Brian then built at great cost a 'Honey Badger Alcatraz' with high concrete walls so that he and his meat were confined to an inescapable compound – or at least, that was the theory…"

Brian: "This is like a game for Stoffel. Every time that I devised something it was a game for Stoffel. He would climb up a tree and onto its branches and swing on them over the walls and out. So we cut all the branches off. Then he dug up all the rocks and he piled them all up high enough for them to escape. He found a rake that he could lever up the wall and climb up that."

Honey badgers are so named because they love honey. They are a disaster for bee keepers and they seem impervious to stings; they have, as Darwin would suggest, adapted so well to their environment that the challenge makes them tougher and tougher.

In the documentary, Brian wages another campaign to protect the bees nest from Stoffel, devising harder and harder challenges which each time Stoffel surmounts. Even when faced with a long smooth metal pole to climb before they can get even close to the honey the two badgers are seen taking turns and looking at each other's technique-plus having a break (sounds like "strategic thinking?") until eventually one of them cracks it through cunning, determination and teamwork.

If we look in more detail at Figure 5.14 we see a number of clusters, for instance:

- *Cunning*: facilitated by a superior brain but also by confidence and enables speed and surprise;
- *Fearlessness*: enabled through the honey badgers' learning capability, its jaws and bite, indirectly through its ferocity, and also its tenacity.

There are probably other interdependent flows that we could draw with lines, but the picture would just end up ultra-complicated.

What is impressive here is:

- The fact that each and every one of these capabilities would be easily and clearly benchmarked relative to most other animals as extra special

- The number of these special attributes
- The *dynamic interaction* of them.

The honey badger seems also to possess some evolutionary advantages; I suspect that were Brian to train the descendants of Stoffel and Hammy then within not too many generations their descendants would exhibit even more impressive capabilities.

I have applied the System of Competitive Advantage model to some other business-related examples for instance to the challenger bank Metrobank, as we will see in the next section, and the results have been most illuminating.

Disrupter case study – Metrobank

Metrobank was founded in 2010 as a "Challenger Bank" in the UK following the model which worked successfully to emphasise superior service.

Banks are notorious for destroying customer value. In 2013 one of the big UK banks, who I had banked with for 21 years, suddenly blocked me from making payments and told me that it was my fault as I had failed the security code three times, which was untrue. It was going to take them three weeks to get me back on the system; meanwhile I had to pay hungry lawyers a very large amount of money to do a major court case. After suggesting that I went to their Bromley branch after it had shut to do a transfer, I set out in search of a nice, caring and competent bank.

After first knocking and then banging on their glass window for five minutes and fearing that security was coming I turned towards the High Street. Like someone from the Bible going to Damascus, I saw the sun glint off a red sign across the street. That sign said "Metrobank." I went in and jumped on the chequebook and statements from that "other bank." Metrobank staff were not put off, sat me down, gave me a cup of tea and converted me. It was kind of biblical.

Metrobank started in the UK only a couple of years ago with the strategy of offering a caring customer experience. They entered the UK market in London in 2010 founded by Vernon Hill, the first new High Street Bank to be registered in 150 years!

They say they want their customers to "love them as a bank." They aim to create a revolution in banking.

I now bank with Metrobank: they are cool. But if you were to ask me "What is the big difference?" I would say that whilst my former bank, RBS "is about control and costs," Metrobank is about "simplicity, slickness – and above all (caring) service". One senior manager in my previous bank had said "We aren't like Metrobank. We are so much bigger so we can't possibly be flexible." Another said – off the record – to be open a lot of our people have gone through a difficult time, as we thought we were going to be sold (to Santander)."

To amplify the point about Metrobank actually really caring, I visited their Bromley store to register on internet banking. I had to set up the password and the numerical pass codes for both personal and business accounts. Now I am a Chartered Accountant and an MBA, so you would have thought that setting all that up and getting it right would be a doddle. WRONG. After 25 years of strategy – "big picture" work – my attention span for random numerical detail kept getting lost. Time after time, whilst Samuel Adetula of Metrobank guided me, I failed to get it right over and over again. Six attempts and 45 minutes later I finally succeeded. Not once did Samuel ever show tiredness, frustration or impatience; he could smile no matter what! If I had been a "mystery shopper" that day I would have been The One from Hell!

Worse is to come: I did make a payment over the internet the next week and thought I had it cracked. Then another week later I tried at home and it wouldn't work! So back I went to Bromley and oh – his unlucky day – Samuel got me again! I remember thinking that I should have worn a Waitrose bank over my head – I had parked there – as I imagined what Samuel would be thinking when he got me as his next customer: " Oh not him again!" But I never saw his face drop, his eyes look up – typical of other banks. He still kept on smiling!

He was even smiling when, almost as soon as we had sat down, I realised I was using some superseded codes that would never have worked! Again, there was no glimmer of a look from Samuel giving away he might be thinking I was a little stupid. Please, please, Metrobank, hang on to that service culture as you get bigger, as you surely will! What are you guys on? Everyone at the Bromley store actually glows with happiness.

I have stress–tested those over four years now. I can be the customer from hell, and I can report no significant defect that has not been quickly put right. Bromley staff were unfazed when (after asking for permission) I did a head stand and said to all "This is Metrobank Standing Banking on its head." I did make a video on Metrobank with *ACCA Magazine*, *Accounting* and *Business Magazine* – see YouTube, "Strategic Insights," not funded by Metrobank.

I have had coffee with their CEO, Craig Donaldson, and their Chief People Officer on two separate occasions and found them both very un-stuffy and down to earth. I work a lot in retail, and they are much more like retailers; they don't feel at all like generic bankers.

I quite frequently run a case study in my mini MBA courses on Metrobank, and when some interesting ideas come up via the Strategic Option Grid I email them to Craig Donaldson. Invariably he emails back his feed-back and within hours – impressive. Sadly, I can't reveal those strategic ideas here as they are, naturally, quite cunning.

I felt it would be a great idea to make a pictorial representation of Metrobank's competitive advantage and what better way than to use the Systemic model as we saw earlier in the case study of the honey badger? Take a look at that model. It is as awesome, if not more in terms of the extent and combined strength of its system of competitive advantages as that for the honey badger itself. (see Figure 5.14).

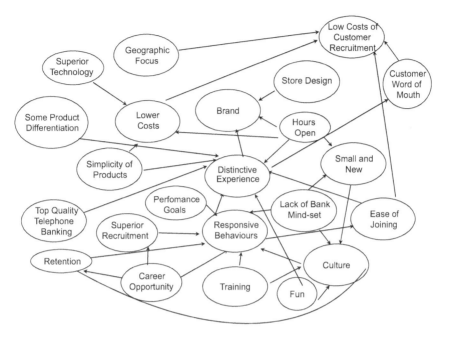

Figure 5.15 A System of Competitive Advantage – Metrobank

Again, this is a dynamic model, as Metrobank was an evolutionary development of the people-friendly banking model in the U.S. Figure 5.14 can thus provide ideas for further strategic development: "where to go next?"

Metrobank

Whilst it is hard to pick out a number of areas of competitive dominance that stand head and shoulders over the rest there are three central clusters that are worth emphasising, as they feed a lot of others and are hard to imitate:

These are:

- Distinctive customer experience
- Responsive behaviours
- Not a banking mind-set.

Metrobank's entry strategy is proving very successful, and whilst not intending to become a big player very quickly or not dazzling with new technology, it is quietly eating away at the market shares of the other UK banks and is a most interesting disrupter. In 2017, they passed the one million current accounts mark. Why shouldn't it now advertise its existence? That would not be aligned to the principles of Sun Tzu.

The Metrobank case illustrates:

- In a market where there seems to be huge entry barriers if you are able to compete in a genuinely distinctive way if you also address customer needs in a way which they see as highly value-added then you can shrink the protection that gives incumbents.
- If you devise a well-informed, well-designed strategy built on a system of competitive advantage then as a disrupter you can have a very real chance of success.
- By focusing a lot on cultural and behavioural factors this makes it very hard for incumbents with inflexible cultures to compete against you.
- Timing is very important for a disrupter. In Metrobank's case, following the credit crunch, where several banks failed and two of the clearers had to be propped up by the Government to save the entire banking system from collapse, the banks have just about the worst reputation for not being trustworthy ever in the UK.

Key insights and learning lessons from Chapter 5

- We can use vector analysis to really bring together the dynamic aspects of strategy – this is a relatively unique approach as previously outside my own literature the only real use of vectors was in change management with "Force Field Analysis."
- Vector analysis gives us a most important missing tool in competitive strategy – the one that got lost between PEST factors and Porter's Competitive Forces: growth drivers. It is as if astronomers forgot to say that the planet Mars was between Earth and Jupiter.
- Both PEST and Porter's too can be represented with vectors and in addition with all three combined to give a grand picture of total market dynamics and attractiveness.
- Even more mobile in form are the variable-over-time curves, where you can plot almost anything whether strategic or not, hard variables like financial versus the behavioural. I do find it odd at times that other strategy writers haven't seen the merit of this approach and that of vectors – maybe that's because I had more mathematical training than they did, or because this was "not invented here."
- Our next port of call was in Game Theory which emphasises the dynamic integration between players in a game and seeing the competitive arena as just that. Whilst business competition generally defies mathematical representation it is still very amenable to soft modelling of psychological behavioural factors.
- At a practical level, there is much merit in pondering then simple wisdom of Sun Tzu both his principles and Game Theory inspire us to study the other players most closely.

- In particular, we found the concepts of deceiving the enemy and of judging "strategic distance" as very useful.
- A third area of additional insight into competitive dynamics over and above vector and "over-time" curves was that of the systemic model of competitive advantage brought alive some graphically by the honey badger case and later on with Metrobank.
- Finally, we saw that disrupters can create their very own dynamic which is extremely hard to deal with, as in the Metrobank case.

Reader exercises

- For one strategic issue what does one of the dynamic "over-time" curves tell you?
- What is your *system of competitive advantage*?

6   The art of alien thinking

Introduction

In the last chapter we focused on the time travel perspective of showing how Strategy can become more dynamic. But an equally powerful way of introducing a different dynamic into strategic planning is through "alien thinking." This was one of the very earliest of the Cunning Checklists in Chapter 4, namely:

> "Number 6: Imagine that you are actually an alien!
>
> Many industries have such peculiar and idiosyncratic ways of doing things that entering into an "alien mind-set" will inevitably generate radical ideas. By re-examining this from an extreme, even an alien, perspective this can give you a very different perspective indeed, too."

In this chapter we look at the "alien experience": seeing industry practices as "Strange"; being an "alien anthropologist." We take a close look at four industries — banking, television production, health clubs, and bars and pubs. We address the question: how does one actually detach from or abandon the industry mind-set through being a pretend alien?

Imagine that you are actually an alien!

One of the most powerful ways of arriving at a Cunning Plan is to just simply put your mind in the mind-set of an alien. (I actually have a fictitious planet in my head: Neptulia!) That kicks me into seeing industries and companies as if I am an extra-terrestrial anthropologist, looking at existing earth strategies as strange. This shift in mind-set seems to propel me into new ways of observing and thinking.

As an alien, I am not anchored in my thinking to a particular industry but am able to access competitive recipes from all the Earth industries I have looked at as if I am an investor. I am also not stuck in the present, as I am able to zap into time travel mode and absorb and transfer learnings from past industrial history, and also to reach forward into the future. So I am able to blend alien thinking and time travel/storytelling.

If you have a struggle with this just watch a few episodes of *Ancient Aliens* on satellite TV. That should do the trick to see what it means to enter deeply into that mind-set!

You don't have to believe what they say on that TV channel, as that would be to give into a subtle brainwashing process at work. Every time they describe something like the Pyramids, stories that we descended from the Stars, cave drawings of flying saucers etc., the soft voice of the narrator asks "Could it be that…" when the answer to any puzzling phenomenon is of course "it's the ancient aliens!" without ever considering alternative and simpler explanations! But that shouldn't prevent us from *imagining if they were really here, how would they see our business practices like an alien anthropologist?*

A second mind-set that one can put into this mix is that of being an alien cognitive behavioural psychologist. A most successful modern approach to human psychological dysfunction is known as "cognitive behavioural therapy," or "CBT." This entails surfacing the underlying beliefs an individual has about the world and themselves. Some of these beliefs are valid and others are not. These beliefs guide our thinking and behaviour at a tacit level. We may not be explicitly aware of what they are, and even less what their influence is. CBT has protocols for re-examining these beliefs, for discarding some of these and for acquiring and testing new beliefs at an individual level.

As an alien cognitive behavioural psychologist, your mission is thus to become mindful and challenge beliefs:

Case Study 1: "Aliens In Irish Air Space"

One example of how I entered deeply into an alien mind-set was a workshop with the Bank of Ireland, when they asked me to help them to come up with cunning ideas for their brand and marketing strategy. To put the managers into a different space I came into the workshop pretending to be out of breath, saying "so sorry I am a bit late: terrible problem landing my 'ship.'" air traffic control in Dublin didn't seem to know I was coming and I clearly wasn't going to be welcomed at the International Airport, so I had to divert to a private runway at Weston Airport 15 miles away West of Dublin!"

I got my laptop out and messed about with all the connections:

"Can I just check with you guys? This is the Alien Workshop isn't it? And you guys are a Bank, the Bank of Ireland?"

They all nodded in some bemusement, as I obviously looked like a very good copy of a real human.

"So let's get started: here are our objectives:

- Look at our brand and initiatives to support it AND take it to another level afresh.
- Prioritise our current initiatives in the light of what we see as being a new brand positioning.
- Identify things that an "alien" would wish to see and prioritise them too.
- Form a new set of marketing breakthroughs to achieve that.

"I understand that you wanted me to come as if I am an alien. Sorry, hope this doesn't disappoint you but I actually AM a real alien from the planet Neptulia. I have been on earth for five years now and really struggle with banks that seem totally unable to understand my uniqueness."

I then proceeded to take Banking apart by opening my wallet and going through my various bank cards and told them stories about how I had just been treated as another customer. Then I said:

"Frankly, having gone to all this trouble – loads of plastic surgery to just look like you guys, *really I just want Earth Banks to treat me as an individual human being.*"

This intervention generated six out of the top 10 very best ideas to come out of that workshop, and collectively these played a major role in revitalising their brand. Indeed, that day's work inspired a very successful campaign on Irish television that played though the new products and services that had been "reverse–engineered" from very well-defined customer segment needs. For example, there was the idea of "Baby Breaks" that would give customers the option of rolling over some or all of their mortgage payments over the period of maternity leave.

Whilst this may seem a quirky way of developing strategy in a formal management context, it does seem to have the effect of loosening mindsets and assumptions about how things have to be done.

Alien thinking doesn't need to be done along with others being there with you; you can play with it when shopping, going to the airport, driving, ringing up a call centre, experiencing train delays. It is like "mindfulness" or very calm observation, where the observer's reference point is one of cultivated curiosity, puzzlement, challenge and desire for better!

Another important part of that alien skill is the ability to understand the human psychology and culture that conditions how Earth markets actually operate. This entails being something of an Anthropologist, where you try to make sense of the apparently irrational decision-making and behaviours that humans exhibit, for example when retail staff seem to take satisfaction from customers suffering inferior services. That is hardly surprising where the same staff are not treated well at all by their managers and employer. They are just projecting that sense of powerlessness onto the customers which is natural and logical for them. That becomes obvious by being in an anthropological mind-set.

The "alien" mind-set that I typically tend to adopt is scientific, ultra-logical, idealistic, and, naturally, advanced and slick. So I am constantly thinking too about applying existing and new technologies to problems. For instance, we are out walking our dog on Shirley Hill, South of Croydon today. I am taking in the view of the City fourteen miles away – "Oh there's the Shard!" My wife grabbed my arm – I feel contentedly reassured – and then she says "Pooh!" as I just missed stepping on some brown material.

I had been telling her about my alien chapter that I was writing and how I would like to emphasise to my readers the importance of using "advanced technology" to stretch your thinking – e.g. by asking "what would aliens do?" I said to her:

"Just thinking about that problem, of how to avoid treading in dog poo whilst still being able to look at the scenery, there has to be a technology to detect that – just like a land mine or a metal detector."

My wife Carolina suggested:

"Well nearly a solution, but wouldn't you wish to detect them without having to bend over, through having poo sensors in your shoes?"

Later, over dinner the conversation continued. I said that aliens would find the present situation at any stage of a walk through a wood that you could step in poo to be totally unacceptable. Yes, it was difficult to detect it reliably but "there has to be a better way," like the Winnie the Pooh Cunning Checklist Chapter 4. The question had to be "at what cost" and "how reliable would it be" and "would it fit on a shoe" so that you didn't have to carry it.

I googled "pooh sensors" and got some interesting results:

- There were technologies such as methane sensors or for methanethiol, gas chromatography for poo detection, although these might have enough fit to the problem to be plausible.
- There were some parallel problems that have been solved of poo detection, for instance there is a sensor that can tell when a dog is pooing, or an app which tells when a human is about to poo, and there are nappy sensors which tell you there is poo: now that might be an exploitable technology for the shoes.
- Was this a problem for a Dyson robotic? (see Chapter 9)

What that short 10-minute search also did was suggest ways of solving it by reframing the problem. For instance, instead of the shoe poo sensors idea you could insist that all dogs wear the sensor that suggested they were going to poo and these would emit a loud noise so that dog owners were embarrassed into always clearing it up. So the poo would never get left by the owners. All dogs in recreational areas would be forced to wear them: don't laugh, it's foreseeable! Someone once invented speed bumps.

Or if we go back to an extreme alien version, all recreational areas are monitored by CCTV or by drones that video any dog indulging in a *laissez faire* poo, and there is alien retribution for failing to comply with the law! The targeting systems would have to be pretty good; also you couldn't target the dog, as everyone knows you should never kill off the dog in a film script.

This leads me to an even simpler solution: if caught pooing, the owner is fined £1000 and loses their dog for two weeks in a kennel – that would teach them (with their owners too?). Big warning signs could be posted in recreational areas and the general public are asked to report any dog pooing and the owner not clearing up and are given £100 for each report leading to a successful conviction. If sufficiently lucrative, there would be poo vigilantes on patrol in heavily infested areas!

So what am I doing here cognitively? I am using the more extreme alien-type mind-set to encourage my mind to stretch my thoughts to the borders of the plausible and a little beyond to create more imaginative space, so that when it goes back to normal I have some useful lines of enquiry I never had before: *beyond conventional, limited, human thinking*. Try it on something!

Case Study 2: An Alien in Knightsbridge: The Wall-to-Wall TV Productions

My next short case study was that of the TV production company Wall-to-Wall, which specialised in niche TV programmes. I had met the husband of its legal director in a meditation weekend in Cambridge, and later got to know his wife too. We all met up in London for a drink later on. After she learnt what I did for a living I was invited to meet her CEO, founder of the company.

He invited me to help them think differently about the strategy, and I recall interviewing some of their clients in the top echelons of TV media. We also had an away day at a very unusual place called "Monkey Island" on the Thames – a conference centre literally on an island. I faintly remember monkeys being around there too.

We had a very productive day, but this case study is more about what subsequently happened. The (then) CEO felt that the whole experience had been a very positive one for the whole management team and invited them all and myself to an expensive Chinese restaurant in Knightsbridge, London's West End.

It was a lively and pleasant occasion, and we had a very large and special round table that around a dozen of us were feasting. I was making polite business conversation and happened to ask someone:

> "So tell me, what does it cost on average for you guys to make an hour of TV? "

The answer was:

> "Oh it is really expensive, where you are shooting a lot on site it can easily be £100,000"

I said:

> "Wow! That's amazing! That does sound like gold-plating."

They then went onto explain that I really didn't understand all the trouble they had to go through to make a really classy programme, and that you really couldn't compromise the original concept.

I wasn't put off, and by now the whole table was all focussed on this issue. So I felt minded to do another challenge:

> "Well if I imagine that I was an alien and landed on Monkey Island and heard that, I would be saying: "£100,000! On Neptulia we could do that for £10,000 tops."

This produced a whole new hubbub of conversation. I sat there observing: listening and watching – the dynamic was fascinating. There were around three sub-conversations, and in at least two there was quite an argument going on for whether in truth you could often get to the same or a similar effect with quite a lot less being spent.

What I had watched was rather like Strategic Magic. I threw a stone into some water and the ripple that went out didn't shrink but grew and grew. Whilst I doubt they ever reduced their unit costs by 90%, I do imagine that they were able to get 10%–20% off at least some programmes.

Case Study 3: How to Get Fit – Cheap Fitness4Less

My third case study involved some strategic thinking in the fitness industry in the mid-2000s. I meet a very good friend of mine, Matthew Harris, for drinks or a curry quite regularly. We met originally, as the accountants BDO asked me to create a Growth Strategy case study for the workshops I was running for them. We lived only five miles apart then, so after a couple of pub meetings we became very good friends indeed.

On this occasion, we met near Heathrow as he was then living in Hounslow West London, whilst I lived between Rickmansworth and Uxbridge in a village called Harefield. I had become involved in a major reconstruction of his Health Club Group, "Topnotch," which at one time had around eighteen clubs and in 2001 had floated at one stage on the "AIM" market. He was running some board workshops to develop the business and asked me to facilitate these.

At the time Matthew had expanded quite rapidly, and his group was carrying a quite large cost base, but he began to face liquidity pressures due to a worsening in the market and the strain of debt. Its bankers were unhappy, and Matthew had to undertake some severe but most sensible cost cutting (which I helped the team work through) and some disposals. Finally, an even bigger reconstruction of the business and financial structure was necessitated, but somehow Topnotch survived. During that process, our attention was rapidly refocused on costs and change – a "detergent strategy."

But survival does not equate with business success, and whilst the reconstructed group was profitable and stabilised, a few years later it was still facing some performance problems in one of his clubs – Bristol.

So we ordered some drinks and after chatting generally no doubt about football – I am an Arsenal fan and Matthew supports Chelsea, so there's friendly rivalry and banter – Matthew mentioned his problem with Bristol. He felt that the club was underperforming, and he told me that he was thinking of actually putting it up for sale. The following is a pretty accurate reconstruction of our conversation.

I thought about it for a moment and said:

> "Matthew, hmm…I am wondering what the other options are. I mean, when you want to sell something is because you think that the buyer will do a better job of making it profitable? I don't really think that a buyer could easily do a lot better than you are doing. To sell it you are going to have to accept a poor deal or be asking them just to take it away for nothing. They will know you are trying to sell them a dog – excuse that expression."

I continued something like this:

> "Why don't we spend half an hour or so thinking about how we might turn it around. Maybe we could try to imagine what anyone coming fresh to the situation might think was possible? Perhaps we should take a look at it *as if we were an alien buyer?*"

Matthew went quiet and reflected:

> "Yes, you could look at it that way, I agree, so how should we do that?"

Tony: "Well, let's think of how we might position and resource the club rather differently as you seem to have done all you can within the present model to do better. What are the variables we should focus on? Then we will generate some options out of that and evaluate them on the Strategic Option Grid."

Matthew:	"Well firstly there are the obvious variables of price and volumes: if we were to reduce the price somehow to under half that of other, similar clubs then we might turn much of that spare capacity into revenue. But I think that we can also address our costs too – that's something I learnt from the restructuring of Topnotch's central costs. Maybe we could do something parallel to that with the club operating costs."
Tony:	"That's true; look at how you slashed the central overhead in the restructuring? Costs should only be there if they add value, a principle of Strategic Cost Management."
Matthew:	"Health clubs including ours do carry a lot of selling costs and that's a constant headache because of the high churn as people get bored coming or can't make the effort and are wasting their money. Now if we could really reduce the price so that the sales pull was very, very strong *then maybe, just maybe, although this is brave, we could dispense with all of that selling cost.*"
Tony:	"That's I think a really strong line of enquiry but let's look at the wider resource and cost as if we were some cost-cutting alien. You remember that I role play being an alien sometimes in banking and retail and nuclear fuel reprocessing? Where else can we make drastic savings?"
Matthew:	"Well, if I was the alien I would arrange for the club to be destroyed somehow and we could start again. We would have much cheaper equipment that looked just as good and things we include free would be now extras just like a budget airline. Of course, this is all in our imagination-right? And we would have applied a low-cost model to the whole business model. Even if we can't throw away the equipment here for cheaper that may suggest possibilities for this new concept for a new club. We can also look at our rent costs too."
Tony (enthused):	"I think we are on a roll. I feel I really want to jump even further into the alien mind-set now, sorry. I'll tell you something: I used to belong to a very, very expensive health club near Rickmansworth which was over £100 a month. They always had in the gym a couple of staff swanning around who never advised you proactively."

"Indeed, there was one guy there who we had come across in another health club 25 miles away and we had problems with him there. Now he resurfaced in a totally new club; was he following us? He was ex-forces

I think, and he wasn't quite adjusted to a more commercial world. He had been appointed "Director of Health and Safety," and he clearly enjoyed that status. He took a very hostile attitude to my doing yoga without trainers on the exercise mats and told me that this was totally against the rules. I explained that if I was doing a headstand, trainers would be a very bad idea and that you couldn't do "triangle" with trainers on.

After a very big argument in the gym I went to the GM to complain that he was doing "Value Destruction" by interfering with my yoga when I was nowhere near the free-weights so there was no safety issue. "Yoga Wars" broke out, and after my meeting with their GM they backed down and their Director of H&S was told by the GM: 'Don't mess with Dr Grundy; he's like handling fire.'"

Matthew laughed at this as he knew I gave yellow cards for poor customer service and red ones for bad service!

"Ever since I have looked at these guys and girls I keep remembering the scene from the spoof comedy science fiction film *Mars Attacks!* by Tim Burton, where the alien ambassador enters Congress and whilst they are all applauding him he pulls out a ray gun and wipes out all the congressmen. So when I see the gym staff hanging around today and chatting I always think: what do they actually do to add value? If you were to start again, why not dispense with them all?"

It was exactly the same sort of reasoning that was the start of the Dyson Appliances Group over twenty years ago, when James Dyson then found that the pores of Hoover bags clogged up, and those customers were being ripped off for something that really wasn't adding value.

Matthew: "Yes, you are right, Tony, I think we can apply that to the whole of Bristol, so assume we have no sales staff, no or minimal staff in the fitness club, a turnstile to come into the club, self-booking of any classes over the internet. I reckon that by cutting a lot of fixed and variable costs there we would really cut our costs."

Tony: "And by making the price really cheap we would be hugely increasing our economies of scale and fixed costs per member could fall by as much as a half just because of that alone..

I then grabbed hold of a paper napkin and we scribbled a quick evaluation of the "before the alien" and "after the alien" on it, lumping the new options together for speed and simplicity.

Tony: "Running through it you would be creating a new and underexploited market and competitive space and establishing a very effective, classic 'cost leadership strategy' so that's a score of three for strategic attractiveness."

Matthew: "And I can see that could be very financially attractive indeed – a score of three too. And it can't be that difficult to actually implement it other than the initial changes – nearly a three."

Tony: "There would be uncertainty and risks but we could do some quick and dirty market research and look at our competitors' prices and offerings and predict what market share we might capture and from whom as well as keeping our existing members to manage that. I am concerned about the potential long term effects of imitation so that's a score of around two out of three."

Matthew: "I think that the really key people are myself and the managers of Bristol who would really like the idea of not having to find a new home for it and also have proved that Bristol could work. And we would have a new model to play with, too."

Tony: "That gives us a score of let's see 3+3+ 2½ + 2+ 3 = 13 ½, as against a score of 1 ½ +1+ 1½ + 1 ½ + 1 ½ = 7!"

Matthew went on to implement the new model, which was branded "Fitness4Less" and was subsequently rolled out throughout his clubs elsewhere. The enormous pull of (at least initially) an uncontested and pretty irresistible value proposition was so great the members flocked in almost purely through word of mouth. Churn was also much, much lower, so there was a snowball effect of a surge in membership and profitability of the new model was very good.

Matthew also found that capacity wasn't such a "fixed" thing as one might assume in peak demand periods as he might have feared. People would put up with it sometimes being so busy by thinking about how much money they were saving. Also, there were a higher proportion of members who were less regular. Because the price was so much lower, they were on average less likely to go really frequently to milk their outlay, and many hardly went at all but carried on their membership just in case they felt guilty. There was also the effort, too, of cancelling their direct debits which was a pain.

I am not saying that we anticipated all these behavioural effects, but we did model the key behavioural drivers, albeit in a softer and more qualitative way.

Matthew Harris not only saved Bristol and made it profitable but also used those insights throughout his business. Inevitably further dynamic effects kicked in and the model was imitated and slowly spread through quite a portion of that industry. He can certainly be credited for inventing the Budget Health Cub sector, at least in the UK. Around the late 2000s, I spent a couple of years as Non-Exec on his board and watched the whole group migrate to the new model; it was exciting and very satisfying.

But there was that spark of alien thinking that day that turned a possible disposal candidate, Bristol Fitness 4Less, into a shining star. I am not sure, indeed I very much doubt, whether we would have been as incisive and challenging without adopting the alien mind-set as successfully as we did.

That conversation took about 35–40 minutes in all; again. a testimony to the fact that strategic thinking can add a huge amount of value in a very short space of time. It was dynamic, it was agile and it worked.

And so we come to our fourth and final case study – Pubs and Bars:

Case Study 4: An Alien Goes Drinking: The Pubs And Bars Industry

I was speaking at a conference in Cambridge on strategic thinking, and after my talk an FD from a large Brewing and Pub plc. came up to me and said how much he was taken with the idea of my alien thinking idea. He was wondering if I might be interested in landing in his market and looking at what issues and opportunities and changes an "alien" would see.

So I suggested that if I had a week's time to do that study, including a debrief workshop with the board, we could do quite an in-depth review that could also feed into their strategic plan through identifying and also doing some preliminary identification of breakthrough options and a first cut evaluation of these. This was all in 2013, when we were still in the surfacing from a recession following the credit crunch.

His CEO was intrigued, and so I got started:

- First of all, I entered into my alien mind-set as the CEO of Alien Direction Consulting, and a trained analyst, and I poured over the macro, the market, and the competitive trends impacting that industry.
- Next I used some of the tools of dynamic competitive strategy to understand the shifts in potential business models, and in the barriers to change and in the industry mind-set past, present and potentially future, with some potential hypotheses.
- I also had around seven half hour telephone interviews with Board Directors with an agenda that they had come into the industry and into the company today (alien-like). They were asked to imagine

what strategic options they could envisage for both the industry and for the company.

- It was then time to go undercover by sampling a number of pubs and bars to understand why people were there and why others were there and what was driving their spending – or equally their lack of spending.

It was a very interesting experience doing this against the clock, with 28 hours of data gathering and analysis and my undercover work I needed to get extremely quickly with some alien insights. As a Senior Strategy Consultant nearly thirty years ago, all the data gathering would be done by a team of more junior "analysts," very bright graduates who were only a couple of years out of university. They would be redundant now as the internet is so rich and accessible.

An unexpected spin-off occurred during my I interview with the Marketing Director. As soon as I rung her to her she said:

"Is that you Tony? When I heard that a guy from Cranfield was going to do some consulting work here I wondered if it might be you: I came on your Breakthrough Strategic Thinking course five years ago, and can I thank you as you intervened in my life?

She continued:

"You helped me with a stakeholder issue on Day 3 and my analysis using the Stakeholder Grid led me to reject buying a cottage in Cornwall and instead an apartment in the South of France, a less favoured option: thank you, thank you, that transformed our lives!"

- Just a little example of the power of just one of the strategy tools!

I thus did a rapid fly-over of the industry, of its demographics, its economics, competitive structure, and an analysis of the main competitors I was able in that very same detached mind-set to say that:

- Whilst the industry was in maturity that didn't mean that it would have to carry on shrinking – obviously the very traditional pub models based on being a social drinking venue for couples and friends would shrink due to substitutes (like drinking at home/restaurant meals/other social activities/other places where you could still get a drink).

- There was (as of 2014) an amazing lack of technology with antiquated competitive and unregulated queuing at the bar (did humans actually enjoy that???) Did they get off on "deferred gratification" (Freud) or find the simulation of scarcity upped the perceived utility value of the drink as queuing made one even more thirsty? The alien was baffled!
- It wasn't a single "industry" or "market" at all – but several: there were the trendy bars, the pub restaurants, the gastro pubs, the adjacent market of cheaper, more rapid turnover restaurants like pizza outlets, and the more traditional restaurants which had effectively some very simple cuisine – or ready-made meals from factories.
- The prevailing mind-set of the industry was one of rationalisation and contraction, with the main focus of the market being a "detergent strategy" where much management effort was being spent in disposals, withdrawal from unprofitable outlets and limited investment and little innovation.
- It was generally assumed that the secular decline year-on-year of beer sales would continue: as it turned out that could be challenged.

I found the experience of going undercover really interesting. When I was much, much younger I was a more regular pub goer. I recall letting off steam after audits at Ernst and Young, the boozy lunches at BP, and Christmas at KPMG. As a family, we used to enjoy a pub lunch until the children became harder to control (!)

Since my overseas tours at BP when I became corrupted by Australian wine I had hardly drunk beer. As an independent consultant, I no longer had colleagues to drink with so I lived in a nearly "post pub" world. So, by 2013 I was the ideal candidate to go undercover as an alien anthropologist in pubs; it was easy to see them as "strange."

What I found was that a high proportion of pubs were in the traditional model that was relatively basic. It was as if not a lot had happened in thirty to forty years! There was hardly any use of technology outside of electronic cash tills, and at that time there was hardly any use of social media.

The hangover caused by the credit crunch had left pub chains with much debt and had inflicted a period of squeezed disposable incomes per capita that caused the major pub chains to have a much more "defender" (where investment innovation and growth are constrained) mind-set, rather than a "prospector one" (the opposite). My alien take on that was that it was partially a self-fulfilling strategy and that whilst the faded, traditional formula was not going to be in growth mode, there were segments of the market that could be nurtured through growth.

One clue to be found was in the rise of trendy, local "craft beers." Indeed, I recalled that one of the joys of pubs when I was in my very late teens and early twenties was to seek out these beers – for example on long cycle rides. Another clue was in the kind of "girl power" that looked to throw off traditional female stereotypes and was driven by young women who actually liked craft beers.

This led to a number of hypotheses – or "lines of enquiry" – that suggested there might be a number of interrelated growth market niches. These other ones were things like having pubs that were fitted out in a clean, modern way but with also ones with not contrived character but very real character too. This was a hard thing to try to bring off, but in some trendy London pubs we were already beginning to see that.

The other obvious ingredient was the gastro pub concept which didn't assume that all of its customers would eat as well as drink but that at least a good proportion would. To create economies of scale to have a decent kitchen and chef required some scale, so this was likely to come off best with relatively big pubs. And in the course of time (the diffusion rate would not be quick) would have a lot more technology – e.g. doing orders by an App).

At a more macro level, to gain economies of scale the "alien" foresaw that there would be fewer players around and the industry concentration would intensify.

Interestingly on one of my visits I went to eat in a rather new model of a gastro pub at a place called Farnham Common in Buckinghamshire. It was an old pub but had been considerably modernised and at the same time had some old "knick-knacks," a phrase for old pans, old books, a genuine Victorian fireplace etc. I ordered some steak and chips and a glass of wine from the waitresses; I didn't have to hang around the bar having to fight to be served.

The waitresses were very friendly, chatty and intelligent, so we had quite a discussion of the way that the pub formula was set up, how it was working and how that went during the week and over the month.

I couldn't help noticing three ladies who were downing pints of local beer and were clearly really enjoying themselves.

In many traditional pubs, the food arrives late and is quite often not that good – with lukewarm chips and plate or just scraps of salad or overcooked meat. Not only was this food hot and fresh and delicious but it was on a stone platter and nicely presented. Compared to restaurant prices in the area, it was remarkably reasonably priced.

I – as the alien – was impressed and felt that I had time travelled maybe five or six years in the future

Reporting back to the board, I think that the alien's report of the strategic position and potential of the industry and the business gave a welcome perspective that things were not all as gloomy as they were seeming around that time. The messages taken were that they should be looking at growth options and opportunities more positively and shift their focus away from the "detergent" aspects of sorting out their property portfolio. Around that time, they had become too preoccupied with an imminent review of competition in the industry around the issue of tied tenancies to the detriment of taking a fresh look at their industry.

Other insights were that whilst they were making some efforts to come up with new and innovative ideas, they should take this much more seriously. Another area for change was that virtually all the Directors fed back that they were so over-busy that just the thought of thinking about strategy when they were already constipated with doing existing strategy was very uncomfortable.

I have met this phenomenon a number of times in recent years, and I do suspect that "strategic constipation" is a much wider phenomenon. From my perspective, whilst I sympathise with that I feel that it might be aggravated by a number of root causes that could be mitigated:

- Have a very clear and lean, "plan for the plan," and planning process so that this doesn't become overly time consuming.
- Detach from the idea that strategic thinking is primarily a "once a year" event, like Christmas, you ought to be thinking that way on small and big things, every day.
- Use some of the tools that are in this book, like the "Optopus" and the "Strategic Option Grid," that cut down the time taken to a fraction of what it would take in just conventionally, talking around the issues.
- Get a much clearer focus on "what business we are in: in terms of roles and value-added" for board activities and for all the individual directors.
- Improve the time management of all the directors.
- Have a better process for project management of strategy implementation.
- Have a narrower set of key priorities and maybe doing fewer big and challenging things ("strategic breakthroughs").
- Work on board behaviours to create a better balance between "getting things done" and those involving more expansive, helicopter and mindful thinking ("Board Cognitive Style").
- Shift the organisational mind-set as to what sort of an organisation we are, we can become and the kinds of things we can achieve.

In conclusion, the "alien in a pub" experience highlights the value of taking a very playful perspective to unfreeze your strategic thinking and one that can also be very productive.

Key insights and learning lessons from Chapter 6

- Another very potent way of looking at your industry and your business is to visualize you are an alien.
- This means entering playfully into the alien mind-set and discarding the industry mind-set, its assumptions, and perceived barriers to implementation and to change.
- Deconstructing and reconstructing the business model.
- Potentially combining that with time travel.
- Imagining the alien has gone to a top business school (like Harvard) and is a very astute, experienced and case-hardened strategy consultant.
- This can be done as a half to an hour's exercise as at Fitness4Less, or as a longer exercise as in the exercise in the Pubs and Bars industry, with more formal industry analysis, interviews by the alien, undercover work and competitor investigations.
- Its effectiveness if one takes the stance of an industry anthropologist uncovering shared beliefs, habits of competing, or of a cognitive behavioural psychologist who surfaces individually held beliefs and questions them.
- Either way it can be done in a short period of time.
- It is generally very effective as it is a route into "strategic mindfulness" were the mind becomes more detached than it ever is in its usual, everyday, operational mode.
- Although directors commonly report perceived severe time constraints in getting around to do truly strategic thinking, my hypothesis is that this "strategic constipation" is largely due to factors that are treatable if done over phases of time so that it is digestible.

Reader exercise

- As an alien, how would you see (a) your industry and (b) your business, and what might both do differently?

7 From projections to scenario story telling

> Why should we think about the future? Because we will spend the rest of our lives there.
> –Anon

Introduction

In this chapter we re-examine the world of the conventional planner, which appears to be based on the assumption that the past rules the future. This is largely a *predictive* model. We contrast that with the world of more fluid, potentially multiple possible futures, which may not be scientifically knowable but are ones that can be explored and sensed. These might exhibit new zones of competitive space that may acquire an organic momentum and evolve and grow.

Besides the other best practices described in this book, for me a central one is storytelling and the world of scenarios where you sense the future. Actually, sensing the future competitive landscape and new potentialities this can enable you to actually visualize a new business model. This can, in turn, actually start off a new competitive dynamic and may bring into being that competitive future!

A classic case study of an organisation that over the period of 1996 to 2016 exhibited some of the very best strategies and strategic thinking, and perhaps some of the very worst – Tesco plc., the giant supermarket retailer that at one time strived to be a global player. Scenarios were used in the most successful phase of its strategic development and could have and should have been used to anticipate its fall.

In this chapter we thus explore the world of scenarios. First there's a case study from World War II in which a novel written fifteen years before Pearl Harbor foretold not only of that attack but also much of the War against the Japanese in the Pacific.

We examine what scenarios are and their value, including concepts, tools, processes and role plays, especially in the case study of Amerada Petroleum's entry into the gas market in the North Sea. We see how it can be used to find new competitive space as in the case of Tesco for Non-Food, Dot.com and Express strategies.

We then look at recent times at the failure of the Tesco Board to detect its UK strategy's turning point in the 2010s and the "Fall." I argue that some, if not most, of that scenario could have been foreseen. I contend that this might have been early enough to maybe have avoided cataclysmic decline, had Tesco continued to use the Time Travelling into the Future in the early 2010s that it had used in the late 1990s.

The Tesco case shows how a number of scenarios actually played a dramatic role in developing four new business areas that probably grew to become around a third of Tesco's turnover – and from very low bases.

But first, what about futures?

The whole idea of exploring the future as a series or continuum of possible worlds goes back to the 1970s, when Shell first popularised the concept of telling "scenario stories" (Wack 1985a, 1985b, De Geus 1988). Here a "scenario" is a coherent and consistent series of events and actions that are set against a backdrop or environment. All of these factors – including the environment itself – are fluid and linked by cause and effect chains.

There is a massive difference between a scenario and a forecast, or a projection. A "Forecast" is basically a set of quantitative assumed outcomes that are the end-product of interacting variables, and then extrapolations of trends that certain decisions – e.g. introducing a new product, seeking entry to a new market – will add onto the financials. A "scenario" is a dynamic series of interlinking events and actions that is the result of sensing a particular configuration of possibilities. It is a "Mini Possible World."

Shell's planners sensed a possible scenario of a very big hike in the oil price in the 1970s through gaming in their head the likely price spiral were the oil-producing companies to create a cartel and milk the fact that oil is what economists call "very low demand elasticity relative to price." So changes in price don't lead to much change in demand.

Scenario stories don't just tell themselves; they need a process and some models – Figure 7.1 exemplifies that – through my "Uncertainty Tunnel" which depicts:

- *Precursors*: what has already gone to prepare for a shift in the world.
- *Amplifiers*: the things that increase and accelerate the effects within the environment.
- *Dampeners*: the things that absorb that energy and tend to push it back to its old equilibrium or a similar one.
- *The first, second and third order consequences*: the turbulent effect of changes over time with a journey from left (one state of the world) to the right (another state of the world).

In a Sky TV History Channel documentary some years ago, I managed to catch a seriously interesting piece on the use of scenario storytelling. This was about the fore-telling of the story of the attack on Pearl Harbor. This went, initially as told in the words of a US victim of that attack:

> All around us the sea spouted and boiled. In only a few seconds I heard a gigantic crash as if a Wedgewood tree had fallen. Another ear splitting crash

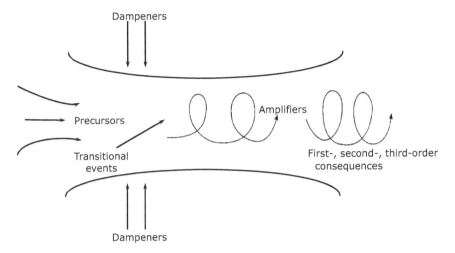

Figure 7.1 The Uncertainty Tunnel

and everything came to an end for me. When I recovered my senses from our boat we could see the Japanese mopping up the rest of our flotilla, shortly before our flagship went down.

These words were written not after the attack (on Pearl Harbor) in 1941, but sixteen years earlier in 1925. The description comes from a work of fiction called *The Great Pacific War* written by British journalist Hector Bywater (Bywater 1925).

I have read *The Great Pacific War* – still available on Amazon – which is an amazing read, as it is not only quite close to what happened, although the circumstances of its ending were not picked up. This is hardly surprising considering that nuclear weapons would have been at best the stuff of science fiction in 1925.

The documentary goes on to examine how these very clever scenarios were arrived at. First of all, Bywater studied the dynamics of a potential arms race and geopolitical rivalry between the Japanese and the Americans that goes back to the early 1920s, when the Japanese occupied some small islands that were closer to the western seaboard of the U.S. than the Philippines, thus posing a perceived threat to the U.S. especially after the Japanese chose to fortify the islands.

The Japanese had become more expansionist and went to war at one stage with China, alerting the U.S. to the possible eastern danger. For their part, the Japanese were worried that the U.S. would cut off their supplies to strategic resources, especially oil and rubber for military and industrial uses from Indonesia. So there were natural precursors for rivalry and conflict that Bywater was only too aware of.

He also modelled the potential dynamics of the balance of military power in the Pacific and even came close to anticipating the formula that was agreed upon between the Japanese, the Americans and the British over the ratios of the capital ships that each was allowed to have so that no side could easily dominate over the other – an effective stalemate.

Bywater also saw that by forging an apparent stalemate in the balance of forces between the U.S. and the Japanese that this was itself a precarious equilibrium as it made both sides – especially the Japanese – more nervous and maybe willing to entertain a pre-emptive strike.

This was further emphasised by another hypothesis that Bywater was drawn, that the U.S. would – to provide a staging post to support the Philippines in case of Japanese attack – build a naval base somewhere between the West Coast and those islands. These two things together created the possibility of a *transitional event*, which is something that destabilises one system and leads to another: in effect, we move from one world to another. (This is the very thing that scenario storytelling helps us to imagine).

The *Precursors* (see again Figure 7.1) were there in terms of Imperialistic expansion, Japanese fear, and a plausible looking plan for a pre-emptive strike.

The *Consequences* were:

- the devastating destruction of U.S. forces at what was to be called Pearl Harbor;
- the Japanese advance through the pacific;
- the waging of a very large battle between the capital ships of both navies, which the U.S. was to narrowly win;
- the massive production of armaments by U.S. industry, giving firepower that eventually overcame the ferocity of the Japanese fighters; and
- eventually the implosion of the Japanese forces as the occupied islands were taken one by one by the U.S. in bloody battles.

The remarkable thing was that this was told by way of a long, comprehensive and coherent novel with ships' names, the names and characters of the commanders, details of the firepower mustered, the battle scenes, the chain of events in the fighting, the losses and casualties, and the strategies and tactics deployed. Whilst deliberately not attempting to forecast the future, by sensing it and by telling it as a story, paradoxically Bywater managed to come remarkably close to actually doing that. I actually call this the "scenario paradox": the less that you try to do a forecast, the more likely that you will!

The other and crucial thing that Bywater succeeded in doing was to get inside the heads of the major players in the conflict: in Chapter 4 we called this the "Out-of-Body Experience." Of course, through his mingling with the military and the politicians during their negotiations of who was allowed to have how many carriers, he would have gotten a keen insight into not just what they thought, but also how they thought.

In turn that enabled him to model their thoughts, anxieties, ambitions and their behaviours and actions over the four years of the war. This also extended to modelling the shift in attitude throughout the U.S. population away from isolationism as a result of a devastating attack on their soil, and the reaction of the U.S. economy to militarise.

Without calling it these things, Hector Bywater brought together systemic thinking, behavioural modelling, Game Theory, dynamic causal sequencing and of course storytelling in his scenarios.

This remarkable "story of a story" is of far more than just some academic interest. As a user of the scenario process embracing these elements, I can attest to many and sometimes remarkable cases where one has literally sensed around a corner or over the horizon through scenarios.

Even when the world hasn't quite turned out exactly as foretold there has been considerable learning. Almost always there were some obvious signals that something might happen in a certain way; it is rare that a transitional event(s) doesn't advertise itself in some way. Of course there might be total "accidents," but even where these happen – as on the tramline in Croydon in 2017 where over 20 people were killed by a tram overturning by taking a bend far too fast – there are invariably precursors, like tram drivers sometimes nodding off with boredom and tiredness.

One of my findings in my doctoral research at Cranfield 30 years ago on the Economic Valuation of Strategic Decisions – relevant here – was that:

> "Uncertainty is often a label for us to stick on things we are too anxious to think about, or just too hard to think about."

But I do think that imagination can cut through a lot of this.

One example of one of my most interesting scenario building exercises was of Amerada Petroleum's feasibility study to enter the gas supply market in the North Sea that the UK Government was de-regulating. I worked closely with its Strategic Planning Department to build a *systemic model* of the main variables in the market: supply-demand balance, likely new competitive structure, new investment, costs, workings of the market, effects of deregulation etc.

It all sounds like posh economics, but I was simpler than that. Although fairly complex, we created a monster map on two flipcharts cello-taped together. This looked at the forces of supply and demand, regulation, competition, long term contracts, the various entry strategies and strategic intent of all the players. These factors were then interlinked with arrows indicating their directional causal flows so that their more dynamic properties could be explored.

Another ingredient was to compile some detailed profiles of the strategic position and intent of each one of the potential new entrants and also of the Government, too. This was then produced as a two-page document with:

* Current resources and capabilities
* War chest
* Strategic options
* Likely leadership agendas
* Likely strategic intent.

We then did a simulation together to pilot the process and to get an advanced view of potential individual moves by the players. Next, we invited some of the senior management to a two day workshop at the Bull Inn, Gerrard's Cross, Buckinghamshire. These managers were allocated into small teams to try to get inside the heads of the other key players.

Facilitating them was no mean feat as there were five groups dispersed randomly through the hotel at different ends. Over a one-day period I estimated I walked a couple of miles, as I needed to check on each one every half hour or so.

We didn't just plunge into the dynamic part of the process – the storytelling itself. We went systematically through a number of steps:

1   Doing a systemic model of the key forces at work in the industry.
2   Rating each in terms of how important these were and how uncertain using the "Uncertainty–Importance Grid" (Figure 2.7).
3   Drawing up a competitor profile (Figure 1.6) which not only looks at position and resources but also strategic options and strategic intent.
4   Evaluating and interpret the planning assumptions that the Strategic Planning Department had collated and compiled.

After a couple of hours, we then let them out of their rooms so that we could then create a dynamic simulation of the scenarios for competing for blocks in the North Sea and then for the competitive environment afterwards.

I had briefed them to role play as closely and as dramatically as they could the actual thinking, behaviours, decisions and actions that they visualized they would do. They did not disappoint me.

The scene was set as follows: we laid out the room with a big chair at the centre where each representative would do a role play. I told them to imagine that when they sat on that chair to imagine they were on *Mastermind*, a TV quiz show where someone who had studied a particular topic to death would answer questions. Typically, this could be as mainstream as the Harry Potter books or as obscure as the historical evolution of the myth of vampires in Transylvania!

So first to go on were the oil majors like BP and Shell. Then we had a niche U.S. oil company who came in, sat nervously down in the chair and fidgeted for a while, mumbling about their strategy, then suddenly jumping up and bolting for the door limping and crying "mummy I have hurt my knee!"

The obvious take on that was that put in the position of placing a substantial bet on entering this market, they had felt out of their depth and the risks and the uncertainties really weren't for them.

Then British Gas wandered in. The person playing British Gas sat down on the big black chair and quickly seemed to struggle to maintain a focus of attention:

> "So what are we really all here for?" mumbled Mr British Gas. Something to do with North Sea Gas?! At that time, British Gas was a denationalised company but one that had taken with it much of the culture of a nationalised utility.

Mr British Gas went on:

> "I do find it rather hot and stuffy in here…in fact…"

Just around that time British Gas seemed to slump in his chair and begin to emulate the dormouse in *Alice in Wonderland* who could never seem to keep awake. Eventually British Gas seemed almost certainly unconscious, and there was a snoring noise!

Finally, I had volunteered to role play the British Government in the form of the Chancellor of the Exchequer. I brought my shiny, nice, red briefcase in and came in muttering to myself like the white rabbit in *Alice in Wonderland*:

> "Oh deary me, deary me. What am I going to do? The Public sector borrowing requirement, headache, and headache. Always borrowing. Who can I raid this year, who has lots of cash? We did the banks last year."
>
> "I know – Oil Companies. Petroleum Revenue Tax (PRT) – that's the ticket!"

And off I went, twirling and singing "PRT, PRT" out of the room.

What was so wonderful about this theatre was that by really entering into the flow and the fun of the drama we managed to simulate a pattern of behaviours and events full of insights and also remarkably close to things that actually happened, particularly:

- There were fewer serious players than had been expected.
- Some potential entrants would drop by the way.
- British Gas, who you would have expected to have been a key player, was really almost out of it, as they were far too slow to put a coherent strategy together.
- PRT might well go up, something that the industry had been assuming would never happen.

The event was not only rich in insights but paved the way for a successful entry into this new market for Amerada. Some years later I did spot that they exited the market for a handsome price, something in the order of a couple of million pounds.

Some months later I was invited out to lunch in a posh restaurant in London's West End by the Strategic Planning Director. He told me that the Government move, which actually materialised to put up Petroleum Revenue tax, had so shocked the other oil companies that they hadn't even begun to lobby against it. Amerada had by contrast immediately staged a major campaign to modify the fiscal changes so that the tax increase didn't put fresh investments, which would bring incremental tax receipts in, at risk.

He said he really couldn't understand the difference in behaviours. I asked him: "well, do you not see the difference?" They had not done a scenario exercise like you did so they would have been in a state of really deep shock and so their reaction time would have been much, much slower.

There are some most interesting lessons from this case of scenarios:

- You need to do a fair amount of preparation to get the basic data e.g. on environmental trends first.
- The industry system model needs to be drawn.
- Using the Uncertainty Grid the most volatile variables pinned down.
- The base positions, capabilities, resources, stakeholder agendas and strategic intent of each of the key players needs to be provided to the team role playing the specific player.
- After each sub-team has got inside the head of their allotted player they then have to place their strategic bet in the competitive arena, having truly had their "out-of-body" experience.
- You need to synthesise the whole lot by seeing what the likely results will be of all the external factors, as well as the interplay between the behaviours and actions of all the key actors.

Finally, there needs to be a "wash up" session afterward that distils the more specific insights, that records the main storyline and draws out the implications and also formally feeds some Strategic Option Grid analysis into the planning and decision-making process.

A more recent systemic model is in Figure 7.2 for the factors driving the global oil price split into three sub-systems: supply, the price itself and demand. This was used extensively on workshops attended by senior executives in 2015 to 2016 in the Middle East and London. At the time the oil price had suffered a massive fall but had bounced back. The causes of this fall were many: shale oil, the intent of the U.S. Government, the strategy of the Saudis and softening demand due to many factors.

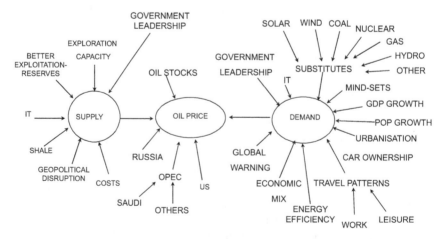

Figure 7.2 Systemic Model for Scenario Storytelling: The Global Oil Industry

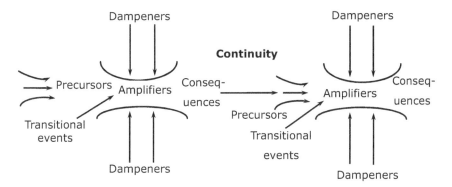

Figure 7.3 Multiple Uncertainty Tunnels

Another important thing to consider is the time scales for the scenario and the possibility of multiple Uncertainty Tunnels and to introduce that as another model into dynamic competitive strategy. Figure 7.3 does precisely this, as we see an Uncertainty Tunnel with abrupt discontinuity that is followed by continuity and then by a period of continuity. **This is then followed by a second Uncertainty Tunnel.**

If you think that the external environment can move through such multiple tunnels what about the internal environment? This can move through a "tunnel" on even shorter time scales as we move through different organizational changes! All the more reason for sensing the future ahead and its potential twists and turns. Witness the Tesco case later in the chapter over the period 2013 to 2016.

So we see a roller coaster effect of change, which we show in Figure 7.4. This might be drawn as either a rate of change curve, which represents the external environment, or the rate of internal change, or combined. Figure 7.4 shows two curves with lags for both the external and internal rate of change. These would be of intellectual elegance were they not so real and scary to managers caught up in the real world. I am certain from where I sit as a consultant on the borders of many organisations that these waves of change can seem like a series of tsunamis!

The astute reader might spot the links between Figure 7.4 and the "Speed Grid" in Chapter 1 (Figure 1.10). In Figure 7.4 the gradient of the curve represents the rate of change of the rate of change!

Many periods of acute uncertainty are characterised by multiple Uncertainty Tunnels. For example, in the War in the Pacific we saw earlier there were a number of fairly obvious Uncertainty Tunnels:

- The invasion of certain strategic islands in the Eastern Pacific
- The surprise attack at Pearl Harbor

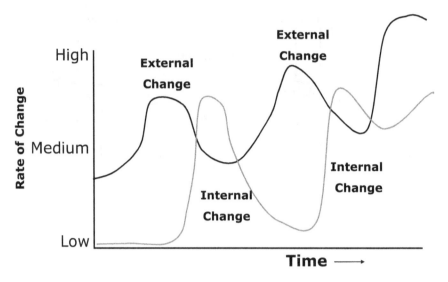

Figure 7.4 Rate of Change Curves

- The battle of Midway
- The battle for the Philippines with the destruction of the bulk of the fire power of the Japanese fleet
- The dropping of the two atomic bombs on Japan.

Likewise, in the Amerada Petroleum case study there were two:

- The bidding for blocks in the North Sea
- The increase in Petroleum Revenue Tax ("PRT").

Or in the case of Brexit there were:

- The Brexit vote itself
- The negotiation of Brexit terms
- The actual implementation, and longer term playing out of, the new political and economic and cultural world
- Potentially, the break-up of the EU itself
- The elections of 2016 and 2017.

So here we would have potentially multiple scenarios: Future 1, Future 2 and Future 3.

Finally, in the case of Tesco we can see two Uncertainty Tunnels (Figure 7.3), both anticipated at least in part using scenario storytelling:

- The Great Discounting War of 1993–1994
- The "Fall" and collapse of Tesco profits 2013–2015.

The up and down story of Tesco

I was involved with Tesco from 1996 to 2000, mainly as a Strategy Consultant and in Executive Development on and off until 2003. I became involved originally in doing some strategic thinking training for up and coming managers at Tesco. I recall that Phil Clarke attended one of my last courses there; I am not sure how much of what I tried to teach stuck with him but at least he did have some exposure to these ideas on the way up to the top. I also coached Richard Brasher, the then UK Marketing Operations Director, who would become Phillip Clarke's number two as CEO of the UK. Richard Brasher and I worked mainly on marketing and brand strategy together.

But my main involvement there wasn't as Tesco's in-company business school but as a Strategy Facilitator. Over 1995–2000 I tried to teach them how to time travel to the future.

Mission impossible 1: Tesco Metro

Tesco Metro was seen as the company's answer to Marks and Spencer foods. Rumour has that it came out of a chance conversation between a Director of Tesco and Terry Leahy as they crossed the High Street of a busy town. One of them said to the other:

> It is a shame that M&S has all the High Street to itself in grocery shopping-maybe we should do something about that?

The result of this was that by the time I came on the scene Tesco had a dozen of them which seemed to have been opened opportunistically – in terms of geography – and without any really clear-ish socio-demographic target.

When I was briefed I was asked to come and help to improve the strategy by doing a "SWOT" analysis, but we went far beyond that. I remember very clearly that when we used the Strategic Option Grid on Metro this led to a very big shift in thinking and to a much cleaner, simpler focused strategy than before. Indeed, it would not be unfair to say that the result was quite an evolution of the model that had evolved as an "emergent strategy."

The outcome of the workshop was a much clearer idea of the ideal product offering, plus the site choice criteria and the target socio-economic and demographic mix that Metro was looking to serve. My sense was that it had not only been a very productive and insightful day, but also that a lot of change had come out of it.

The next day I did a quick call with the business leader who was running it then: how was he feeling? And the answer that came back was that he was absolutely shattered! He put it this way:

> I often commute around a hundred miles each way from the South Coast round the M25 to Tesco's Head Office in Cheshunt and back again. This morning I felt a lot more tired than normal – I don't know why that is.

I then said:

> Well, yesterday what happened was that we rearranged all of your strategic
> furniture and besides throwing out a few things we added some quite new
> ones. So that was probably cognitively and emotionally very disturbing and
> tiring.

This experience taught me *that clients often need as much time to reflect on and to
emotionally digest some new decisions as they need to come to making those decisions.*
That argues for not being so stingy with the time you allow for a workshop.
It depends on the situation; a day was probably not enough on that occasion.

One of the things for sure was that the strategic thinking process – even in
these very early iterations – was able to hugely accelerate the development and
implementation of new strategies, ones that are highly visible today.

Mission impossible 2: will Tesco Express ever succeed?

An even more impressive was some extended coaching sessions that I did with
Liz McMeikan. Liz was then given the job of project manager of Tesco Express,
then amounting to just two rather isolated stores which had not been particularly successful to date. Like Tesco Metro both sub-brands were truly "question
mark" strategies around this time and Express might so very easily not have
made it!

Liz and I began to realise that if we rethought the business model of Express
there were the potentially overwhelming competitive advantages that might
come through the Tesco branding, from greater economies of scale as a national
chain but with local catchment areas. Corner shops would struggle against
Tesco Express, as it would be quicker to do a shopping trip there than in a full-
scale supermarket, and it would be cheaper and more consistent quality.

I imagined time travelling way into the future some years down the line,
and the picture came up of *not just tens of stores but hundreds,* all in new sites,
too. And I said: *"Liz, Tesco needs to totally ahead of that game to gain real first mover
advantages."*

I couldn't have been more correct. The Tesco Express formula became over a
thousand stores – they sprouted everywhere. After a few years, Sainsbury eventually entered the market with Local. ASDA never entered that market, and by
the time it had become a significant part of the market it was too difficult for
them to enter. Indeed, I was really surprised at the slowness of the imitation
effect.

The work that I and Liz did locked away over two days maximum was very
much inspired by relatively simple scenario storytelling, and mental time travel
into the world post-2000, then about five years into the future. Having time
travelled to the future environment and our position, there we were then in
a much better and easier position to tell how the strategy developed going
backwards.

Whilst I had placed Marks and Spencer as being possible entrants to that market as early as 1999 – as it had a strong brand and a very strong convenience food business – it was quite a few years later that they entered that market both with ones in petrol stations and ones at places of high footfall, like near very big train stations. These did not seem to be a success, and it has been said that they overpaid on their rentals, especially in the second category. Eventually they were to do larger food only stores, and that turned out to be a much more "natural strategy."

Indeed, it is interesting that although there was an accelerating dynamic in that market its rate of change was decidedly less than what we see in more contemporary retail and similar markets.

By around 2010, however, Tesco had lost its local store edge with both Sainsbury Local and the revamped Coop chain offering viable alternatives. In addition, the discounters – Aldi, Lidl and Netto – also had smaller, local and quicker to get around shopping experiences than the larger supermarkets. Also, as Tesco charged a price premium over its "mother ship" bigger stores – a return on the convenience (sorry guys, but the idea of differential pricing came originally from me, starting with petrol there!) – they were now seen as overly pricy. Nevertheless, it would have been hard for them to sacrifice margin for retaining and increasing volume.

So with the convenience stores, Tesco faced a competitive incline that was harder to climb. That was mirrored in the dynamic of other, newer parts of its extended and stretched business model.

Mission impossible 3 – "What is non-food?" asked the alien. "Something (or someone) I shouldn't eat?"

The third area of Tesco's strategy that I provided input for was Non-Food. Whilst Tesco Express grew to several billion pounds sales, Non-Food climbed at a stellar rate to over 10 billion pounds turnover. Yet it is probably forgotten what its modest beginnings were. When I was asked into that business I found – as I had at Metro and Express – the strategy to be something between an "emergent" and a "submergent" state. I found the starting point to be: we didn't have a clear definition of what business we were in, where in the market we were trying to dominate, and no real clue how. There was also, not surprisingly, a general lack of confidence surrounding all those who were involved.

So with Non-Food (which was anything basically that you couldn't eat, other than household cleaning materials and washing powders which although you can't eat, weren't classified as that!) these products were limited to a few pharmacies, health and beauty, some Videos and CDs and flowers, and of course, petrol. On the agenda was to consolidate these as a Non-Food business and to diversify.

Again, deciding what the process would be was the key to developing the strategy and not jumping in and grappling with the issues. I felt that we were talking about latent strategic and "competitive space" (see Chapter 10). At the heart of it was the extent to which the natural pull towards convenience, choice and lower pricing outside the High Street environment would make large supermarket stores a plausible substitute.

We also needed to model the potential rate of market growth drivers within the context of the macro-economic environment; that picture looked positive as the UK had come out of a very deep recession and was about to grow with only one pause through 1996 to 2008. I did look at what the Henley Centre for Forecasting suggested about that market, and the wordy stuff that was coming out confirmed the positive picture that came out of my Growth Driver picture, which depicts vectors for things increasing growth and things decreasing it (see Figure 5.3). The Henley stuff was useful but essentially the core thinking on that dimension took maybe an hour.

The two other parts of the jigsaw picture were the customer experience and competitor capability.

I had carefully articulated a "plan for the plan" (see Chapter 11) that would take us step-by-step through three whole days. We allowed a couple of hours to do some competitor visits. With hindsight, we might have spent more time on the customer value added. But the competitor visits were useful in deciding that we were going to avoid their mistakes. I was despatched to be a "mini Espionage team" and went to an ASDA store – I think it must have been the one at Bishops Stortford, as we were staying in a hotel somewhere near Stansted Airport. It was a good thing to go off-site.

I had been expecting ASDA to be more focused in their Non-Food business, but what I saw was not in my view that good. We used a variety of strategy techniques, including growth drivers (Chapter 5), competitor profiling (Chapter 1) and the Strategic Option Grid (Chapter 3), but that was about it. I broke them down into business stream groups like pharmacy, clothing and leisure, and I got them to follow a parallel process, feeding back in a pool and using that to critique and refine their ideas alongside my input etc. Over the three days we covered a lot of ground, and as they presented the output I was furiously transcribing it as I knew that much of their tacit views would be lost over the weekend. It would have been better to have someone "in the know" to have done that so my hands were freer. It was a three-day strategic workshop.

At the end, they all looked quite exhausted but satisfied. I did my summary of where I saw them and the strategies that we had broadly all agreed on, plus the areas to be investigated further. Then I asked them:

So what are you all going to do now?

And there was a curious quiet that fell over them in sharp contrast to the energy and enthusiasm that we had all mustered throughout the three days and slightly boozy evenings. Not only that, but the faces seemed to have worry written all over them.

It was as if I was a football striker with possession of the ball under 25 yards from goal, so I just kicked the ball and it sailed over the keeper curving into the net. I said to them:

> That's a very, very curious silence. You know, from that reaction, *I don't believe that you believe that this is actually possible.* Maybe you are just looking over your shoulder at the last failed attempt to do Non-Food. Wasn't that in the early 1970s and someone "up there" had that memory passed onto them?
>
>   Well, from where I stand here, now, looking at these potential strategies and the potential future that we have sensed out there, I am very confident that you have a fabulous opportunity. It feels just like getting on the bottom of the M1 at 4am on a Sunday morning. It is an open road; it's Birmingham in 90 minutes. Who are you? ***You are Tesco – and you now have the vision, the strategy, and the beginnings of a team and of a potentially awesome brand – just go for it!***

And it was just like the ball had bounced into the net. It was a defining moment that was to see Tesco build a business of over £10 billion a year that was there for the taking without the self-doubt.

I dwelt at length on the case of Non-Food not merely because it was, as they say "Epic" in terms of its business significance, but also because it illustrates a number of really important dynamic factors, namely:

*   *Cognitively*: building up shared cognitive maps of the present and future business positions and environments, and of the competitive dynamics on the way.
*   *Emotionally*: letting go of the fear of failure and insecurity and identifying with the desire to make this happen and to win and win together.
*   *Procedurally*: getting on board a very novel process and used to and trusting in their strategy guide – a part Business School Professor, part strategy consultant, and part whacky thinker who would shake mind-sets and assumptions like a wind shakes apple trees.
*   *Politically*: for all to feel they had the freedom to make this journey and to look to their leader to take that ball from me, Tony G, and to take it and score the next goal, and the one after that.

Interestingly, when I decided to come onto that free ball and kick it myself it was not really my job! It is the leader's. When I actually kicked it I had in my mind an old story. I don't know where I heard it so apologies for not attributing it. It goes like this:

> A CEO was thinking how he could get his people to think differently about their strategy and going off-site in the UK was going to be expensive and they had done it before. He heard about a Swiss hotel that was

really nice and cheaper than the UK. It was high up a mountain which would help them symbolically enter a more strategic thought space than a crowded, crumbling and creaking training centre near Oxford.

Unfortunately, the plane ran into a really bad storm after I had developed some problems in one engine and actually crashed in the mountains. Fortunately, the pilot found a relatively smooth and quite soft and level piece of snow in a mountain valley and all escaped save for minor bruising. The managers crawled out and once gathered the question arose as to which way they should go.

The co-pilot had been trying to keep track of their position in the last 20 miles of the descent, and he drew a map of where he thought they were and where they should go.

So it was they chose to head over a ridge and down. As they descended they eventually saw lights and eventually came to a small village and they went into the nearest bar.

The Marketing Director ordered a round of drinks in German but the barman answered in Italian. The Director couldn't believe it and asked: "Where are we? Switzerland, yes? The Alps?"

The barman replied: "Actually no, the Dolomites, Italy."

A possible moral to this story is:

It might be even more important when people are frozen to have a map even if it's the wrong map (For "Map" read "Plan" here).

Of course, one really must not endeavour to have the wrong plan and a Cunning Plan to boot, too. But should you not have any plan at all that you can actually identify with rather than freezing with indecision, that's worse. And what Tesco had now was not just a map, but a plan and at that time, a Cunning Plan.

Mission Impossible 4: how to sell direct through the internet without cannibalising ourselves

The final example of strategic workshops with Tesco, which were collectively to play a role in kick starting their aggressive growth and their success from 1998 to 2008, was Tesco Direct, that was subsequently renamed Tesco.com. I got a call one Monday asking if I would like to facilitate a one-day session to re-examine the strategy for home-shopping. In common with Tesco Metro, Tesco Express and to a lesser extent, Tesco Non-Food, the home-shopping operation was when I found it, lacking a focus, without any really clear idea of how it was going to compete better than its competitors and what value it would be bringing to customers, and indeed who they would be.

It was also unclear as to what their product offering would be and how logistics and IT would work: it was an "emergent strategy."

Unlike Tesco Express, which was based on existing technology, Tesco Direct (now Tesco.com) was definitely a bigger step-out. There was really nothing around at that time, so the element of future thinking was even greater – and ditto for Non-Food. So it seemed a natural choice to use some scenario storytelling to explore the future and to generate and flesh out strategic options. We were then in 1996, and the Dot Com market was still embryonic. Indeed, the boom in Dot Com was around the turn of the millennium. Amazon was just two years old then!

The starting point, or the "current position," was that Tesco was home delivering a few rather random products to a few random people – at that time things like gift cards and flowers. Indeed, in this case whatever they were doing then was a distraction. So I asked the two sub-teams who worked on the issues to imagine we had a zero base – in effect to think of this as a start-up.

First of all, we tried to time travel five years into the future, and that proved very, very difficult. Basically, even if we tried to take orders for most if not all of Tesco's products (that's another issue) as a mass process we had to make it operationally do-able. When I enquired how they were currently doing it and might do it in the future the answer was: "well to start with we were taking orders over the phone as we were only selling a few things, *but we think we will have to get people to fax it in when they need a proper shop*". Looking back only 19 years, the primitiveness of this seems unbelievable! But that's not a criticism.

I didn't allow myself to be distracted by that assumption. I asked: "So what do you think we will be doing to take orders much further into the future?" The answer was of course that people would be eventually just as used to using the internet as going into a shop. It would need to be low effort and lower cost for both customer and supplier, as they would be making shopping purchases from home that would require a home computer, and better still a laptop for armchair shopping.

So I hypothesised that at some future stage a laptop would be used by a sufficient number of consumers in order for grocery home shopping to really take off. But by when would that happen, and was there any transitional event that could bring it closer in time?

At the time, home computers and laptops were still quite expensive at around £700-£800, but I felt that if that were to drop say by a third to be around the price of a half decent colour TV, then the market would take off. So then I asked: "So what might bring that about?" There was a very plausible event: one of the big pc manufacturers would drop prices by 20% or more and go for volume so that they would rapidly recover to profit, maybe an IBM or an HP.

I then visualised that happening within just two years, which would be perfect as that would be around the time Tesco would have established critical capabilities and a critical mass. With hindsight, that all happened about 18 months later, and there was a further boost to demand as the internet became talked about, trendy, and began to really change all our lives in a steeply rising and non-linear curve. The rest is history.

This chain of reasoning happened in about 45 minutes – sometimes a scenario comes through very quickly. And the crucial breakthroughs in thinking were there in around 5–10 minutes. So we had a most productive one day's strategic thinking to lay the foundation for Tesco.com, now a huge business. But was that enough? Well, probably not, or at least there were some loose ends. Towards the end of that day I shifted from my "build" approach to a more "challenge" approach. The latter is typically done either systematically using the Uncertainty Grid from Chapter 1 or more on the hoof with questioning on:

"So what's the one big thing we have forgotten?" Or;
"So what's the second big thing we have forgotten?"

There is always the first, and usually there's a second. The first one was that home-shopping would cannibalise existing business. I raised that point and also asked who would be our targeted customers? They said, "well, Tesco's of course," which I strongly challenged, as that would not bring much to the business other than more non-food sales. I also warned that Tesco's Group FD might challenge a business case which was a significantly value diluting or destroying element, but I wasn't sure that they really wanted to hear that.

Another unanswered issue was how the logistics would work. In my challenging I did get them to think about the role that pricing of deliveries would take in the competitive combat. They assumed around £5 a delivery. Two days later I was Dyson-ing at home and the thought surfaced: "hold on – what happens if Sainsbury's deliver for £3 or £2 and free for over £100? The margins will be blown."

But the real killer area that I did probe on (but didn't get fully to the bottom of) was logistics. Again, I asked: "So how're the logistics going to work then?" – to which I got thoughtful faces, but no real answers or suggestions. Probing again, I said: "so can we assume that we will have a dedicated logistics facility?" Again, I got no clear response. I do wish that I had really dug in here, as I often do when I morph into a more "Lieutenant Colombo" detective role. With more time, the Uncertainty Grid would have surfaced these uncertainties (Figure 1.7). This is a reminder not to skimp on time and consultancy costs.

Little did I know that Tesco's mind-set was that they were going to try to pick everything from an existing store, thus replicating all the inefficiencies of the customer picking for him/her. This meant that there would be errors, gaps in what was picked and time inefficiencies. Also, how would the financials work out whilst the fixed costs of the store would be paid for by the usual retail business, assuming little overall cannibalisation effect, would that be sufficient to pay for all these incremental picking costs plus the delivery costs?

Whilst my questioning was solid this just shows that you often need quite a bit more time; a second day was needed here at the very least to do a thorough "deep-dive" into the issues, particularly of the "how" and the way a business/operating model would actually work.

Even the delivery strategy was nearly skirted over. But fortunately, I had done some preliminary research before the workshop. I went in search of my then-wife, who I found putting the washing out in the back garden. I asked her: "Ann, what would you pay to get the Tesco shopping delivered to our home?" Answer: "I don't know." Next: "What would happen if the delivery were late?" She stopped and thought for a few seconds and then replied: "I wouldn't use them again. If for example they were late and it was the school run then I couldn't be late, as your son James would go mental!"

When I challenged Tesco on this they admitted that they had not thought at all about the problems of meeting delivery slots. I am told by a manager in a big grocery store that such things are a real operational problem today.

Another area that I tried to probe, which was resisted, was whether they should offer part of their range or all of it. I suggested part, but they insisted it must be all. They wanted to satisfy *all of their customers' needs*. Laudable, but would that ever be profitable?

Were you only to have an order for potatoes, for example, that would be a loss-making business. I am not saying I was right and they were wrong to offer everything, but there were other options and business models. Looking back – just taking for the grocery deliveries – the combined effects of doing the whole range, and not trying to mainly target competitors' customers, the heavy costs of picking would almost certainly resulted in a value-diluting business model.

A final "one big thing that we missed" was the longer-term competitive dynamics which might play out between substitute business models here. Remember that Tesco Non-Food had an edge in some respects like price and convenience versus the High Street – e.g. on clothes.

In a workshop only some months later we foresaw the future rise of the internet and home-shopping. Eventually, after about 10 years – around 2007-ish – this would begin to corrode demand for Tesco Non-Food items such as clothes and electricals, too. So the "click retailers" and even Tesco.com would actually be eating into Tesco Non-Food! I confess that I didn't get that one, but to be fair we were certainly not operating with 10–20 year time scales that day. But with hindsight, one might argue that someone should have seen that coming however by around 2007.

Was the apparent unwillingness to probe the potential downside wrapped up in optimistic cognitive bias here?

Lessons from the Tesco.com case are that:

- Scenario development can be very enlightening and is especially powerful where a market is latent or emerging.
- The process can be surprisingly quick.
- You really need to do some thorough, detailed investigation with some "deep-dives" when trying to generate strategies and business models out of that, and you may need to allow more time for that.
- You have to really probe the downsides and ask a number of times: "So what is the really big thing that we have missed?"

- Beware assuming then that you have got the complete picture or that once done, you won't have to redo or extend the time horizons, nor that the emerging strategy is then something that never needs to be revisited.

So by the late 1990s, Tesco had a number of really strong things going for it which underpinned its ascent not just in terms of growth but also profitability,:

- It had realised that its brand was a real strength based on its customer service excellence and product quality and its fresh store layout (both areas I had the luck to work on).
- It was reaping the rewards of Retail Format innovation through Metro, Express, Non-Food, Dot Com Services and Financial Services.
- Maybe a mixed blessing, but they were beginning to make the international business work.

In a nutshell, they were on a roll. Around 2004 Tesco broke through the £1 billion profit barrier. At that time it was said that "Tesco has one foot on the accelerator and the other foot on Sainsbury's throat."

This momentum built and Tesco could seemingly do no wrong. Based purely on data available from the public domain and from general observation, to understand the evolution of its business model I drew a "business value system," a tool that I had developed around 1995 in the Football business of the network of value generating activities that were interdependent (see Figure 7.5), depicted in the arrow lines there.

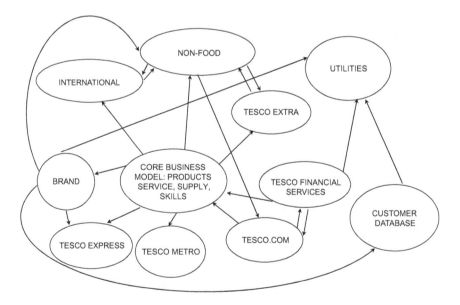

Figure 7.5 Business Value System – Tesco's

There were at least two ways of looking at this model, which shows the Tesco brand feeding into the new formats, online and Financial Services, as well as into International. One take on it is that it was an impressive network of synergies. Another was that it was becoming very complex and given the rate of growth plus the effect of having a much more unwieldy (and possibly political?) organisation that it would become very hard to manage. You might say that this is a view taken in hindsight, but even from the outside there were a number of signs that this strategy was beginning to be a "bridge too far."

This earlier drawing is of the model around 2005 to 2010, and since then a number of only partially related acquisitions were made that made this even more complex and unwieldy.

It would be hard to believe that when it's CEO, Sir Terry Leahy, stepped down in 2010 he didn't see *absolutely any clouds* on the horizon. According to a Strategic Planning Director of another large plc. referring to his surprise departure: "Terry's sense of timing was amazing." Terry had taken Tesco's UK market share according to some sources from 20% to 30% in fourteen years. With the exception of Tesco's predicable failure in the U.S. with a new brand – "Fresh and Easy" – Terry's record was not only exemplary but unblemished. But many shoppers around that time, including myself, were already feeling that Tesco was losing its way. Some were more vociferous in suggesting that Tesco had gotten too big in the UK and a few even called it a "Tescopoly."

A dynamic turning point

Terry had lived through the recession of the early 1990s and had experienced what happened when a slump in disposable incomes finally affected retail grocery sales and competition and margin with the impact of the discounters. Could it be that the knock-on effects of the credit crunch and squeeze of the UK economy plus an even more aggressive attack by the discounters play out that kind of scenario again in the 2010s?

On top of that, as a loyal customer of Tesco I observed a marked decline in customer service which had been "very good to excellent" in my opinion in the late 1990s, to "good" up to 2005, and then "average," fast turning into "weaker" and then "weak" by 2010. As put by an ex-Tesco senior manager: "so much investment headed overseas and the UK network was underinvested and lost ground."

Terry went out on a high in 2010, and at the time I was unsure that the team that took over from him realised the extent of the challenges that were before them. I did not see a sense of urgency and the view at least in the UK was that the strategy was fine. I certainly did not feel it was fine, but around then there seemed little eagerness to listen to outsiders.

I am not sure what really went wrong organisationally after Philip Clarke took over the reins as Group CEO. For sure Tesco didn't feel like the robust, family type culture that it had been in the mid-1990s. But it is not uncommon to find that after a very long period of success that complacency sets in and that when things do start to go wrong a spiral of reactive behaviour sets in. There was a lot of talk about boardroom acrimony in the press around that time, and where there is so much smoke there is probably a fire somewhere.

If we thus look at the dynamic that was being played out, there were thus:

- Changing economic conditions in the UK
- A re-mobilisation of the Discounters who in the case of Lidl were starting to build a reputation for quality. They were achieving double digit growth rates.
- More internal organisational and political rivalry
- Competition generally becoming much more difficult
- Non-food being hurt by the internet and resulting in overcapacity
- Over-saturation of supply making Tesco's property valuations look excessive and its land bank of undeveloped properties and land rather surplus, making improvements in Tesco results would become increasingly difficult
- Decision-making becoming slower and more politically difficult in order to prop up sales and profits; desperate measures became things like: discounting vouchers by 12.5% (£5 cash back for £40 sales) – you don't have to be an FCA and an MBA to work out if margins were 5%, that's potentially throwing away over double that!
- Fraudulent accounting for supplier rebates to the tune of around £250 million. This smacked of desperation to report acceptable results and was a very clear and astonishing Governance failure.

From stardom to The Fall

I think of this phase of the trajectory as being "The Fall." In mid-2014 the wheels came off the wagon and Tesco made a profit warning. Its shares started to slide and that process got worse and worse. In March 2017, even despite the valiant efforts of its new CEO to turn the business around, the share price was still around half the level it had been before Clarke first posted the bad news.

I do find it remarkable that the market and the analysts did not see that the fundamentals of the business and the organisation were not right. You only had to be a customer of Tesco, or a supplier of Tesco, or have seen Philip Clark's personal criticisms of Tesco's own products on social media, which were highly revealing of management style to get a feel that this organisation was losing its way. This is sometimes known as "strategic drift," which is one of the few (existing) tools in strategy that are truly "dynamic." (see Figure 7.6). In strategic drift, the rate of change externally is accelerating whilst the internal rate lags that. Rather than recognise that fundamental strategic change is needed, adjustments are incremental. In Tesco's case, one might even suggest that deterioration in customer service represents negative internal shifts, so the bumpy internal change line actually goes down!

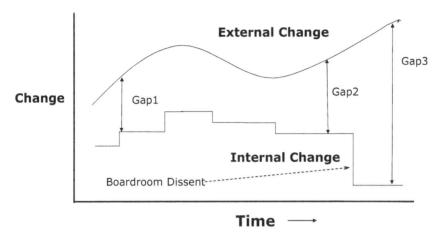

Figure 7.6 "Strategic Drift"

Rapidly the position of the Group CEO Philip Clarke became untenable and after a stream of profits warnings he resigned in July 2014. Tesco head hunted a top manager from Unilever known for his turnaround and change skills – David Lewis – to save Tesco, and his start was hugely accelerated due to the seriousness of their situation. (Lewis had to cancel his holiday and start a month early as things were that dire).

Figure 7.7 is a close approximation to what was happening to Tesco throughout 2008 to 2014; from being a quite a benign market supermarket, retailing became a much tougher and more hostile place. Tesco had been an amazing success. It had gone from £750 million profits in 1997 to £2 billion by 2005, and then £3.1 billion by 2010. Its turnover at its zenith was over £60 billion, and a substantial amount of turnover was outside the UK and there was a separate international business. I did try to suggest in one encounter at very senior level around that time, framing it most positively, "there are huge opportunities in customer service," but that suggestion never went anywhere, although it was supported by an email several pages long.

Looking back on that from the outside, I think that much of what went wrong was to do with on the one hand Tesco having gotten too used to its own success, to underestimating shifts in the market and increased competitive pressure and the effects of economic slow-down. And on the other hand, when results started to slip this would have resulted in panic measures and when these didn't work, pure shock. Had Tesco top management done some scenario storytelling in 2010 (or earlier), then it might have alerted them to the need for strategic change in 2011, and the super-tanker could have steered a less damaging course. *They could have done that.*

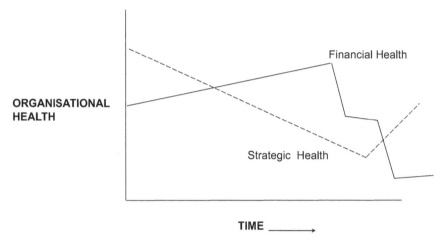

Figure 7.7 Strategic and Financial Health

David Lewis put in place a number of key things mainly as a "detergent" strategy:

- Mothballing some stores that were partially built (a very brave but necessary decision), and the closure of 60 existing stores (half of them smaller stores).
- Disposals of non-core businesses including its South Korean business "Homestore" for £4.2 billion and also: Giraffe restaurants, Howes and Hoole coffee shops.
- Disposals of its five private executive jets for £66 million (who at Tesco bought them? When and why?).
- Attempts to improve customer service by increasing staff numbers (personally I have seen very little real difference in our local store: I had to get the Regional Director down to the Elmers End store to get proper signage for customer service – which usually has long queues).
- Price reductions on staples like vegetables and also off popular brands.
- Marketing campaigns to help provide a pull to customers and to help repair a tarnished brand reputation.
- Accounting write-downs amounting to over £6 billion, so that all the bad news had been taken – making it always so much easier for earnings to bounce back.

I find it slightly astonishing that Tesco embarked on a series of acquisitions pre-2014 without an apparently clear and realistic strategic idea of how it could add value to them. This happened precisely around the time when there were not just "weak signals" from the environment. Actually, there were really quite strong ones from a) major shifts in the structure of demand were happening and b) from the discounters were a lot stronger and better organised than in the mid-1990s. **Maybe this was a case of: DGLFNU: "Don't go looking for nasty uncertainty!"** Is that a form of cognitive bias?

By late 2016 Tesco reported improved sales and market share and it was now ASDA's turn to be facing a competitive and financial squeeze as the discounters pressed home the attack, as ASDA had a price positioning characteristic of a "cost leadership strategy" and was maybe more vulnerable to them than Tesco.

Postscript

Tesco made an approach to buy Booker Foods for £3.7 billion, a large cash and carry supplier with many convenience stores, but this was likely to be scrutinised closely by the regulatory authorities. The strategic logic is interesting, as clearly Tesco saw much of its future in smaller and more convenience stores. So even though our vision 20 years ago for Tesco Express was radiant little did we know that that tiny "tail" would come one day to wag the entire Tesco dog! What better a case for scenario storytelling and time travelling into the future?

In April 2017 Tesco also reported operating profits (before exceptional items) up by 30%, clear evidence of its turnaround.

Meet the new enemy: Lidl

Nothing stays still in this very dynamic game. Funnily enough we used to have an Iceland frozen food store nearby in the posher London suburb area of West Wickham and it was closed down to make way for some new flats. One day I noticed that underneath it a new Lidl had appeared there, so I thought I would give it a try, particularly as I have become allergic to the experience of customer service and the difficulty of finding things in Tesco Elmer's End in South London.

I parked very easily only meters from their front door. I was very surprised to find it well and cleanly decorated with nice displays and signage, trolleys that actually worked and I could get 85% of our weekly shop there and almost 100% of fresh food. It was actually quite spacious inside, rather like a Doctor Who Tardis time machine. The vegetables were fresher and tastier than Tesco's and much, much cheaper. Indeed, the prices were astonishing. I felt I had time travelled backwards price wise by at least 10 years!

There was also some wonderful fresh bread that for the quality was a very good price at the back of store. I could not only get almost all the staples but also some treats like Eton cake deserts for around two pounds and a very generous helping of high quality smoked salmon for around two pounds fifty!

The core advantage of Lidl is that it magically manifests often higher quality products at a substantially lower cost. I was queuing recently and noticed that a

Chinese man was buying some deluxe, tender, long-stemmed broccoli; he had three of them. I pointed to them and said "you like?" His reply was:

> "Lidl good! Lidl much good! Look. This. Cost me 50 pence more Sainsbury, same thing."

Me: "No, we had one recently, *better.*"

Our family now do 70% of our grocery shopping at Lidl and use Tesco and Sainsbury almost entirely for branded and specialist items. We save money, mileage, time (travel and in-store), and masses of frustration, and we get better overall quality and interact with very helpful and nice staff.

As an example of frustration: recently I had to campaign at the Sainsbury High St West Wickham for the light bulbs to be replaced in the Deep Freeze fridges and was told by staff that the contractor just didn't seem interested in repairing it; there was nothing that they could do. This had gone on for weeks and you couldn't see the frozen food! I told them I was going to fix it myself with Head Office and was met with the attitude of "well, go ahead."

When I rung Head Office to complain, they spent five minutes denying that they even had a store there (they actually have two!). It was only as I was insistent that if that were so I would have to visit and tell them this was a fake store that they checked I did mean West WICKHAM, Kent and not West WYCOMBE, Bucks, near High Wycombe! This issue is just one of countless examples of "hygiene-factors-not met" that on top of lack of price competitiveness will continue to leak business and market share from the large stores.

Ten days later after my complaint the store had done absolutely nothing: yellow card

Such cherry-picking shopping patterns that our family exemplify are not that unusual now but common, and Lidl is exploiting that: why carry all the range if the big superstores will do that for them? My cheeky strap-line and Cunning Plan for Lidl would be, paraphrasing Tesco:

> "*Every Lidl Bit Helps.*"

The Lidl check-out staff were extremely fast and helpful and they were happy and did not seem depressed, as often they seem elsewhere.

In terms of a strategic change, dynamic things like Lidl and the discounters suggest that the CEO David Lewis will have a considerably harder time shifting the Tesco culture than his detergent strategies, like disposals and closures: I don't think five years will be enough.

Indeed, Figure 7.5 sums up the dynamic of Tesco very well: you can continue to look pretty good financially (profits, returns, cash flow etc.) whilst strategically your health is dropping. Then suddenly customers drop away, maybe the market loses its shine and competitive pressure goes up. The result is a stepped profits collapse at Tesco. This is often followed by a big reversal in cash flow. Whilst turnaround attempts are made, there is another lag before this kicks in financially. Often short and medium improvements are not sustained as shifts in strategic health are insufficient. This is yet another reminder to focus on the dynamics of competitive strategy and organisational change and to read the future to do this.

Final note: here are two suggestions for Lidl:

- In busy times have a fast track till for a small number of items.
- Have a customer voting scheme for "We Want It Back!" for products only there for a week – e.g. the Blackcurrent Sorbet, May 22–27, 2017.

Some useful lessons on the Tesco case study

After this little "deep-dive" look at contemporary Lidl, let's go back to the story of Tesco, which was the main focus. This case study underlines in so many ways the way in which dynamic effects permeate strategy through:

- Scenario storytelling; this makes it actually really not that difficult to see over the conventional planning horizon, to see around corners and to penetrate the fog of market and competitive uncertainty.
- This makes it easier to detect when an organisation is beginning to lose its way and the behavioural dynamics that can result from complacency followed by denial, shock and then panic.
- Looking down on the competitive battlefield from a helicopter or even an AWACS aeroplane perspective enables us to see how the competitors are likely to move and interact with each other in a cycle of competitive gaming.
- Scenarios, which can also be used to sense how top management will behave in a situation of crisis and the behavioural dynamics which will then have a pivotal influence on the first, second, and third order consequences.

> *After the 2017 Manchester bombing I did put it to the UK intelligence authorities that scenarios with role play games to surface what terrorists might do, when, where and how, could be fruitful, particularly through the "out-of-body" experience. Hopefully the idea will get picked up.*

Key insights and learning lessons from Chapter 7

- Much perceived "uncertainty" can be dissolved or reduced through scenario storytelling.
- Whilst it is not the objective to predict the future scenario story-telling can be remarkably on target.

- It is underpinned by systems thinking, and there are also other strategic tools that can help provide a background – e.g. the "strategic onion."
- Even more dynamic ingredients are understanding potential strategic and stakeholder intent, role playing and spotting transitional events and working through their knock-on effects.
- Scenarios can play a very big role in guiding strategies as in the case of Tesco's new businesses.
- Have a time-frame and this may be followed by another bout of discontinuity – e.g. the extra pressure on the big supermarkets through the 2010s from the economic stagnation and fall in consumer disposable income, the effect of the discounters, changes in shoppers' habits and the impact of internet direct sales on non-food items. There can be multiple futures and Uncertainty Tunnels.
- Reluctance to revisit and refresh these scenarios, and to review strategies, can be caused by complacency and fear and politics, and it reflects poor governance.

In Chapter 10 on stakeholders we look at how scenarios can be applied to stakeholder dynamics and strategic influencing.

Reader exercise

- Using the Uncertainty Tunnel, or the Uncertainty Grid, or both, try to tell some scenario stories for a business or personal issue?

8   Emotional value

The key to competitive advantage

Customers are often the best and the cheapest strategy consultants that we can find anywhere.

$$-\text{Tony G}$$

Introduction

Another dimension of dynamic competitive strategy is how customers feel products and services at an emotional level. "Buyer power" from Porter's five forces is very much governed by emotional value. To examine this deeper we look at customer's perspective first through "motivator – hygiene factor" analysis. We look at a number of examples including BMW, Travelodge and also hot Bikram Yoga, also at the value-over-time curve and then the System of Customer Value. We then translate emotional value into economic value.

We then explore how customers can suggest ways to develop our future strategies, maybe by time travelling into the future with them to examine the art of the possible.

"Motivator and hygiene factors" not met

One way of understanding the key drivers of relative customer value added is the "motivator-hygiene factor" analysis (Grundy 2002). To get a true handle on "competitive position" we need not just know of our general relative value added in the market (the competitor profile) but also what customers think of us. Customers are often the best and the cheapest strategy consultants that we can find.

"Motivators" are the things that were such a turn on that customers would switch from other competitors to get them, as they add a huge amount of value. Or, they are so much of a turn-on that as long as they were there it would be extremely hard to switch to a competitor. "Hygiene factors" are things that you would just assume would be there – you don't get any extra "brownie points" for having them – but if they are not met that is a major turn-off. These are both drawn as vector lines in proportion to their importance and strength.

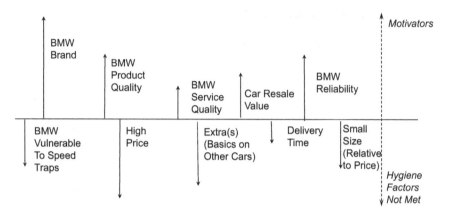

Figure 8.1 Motivator-Hygiene Factor Analysis – BMW Purchase

In this example, we depict the customer value for a fairly frugal but aspiring businessman thinking about a possible purchase of a BMW Three series. Whilst there are certain things that are a very real and distinctive "turn-on" that could either lead to switching to a BMW, or which would make an existing customer reluctant to switch out of that car, these are major things, not minor things.

Hygiene factors are things that if they are met they don't appear on the picture at all. Alas, distinctive value ("motivator factors") are often negated by hygiene factors not met. In the case of the BMW, things like the car being relatively small compared to the price and the fact that you tend to have to pay a lot more for extras can be huge drawbacks – maybe "stoppers."

I was once using this technique with the London Metropolitan Police in a workshop. As I was explaining the technique (with the picture on the BMW in Figure 8.1) when many of them started inexplicably laughing. When I asked them why they were laughing the (then) Deputy Chief Superintendent at the time (a kind of the "Son of God" there) said:

> "Oh, we are all laughing because We Totally Agree With You that BMW's *are more vulnerable to police speed traps*, as we prefer to catch them for speeding than any other car."

It also appears that such duties were rather boring, so to provide more meaning sometime officers would sometimes play a snooker-like game where they got not only more points for catching a BMW but also more too for a red or black one!

The lesson of this story is that different cars were more vulnerable to speeding! I doubt BMW knew this, but this was still a hygiene factor not met!

Motivator and hygiene factors are typically heavily influenced by emotional factors and are a huge potential source of competitive advantage. These emotional elements are dynamic, systematic and only partly visible; these invite psychological investigation – a skill foreign to many if not most hard-nosed, commercial managers hygiene factors are an everyday occurrence.

Now let's take a look at a more complicated example (Hot Bikram Yoga) to explore the customer value Optopus.

Hot Bikram Yoga is a commercialised yoga developed by an Indian named Bikram Choudhury, who created a network of franchised yoga studios around the world – actually over five hundred! This particular yoga is challenging in terms of its strengthening attributes, its emphasis on balance *and the fact that it takes place in a large studio heated to over a hundred degrees Fahrenheit*! The theory of the heat is that it enables the body to be more flexible through warming up the muscles. There are 26 set postures in the fixed sequence, many of which are cardiovascular.

For more on this product have a look on YouTube – e.g. my videos for "Strategic Insights" with the *Accounting and Business Journal* called "Bikram Yoga." See: www. youtube.com/playlist?list=PLhCTkN6YWdPm0bwXix7TXmGQXUBdf-z6N

I did my first Bikram yoga classes in 2000 and am a veteran of 17 years and probably around 600 classes lasting around 900 hours. In 2011 I interviewed Olga Allon, who still runs a studio at London Bridge and also one at Fulham on how that market was changing and what strategic options might be available (see the case in *Demystifying Strategy* Grundy 2012). In that study, I highlighted that:

- The model had been underdeveloped and was amenable to being mixed with other yogas.
- There was a rising threat from "substitutes" in the form of generic hot yoga – e.g. "Breeze" – in my nearby Beckenham.
- There was much more that could be done to refine the experience, to communicate its value and to market it better.
- Individual clubs needed to innovate in the face of an increasingly dynamic but mature market.

Since then Olga led many innovations in bringing in a more varied experience and classes and has been at the forefront of freshening up the business model.

After meeting Olga on a more recent occasion, I suggested using the Optopus model to break down the distinctive value of Hot Yoga taught through the Bikram model. Olga changed my words a little on her website but in essence it is unchanged from those earlier discussions that we had a few years ago. In Figure 8.3 we see eight key distinct areas of customer value:

- Fitness
- Weight loss
- Strength of mind (I called that "determination" and "concentration")
- Healing (of strains and bad joints etc.), and immune system
- Body strength
- Relaxation
- Detox (through the sweat: typically you lose at least a litre of water)
- Skin: it is absolutely true that your skin is smoother.

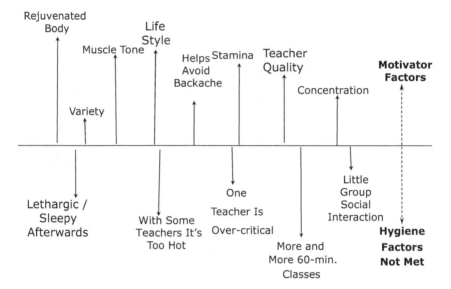

Figure 8.2 Motivator-Hygiene Factor Analysis – Hot Bikram Yoga

The idea behind this was that Hot Bikram Yoga was a one-stop shop which had some of the physical fitness aspects of a gym-type experience and a lot more – including more internal benefits – concerning physical joints, muscles and mentally and emotional health.

Not only is this a very powerful model of how you can build distinctive customer value but also how you can communicate it too. I had visualised these eight characteristics being put on a colourful chart and made into posters – the studio walls are quite dull, just painted white (Mr Bikram's picture seemed to disappear five years or so ago!)

Looking back, I would say that all of those prognostications have come to pass, possibly hastened by the loosing of control from its founders due to reasons that can easily be discovered on Google. Many clubs have dropped the Bikram name, although Bikram yoga is still taught as before – for example, Olga's clubs are called "Hot Yoga Societies" and her former Balham club, which I go to, is now a part of Hot Yoga South.

Despite these changes, the totally packed classes of five years ago with nearly 70 people paying on average over 10 pounds for an hour and a half are not as common, and there are frequent "flash sales," so clearly marketing efforts are a lot heavier.

Let's look at a motivator-hygiene factor analysis of my recent experiences of the practice. I am very aware that these are perhaps idiosyncratic, as I am a long term user and I don't like the cut down 60 minute classes that have been introduced alongside the 90 minute ones – for the time poor – since I feel part fed after these and at the same price as a 90 minute class they are 50% more

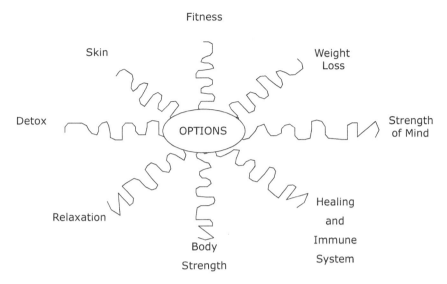

Figure 8.3 The "Value Optopus" – Hot Bikram Yoga

pricey! As I travel nearly 90 minutes there and back (yes, I am an addict!) to do just 60 minutes, the class is barely worth the effort.

Also, whilst I actually encouraged some non-Bikram yoga hot yoga classes, that means I have even fewer Bikram classes to choose from. My motivator-hygiene factor analysis is on Figure 8.2. Whilst there are some very strong positives that haven't really changed over the years, there are some hygiene factors not met *that have changed*:

- The many 60 minute and non-Bikram yoga classes (with the latter I could do those more locally at room temperature of by myself).
- Some teachers do over-cook you and you do feel really lethargic later that same day if they don't open the doors for more air!
- Although I avoid the "one over-critical teacher," it is still a hygiene – factor – not met, as it diminishes choice. Having said that, the quality of teaching is outstanding and I would really miss that.

When I did this analysis – actually as I was recovering from an excellent class: thanks Eugene (Sabala) – I found it interesting that it probably wasn't as over-whelmingly challenging as, say, five years ago. I think that is probably because five years ago I wasn't going to the gym, nor Kundalini Yoga (which is even more challenging), nor doing Pilates as I am doing now, so there is an impact from "other substitutes".

So not only does this illustrative analysis highlight the dynamic shifts that happen within customer value (much of it emotional) over time, but also the importance of dynamic interdependencies between different variables of value and with things outside this, like substitutes. And it is the emotional dimension that is the glue of the value experience: a key message from this chapter.

The value–over–time curve

Let's now turn to another technique that I one invented at an Arsenal game around 1996 called the "value-over-time curve." I hadn't been to a foot-ball game since I was about 15 and went to see Manchester United play. Originally, I was a Bolton Wanders fan, and one of my specialisms was to run on after most goals. I was very quick and always got away, but at Man U I found my match. A police officer intercepted me and picked me up and threw me over the fence and I landed on the concrete! This was something of a trauma, so I left football alone until my son James asked if we could go to see Arsenal.

A then (in the UK) unknown Frenchman named Arsene Wenger became the new manager, so with anticipation I saw my first ever Premiership game. Arse-nal seemed to struggle a bit and actually let a goal in so I felt that as a negative value. Then at around 85 and 80 minutes Arsenal struck twice – I think one was from Ian Wright – and the crowd was in ecstasy. Sorry, Bolton, but I became a convert, an Arsenal fan.

When we were on the way home I drew the first "value-over-time curve" with the initial positive value gradually falling off and then going negative on the Bolton goal, then surging upwards in the last few minutes. *Overall, the areas of the curve relative to the y-axis are positive:* so net value had been added (see Figure 8.4).

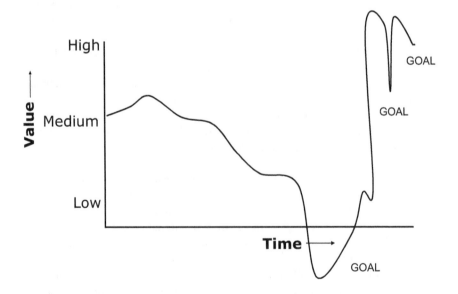

Figure 8.4 Value-Over-Time Curve – Arsenal *v.* Bolton Wanderers

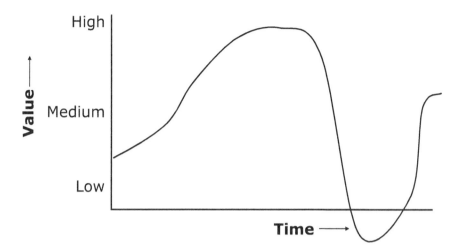

Figure 8.5 Value-Over-Time Curve – Hot Bikram Yoga

Looking at the experience of Bikram yoga (Figure 8.5), this climbs steeply and then comes down and in truth is negative after the session when the tiredness kicks in after around an hour. This needs mitigating with water, food, a couple of oranges and maybe (shock!) a bag of crisps to replace the salt. This analysis – new for this book – was really interesting as the act of drawing the curve made me realise just how that did affect me. Moreover, it also flags an opportunity for the studio to sell more things that can replace energy and electrolytes rather than just letting it fall to customers to deal with.

Clearly the Motivator and hygiene factors and the value-over-time curves are highly complementary and can be used with each other. Emotional value, which at its core is complex and systemic as we will now see with weddings.

Systemic customer value – the case of Sandals weddings on *Back to the Floor*

I was once lucky to see a very funny and interesting documentary on television on a series called *Back to the Floor*. In it, an "employee" who was "new to the company" set off for Antigua in the Caribbean to spend some time as a "Trainee from the UK" called Gali. The programme was called "*Back to the Floor*," which is a hint.

He was about to learn the trade of being weddings coordinator. Each wedding package cost around £5000, and with 500 weddings per year on that site and with 10 sites that is the order of £5000 × 500 × 10 = £25 million a year (excluding any revenues): that is around 12.5% of Sandals' estimated turnover, at that time roughly £200 million, so the weddings operation was substantive. Weddings were promoted in newspaper and TV adverts as being idyllic, romantic and personalised.

The "trainee" Gali is thrown, deep-end into trying to make the best of a bad job. The local operation is laid back in terms of its organisation, with the administrators, the kitchens and the photographers dictating the process which, crammed into a short time each day and each week, results in predictable chaos.

Commentary on TV: "It's one wedding after another"

Gali: "I am trying to find a bride, where would you find a bride at this time of day"? Now there's (loads of them!), (there's) a meeting of the brides. In the heat of the day there's lots of weddings going on all the time. It's ever so hot and there's no water on the table. But there's no time to dwell on that – the table needs setting for the next couple."

Gali tries to coordinate two weddings, both of which the outcome is "not good," with the second being even worse than the first. Now obviously this is a very small sample and many things have no doubt changed, so I am not suggesting anything at all about what they are like now. But on the basis of that experience, it is possible to draw up as many as thirty-five root causes on a fishbone analysis of "why these two weddings were not good."

One of the most notable of the root causes was that the bargaining power of the buyers was low; it is hard if not impossible to complain about a bad wedding experience on account of the fear of making it worse, and you can't just change your mind and say "we are not doing it at all here!"

Gali: "On days like this when we have to do five or six weddings, do we have to too and fro like this to do the washing up of the glasses?"
Lydia: (Weddings administrator): "Yes."
Gali: "I have noticed that the weddings coordinators are involved in many things like picking up telephones and doing things that other departments should be doing. I think that they should be concentrating on talking to the guests, checking what's going to happen, making it special for everybody."

Later on, Gali is asked to sell some extras to his first couple, Martin and Suzanne. He sees them in the gift shop and makes his pitch:

Gali: "I have been looking through our catalogue of things that we have to make your wedding special and I came across something good, called a midnight escapade. It involves decorating your room with flowers, petals on the floor, candles, balloons – really romantic, and the price is only $100."
Martin: "I don't think so, not really." (*Laughing*).

Gali is drawn back to the logistics of organising a stream of weddings, like planes taking off one after the other at Heathrow Airport. After the first wedding, he reflects:

"There was that magic moment (when the photographers signalled prematurely it was time to start) when the table came out to be laid down at the same moment as the music 'here comes the bride' started. I think I will remember that moment as long as I live."

Wedding two: Gali goes to collect the bride.
Commentary: "But some things he hasn't had time to change."
There is tinny music playing on a mobile, cheap looking cassette player. We hear deep, loud, rhythmic music in the background over that.

Gali: "I think that music sounds like it is coming from the pool – that's a pity."

It's not the only distraction, as a laundry trolley rolls past very noisily bumping along the cobbled path only 20 feet away from the couple just taking their marital vows.
   Gali reflects: "What I am seeing and hearing is that we work to a format that isn't aligned to the couples' needs but is for the convenience of the videographer and the photographer – *why don't we do it for the couples, why can't we make it individual?*"
   A video of the wedding gets shown afterwards to the couple. At the start, it comes up as "Mr and Mrs Blake" which is greeted with shrieks of laughter by the couple who say, "you got the wrong name!"

Gali: "Sorry about the crackly noise too – it's the machine. Someone put the wrong video in with the wrong format and it hasn't been fixed."

And finally, Gali takes the two wedding administrators to one side and tells them:
   "I have a confession to make girls, I am actually the MD of Sandals the rest of the world – I have come…*back to the Floor.*"
   The weddings administrators, hearing this, feel tricked and pour cold water over his head!
   Later, Gali takes the local management team back to the weddings location – like the "murder scene" – and makes a meal about how bad the experience and the set-up is, effectively throwing away all hope that they will change much once he has gone back. He helps build a shelter, adds water to the drinks and tinkers with some other minor things. Yet he fails to see the opportunities of complete customer value transformation and a potentially profitable business. I had my doubts watching it whether he was going to survive.
   The consequences of these "not-so-good experiences" were that:

- There might be damage to the brand by dissatisfied customers telling others when they get home.
- Other customers witness them too.
- It might make it very difficult to expand or develop the business to be more premium.

Figure 8.6 represents the very simple areas in which value was being added over customers around that time: a very basic and underdeveloped model.

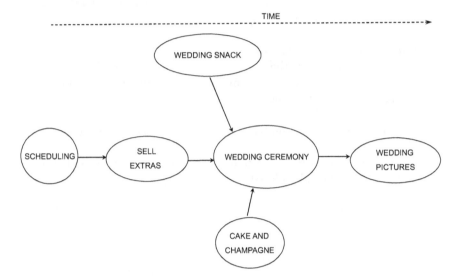

Figure 8.6 Customer Value System at Sandals Weddings – "Before"

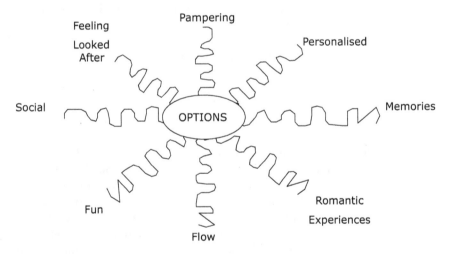

Figure 8.7 The "Value Optopus" – Sandals Weddings

Standing back from this situation, if one used a systemic model of customer value as in Figure 8.7, there are so many other dimensions of potential value to be exploited, including:

- Pampering
- Personalised
- Memories

- Romantic experiences
- Flow
- Fun
- Social (e.g. party with other married couples, being at the same reception)
- Feeling looked after.

Now if we bear those things in mind and reconstruct a possible flow of experiences into a very different model, we might just come up with Figure 8.8, which also has:

- Personalised wedding planning and consultancy starting in the UK
- Packages with discounted business class travel (with alliances and bulk deals) both ways
- Limo pick up
- Proper reception
- Many other special honeymoon/romantic experiences before and after the weddings
- The journey home not neglected
- More relatives encouraged
- Limo back to the airport and surprise reception back at airport in the UK.

With a re-engineered offering, the experience could be much more premium and expand by having separate sites for the actual wedding, maybe with the average prices at £8000, and with 50% more weddings that's:

£8000 × 750 weddings × 10 sites = £60 million a year

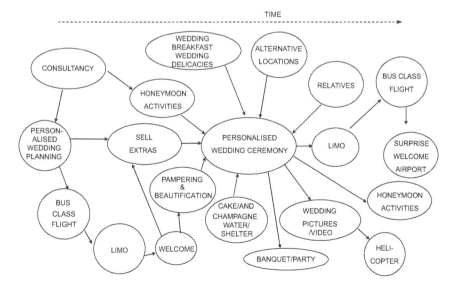

Figure 8.8 Customer Value Systems at Sandals Weddings – "After"

with even better margins too. Plus, in addition, improvements would have also enhanced the revenues from relatives (and friends coming on holiday) as well as the couples themselves.

In a stroke, we have not merely turned Sandals' then ailing wedding business around but also totally reconstructed that business model backwards from the customer and from the couple's emotional value. There was huge emotional value not just not being captured but in part destroyed on such a very special occasion.

At that time, the average cost of a wedding in the UK was around £15,000, and what with both general inflation and the trend to make this an even bigger and bigger event there ought not to be too much of a price ceiling. Usually couples plan an expensive honeymoon, so if that budget is available there ought to be stretch. Also, some of the bulk discounts obtained from airlines could be passed back to the couples.

The Sandals case study is particularly interesting as it shows how mapping the dynamics of customer value can unlock some most interesting and value-added strategies with high returns, especially where there is a lot of latent emotional value. Obviously, you might not wish to stretch that premium pricing too far as it might set about encouraging new entrants, so their potential intent might need to be modelled as well as scenarios for how this might evolve as a global, multi-player business.

It also emphasises that even once one has a new model there is quite a lot of work needed to commercialise it – pricing, marketing, product development, resource deployment, marketing and pricing, profit planning and budgeting. Value capture requires much effort!

Using pictures like this, you can map out how one element of value enables another. By showing this as flow over time from left to right you can generate an entirely new business model. Later, as it is being implemented, you can track the value as it is perceived by customers' using the value-over-time curve.

Putting an economic value on customer value

In my PhD research into linking strategy and economic value, I learnt that "intangible" was a loose and lazy label for many things that were hard to value. These areas of value often had not only very different characteristics but were also difficult to evaluate.

Some were about the future, and some about the now. And others were part of a "set" whose value couldn't easily be extracted out, so they were complex and systemic. Finally, there were some that were generally shrouded in impenetrable uncertainty, and others existed where we just hadn't bothered thinking about them deeply enough or hadn't gathered any real evidence on them.

In short, they weren't a singularity but a diverse family! So rule number 1 needed to be to ask the following:

- What kind of an intangible is it? Is it a "protective" one (avoids cash outflows), an "opportunity" one (dependent on investing afresh and taking risks), or a "contingent" one (requires the alignment of a number of factors)?

- What makes it hard to quantify and why?
- Where are the different pots that its value can be found in?

The last question leads to our introduction of "value drivers". I define a "value driver" as anything in the business internally or externally, directly or indirectly, now or in the future leads to cash inflows.

These Value Drivers might be different for different stakeholders, of course.

Before we get into my more theoretical approach to valuing intangibles, that few, remarkably, have shown much interest in, I would like to flag up one exception to that in Eduardo Porter's book *The Price of Everything* (Amazon. com 2011) that looks closely at anomalies in pricing, especially in the U.S.; it's worth a read.

I particularly liked his linkage of emotional value and pricing, especially in the context of the different pricing regimes operated by some religions. It seems that obtaining a high level of financial subscriptions for membership of a church, in parallel with having severe penalties for ceasing to believe, and high rewards (in the afterlife) for continued faith, *seems to procure far stronger believer loyalty. The lower the price and the more dampened the pay off, the lower the loyalty.*

"Emotional value" is of great consequence in the business-to-business market too, and it is a rich source of competitive advantage. Even in a very competitive market there are often differentiators of an emotional nature to capitalise on. If we add in the techniques of stakeholder analysis that we will cover in Chapter 10, this is an even more powerful combination; *this is a very important point indeed.*

Valuing strategic thinking – and strategic interventions

One intangible that is particularly interesting is the value of strategic thinking (Grundy 2002). From research with both managers and academics, I discovered that its value was generated in many, many ways. I arrived at five big clusters – the "macro-value drivers" of:

- Thought value
- Business value
- Creativity value
- "Soft" value (a combination of confidence, clarity and reduced personal anxiety) and,
- "Personal" value.

"Business value" is figured into:

- Options (including flexibility)
- Decisions (and then splitting this into their protective, emergent, detergent and contingent values).

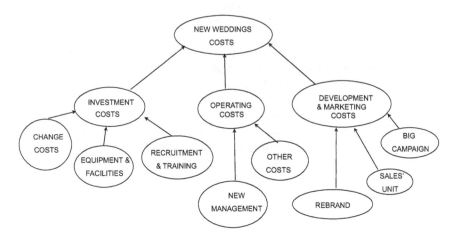

Figure 8.9   Cost Drivers – Sandals Weddings

So if someone were to ask, "how would we assess the value of one of your strategic thinking courses?" then you would have a refined framework for looking in a really good selection of value spots (see Figure 8.10). Effectively this is first segmenting the value, making it then easier to establish some more specific value indicators and also measures, as a step-by-step process.

For example, we could look at whether any difficult decisions of a strategic nature were made much better, quicker and easier relative to the ex-ante situation. And what was it worth, approximately, to make them well and avoid screwing them up? Or, was the level of anxiety down by 50%? Or were there many more options generated than would have been expected normally and what is that potential opportunity stream worth around? Were those options to be forgotten? What would you pay to get them back? What is their "Regret Value?"

Although this is not easy, using these valuation recipes with the exercise of judgement, sensible "what ifs" and, where appropriate, some "hard" evidence collection, economic assessment is usually doable.

Sandals' new projections and incremental profit

Old profit:

Sales × margin% = £25 million × 10% (assumed) = £2.5 million

New Profit:

Sales × margin% (for the couples) = £60 million × 15% (assumed) = £9.0 million

Sales × margin% (for their relatives…3.75 million × 8% (assumed) = £0.3 million

Total £9.3 million

Net increase in profit £9.3 million–£2.5 million = £6.9 million

Over a 5-year period of sustained competitive advantage 5 × £6.9 m = £34.5 million

Extra investment outlay £4.0 million (to upgrade facilities and equipment)

To arrive at a "Value to Cost Ratio" (or "VTCR") – a useful ratio:

Divide the profit increase over 5 years divided by the outlay £34.5 million/£4.0 million = 8.6 times!

Note 1:

Relatives: assume extra one couple per four weddings or
5000 weddings × ¼ × £3000 × 8% (lower margin – as excludes wedding premium) = 0.3 million per annum

Note 2:

Investment in better facilities and new staff £400,000 per site × 10 = £4million.

The mirror side of value drivers is of course "cost drivers" which we define as:

"Anything in the business internally or externally, directly or indirectly, now or in the future leads to *cash outflows*."

These would then need to be broken down into a cost driver tree rather like the one for value, maybe with a structure of: investment cost, operating costs, and marketing and development costs (see Figure 8.9).

One would do Figure 8.9 in depth to arrive at the detailed outlays assumptions and the ones for new costs and new margins.

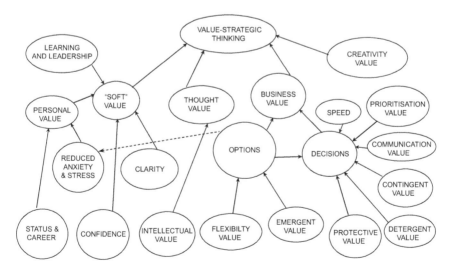

Figure 8.10 Value Drivers – Strategic Thinking

What the Value to Cost ratio above suggests in this case is that, ignoring for simplicity and the time value of money, there would be a big and quick return from the investment, assuming that the strategy was well executed (and also there was equally excellent change management!) With a more conservative view one might assume a gentle build-up of sales and margins over years one and two, and maybe a two-year period decline in margins and sales after then.

Value sharing and Porter's Competitive Forces

To value the strategic thinking that leads to a strategic decision, like the one to change the strategy of Sandals weddings, leads us to consider how value created by a supplier is shared between them and its customer. There was long ago a concept in competitive strategy, no doubt taken from Utility Theory in economics, that there is a thing called "use value": what would be the maximum I would pay for something were it not fairly easy to get something more or less as good from a competing source.

So, if the only restaurant that existed in Croydon (let's suppose Croydon has now become an island – I wish!) was the excellent Koz Turkish Mediterranean restaurant where I live in Shirley. What would I pay for one of their beautiful two course meals and wine? Well, I would pay £85 for a special Koz experience. But what do I actually pay? Well that's £55, so at that price I am getting surplus value of £30 (see A below).

Another benchmark is that at that price I pay maybe a premium of £30 for each meal for two, incrementally as it would cost us £25 to do a similar meal at home with wine, which isn't much.

Let's assume that (ignoring VAT), for Koz to make and serve that £55 meal costs them £45, so their net margin is £10. Then as the value to the customer (us) is £85, the extra underlying value created by Koz of £85–£45 is £40 in total. This £40 made up of our £30 (see A above) plus Koz's £10 margin.

Therefore our share of value created is about £30/£40 ×100% = 75% of the value, and they get 25%. To understand this, it is maybe better to look not so much at the numbers but at a picture – see Figure 8.11. I think we are getting a pretty good deal out of that! Of course, competition helps create such a high share of value for us. Croydon is not an island, and there are many restaurants.

Of course consumers, especially at the end of the chain, may not be able to think consciously about such economics when making their buying decisions. But that doesn't mean that they aren't somehow estimating the economics unconsciously. Also in the business-to-business market buyers are a lot shrewder, and this is all driven strongly by Porter's Competitive Forces, particularly those of buyer power, rivalry and substitutes. Indeed, these all weaken the supplier's ability to get more than half of the utility gain of the customer. Obviously, the stronger emotional element there is in the customer value mix the more the effects of competition is dampened!

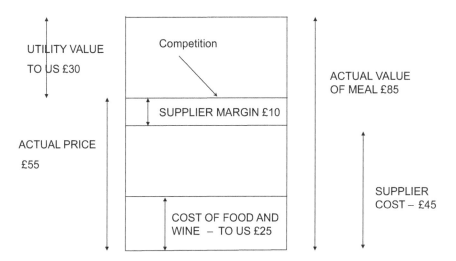

Figure 8.11 Value Sharing – Koz

The final, very important element within this interplay is price mind-set. This is:

> a general perception of what sort of prices things are when set in particular pricing contexts.

So that is not just a function of what it is anyway, but also where you found it. For example if you see a sandwich in Harrods in London you are not going to be shocked at it being £7, or a coat at £4000 etc. You might be shocked to find Tesco selling a data stick for around £10 – I was! – when a similar one on the internet would be £5, or a bayonet light bulb in Sainsbury at £4, but a £1.70 on the internet! Within each and every transaction there is a dynamic of competitive strategy being played out.

Going back to our earlier example of putting a value of the strategic consulting at Sandals weddings, how would we assess how much the consultants should be paid for their successful work? The question is: what value might one attribute to the strategic thinking that sparked that off? You can't say that 100% of it was down to that, as strategies have to be mobilised, executed in full and sustained. So crudely, if we said that the strategy formulation is 20% of the value added in that process and that half that value would have had to be added through the intact team turning the ideas into detailed plans, that leaves still 10% value as attributable to the consultants who brought that thinking to the party.

Such a calculation, albeit approximate, is of interest to clients hiring consultants in deciding whether they are getting fair value or not. If I were a client

I would probably not want to spend more than 5% of the net value generated by a strategy on the initial consulting advice. So if the fee were say £3 million for help say with a strategic review of a notional £1.5 Billion company, then you would want the net value added to the client to be at least £3 million divided by 5% = £60 million! (Fortunately, I am a lot cheaper than that, so if my pitch is of a similar payoff but a fraction of the fee then my relative attractiveness compared to a big "firm" is a no brainer. Such illustrative estimations lead precisely to competitive advantage in B to B (business to business)!

Once upon a time it came to my attention that there is a market in getting advice on hiring consultants! Around 20 years ago I was asked to quote for a big piece of consultancy on the Economic Value of Strategic Decisions in a big energy company. I declined, saying that I didn't want to only get on average one in five pieces of work when I could then get clients without competitive tendering, so I wasn't in that business. My client said: "oh that's a real pity as we thought you have a really good chance?"

I did some quick thinking and said: "It's also rather too big for me, so I really don't think so, but tell you what, I could help you choose the consultants!"

So that's how I got on the panel choosing between these expensive consulting firms, and a few days' most interesting work! I will always remember the day of the bids. The panel was due to meet in London the next day and they put me up in a hotel near Victoria, London. I had just read the bid quickly and was about to go to the bar to meet up and the phone rang. My client asked me if I had read the bids. I said I had skimmed them. He asked: "have you seen the one from GDF consultants?" I said "yes, it's £900,000." He replied: "but that is just for the first stage!"

I imagine as that was the initial scoping of the work that the full fee was at least £4 million or £8 million at current prices! That's unreal!

We eventually gave, as a panel, the work to a less glitzy consultancy which, although solid, still needed a lot of steering, and I was retained to help in that process. Ironically, as the project progressed I began to regret not bidding for the work in the first place.

As we are very much on the subject of customer value, and emotional value in particular, taking the example of strategic consulting input a little further we would probably highlight several areas as per Figure 8.10 to emphasise the following:

- Confidence
- Clarity
- Reduced anxiety
- Reduced stress
- Learning (I particularly focus on the transfer to of learning vis a vis the strategic thinking process)
- Personal value.

But in addition, in the context of strategic consulting there is also "one big thing missing" from that picture and that is:

- Political value.

It is not surprising that neither senior managers mentioned this, as that would be hard to admit, nor the academics who were strategy teachers as opposed to organisational behaviour specialists! This is important here because when you get a cluster of such entangled emotional value then it is a field day for slick organisations to position themselves as some kind of Strategic Mission Impossible agents that will turn a problematic strategy onto a rosy vision and plan for transformational change that they are never going to be around to implement.

As this is set in the context of the fact that they will not be paying these big bills out of their own Directors fees and bonuses, then there can be a much-dampened control over costs and the buyer's mind-set that goes with this – not always but often.

You will see the effects of emotional value leveraging margins and returns in so many parts of everyday commercial experience, from buying an IPhone, a Dyson, a ticket to an Arsenal game, a funeral, an IVF treatment, a Sandal's wedding…the list is endless. From a dynamic competitive strategy perspective, clearly this presents a huge opportunity to reap the benefits of imperfect market competition, but it is not without its risks, as over-milking of such opportunities may attract disruptive new entrants.

Of future customer value

One of the very best contributions to strategy over the past 25 years has been Hamel and Prahalad's *Competing for the Future* (1994), as it emphasises thinking much more about future markets, competitive structures, customers, future customer value, future competitors and future competences ("competitive advantage" broken down), rather than present ones. This is such a simple thought and one that might, on occasion, reverse the conventional model of thinking strategically by thinking about the present first ("Model A") and instead start by visualizing the future ("Model B"), then working out the strategy second.

One option is to time travel into the future and journey to meet future customers – that isn't crazy at all! On one occasion, a senior marketing team at that very large UK life insurance company – the Prudential – wanted me to take them on a journey 10 years into the future to visit future markets, future customers and future customer needs. The goal was to develop some new ideas for products as well as to gain other competitive insights. We actually defined some assumed market segments, and certain members of the team then went off to rehearse role-playing specific individuals who had names (fictitious) jobs, incomes, family circumstances etc. It was really sophisticated and very clever.

This was carefully built up over three days in the basement of a hotel near Euston Station in London (a mistake, as without natural light they are wilting by day 3). Anyway, there were some rich insights and ideas that came out of the customer role-plays by day three, and when we eventually surfaced on that Friday afternoon it was with a new market and competitive context.

Ideally, we would have paid some real "out there" customers to do a one day focus group to be more authentic. So don't be afraid of engaging your customers in how they see the future; actually involve them in any of your strategy development. As I have already said, customers are often the best and cheapest strategy consultants. Not only is that true, but they are almost certainly going to love you for asking them!

Key insights and learning lessons from Chapter 8

- Customer value can be understood using the motivator-hygiene factor analysis to get a handle on how customers see the world and view customer-facing competitive advantage.
- Often companies ruin it for themselves through not meeting hygiene factors rather than failing to be special.
- The profile of these motivator-hygiene factors shifts dynamically over time.
- The Customer Value Optopus is a great way of targeting what you are going to do for the customers that is just *That Special*, and for also communicating that with them.
- Alongside motivator-hygiene factors, the value-over-time curve is a revealing and dynamic representation of the customer experience of value: both can be used to re-engineer a business model as we saw so graphically at Sandals' weddings.
- Further work is then needed to fully commercialise that business model;
- Whilst putting an economic value on customer value can be a little tricky, this can be a most valuable piece of strategic thinking. To bring that off requires an understanding of customer value sharing and the valuation of intangibles, which we saw in the cases of valuing consultancy input on strategy at Sandals and also in the case of the meal at the Koz Restaurant, Shirley.
- This can also be deployed as a weapon in securing competitive advantage at the sales interface.
- Finally, taking all that further we explored mental time travelling into the future to role-play future customers and get their input as cheap if not free strategy consultants to your strategy.

Reader exercises

- What does a motivator and hygiene factor analysis and a value-over-time curve of something you have experienced in business or personally tell you?

9   Case study: Dyson appliances

Introduction

Dyson Appliances is a successful and profitable British company with international operations and sales. Its core products are vacuum cleaners and it also makes and sells a number of products that rely on very rapid air movement-like hand dryers, fans and hair dryers. This case study describes the competitive dynamics of its evolution and looks at prospects going forward.

The case emphasises not just future dynamic, but also that within dynamic competitive strategy we should emphasise the historical dynamics including the history of our past external environment relative competitive positioning (and strategies). The case is based on data from the public domain and personal interpretations and thoughts.

A short competitive history of Dyson

Dyson Appliances was founded in 1991 by the British designer and inventor James Dyson as barleta Ltd in Malmesbury, Somerset, England. In 2015, its sales were £1.74 billion and its profits £448 million, which is an astonishing 25.7% return on sales – an economist's dream. But the real story came earlier with the invention of the first bag-less vacuum cleaner by James Dyson in 1974.

James had always had a passion for designing novel inventions and had already invented a light and very fast military patrol boat and the wheelbarrow with a cylindrical wheel (that wouldn't get bogged down in the mud). But these were tiny as compared with his re-invention of the vacuum cleaner. It was in 1974 that he bought a Hoover junior vacuum cleaner, and though new, it rapidly became less efficient as the Hoover bag was used more which in theory shouldn't have been happening. James became frustrated and ripped a half used bag up and found that the dust from the bag had clogged the pores of the bag.

He visited a sawmill and observed that sawdust was cleared away through using a cyclone and twigged that maybe a cyclone motor was just what he needed. So he made one with some cardboard and other materials and found that his new vacuum cleaner seemed to work well.

Between 1979 and 1984 he tested 5127 prototypes until he felt he had a model that he could take to market. So far so good, but this led to a long and very frustrating phase of trying to commercialise it, which proved very difficult and fraught with uncertainty. The first product to be sold was made by a company that he once worked for called Rotork. The Rotork Cyclone sold just 500 units.

His first attempt to commercialise was with the U.S. corporation Amway in 1984, but that turned sour in months and James was forced to pay to recover his patents.

In 1986, he sold the product via Apex Ltd as the "G Force" and that joint venture didn't really work out. The next step was that Phillips Plastics produced his first real Dyson and was sold for £200, but that didn't work out well and James severed the agreement in 1993 and set up his own plant in Malmesbury to produce the "DC01."

In 1996, his product was featured in one of the Money Programme's best editions, showing him pitted against his adversaries. *By that stage he actually claimed to have wrestled market leadership from Hoover.*

In the second half of the 1990s Dyson broadened its product range with cylinder models and with ones aimed at picking up animal hairs. In 1999, it successfully sued Hoover for patent infringement and in 2001 the company was renamed Dyson Appliances. Around that time Dyson launched a robotic vacuum cleaner and a purple premium washing machine, beginning its move towards related diversification.

In a shocking move, Dyson moved its manufacturing operation to Malaysia, which drew a lot of bad media commentary due to the loss of jobs. Wikipedia records this as bringing down manufacturing costs by 30%, and the fact that Dyson's margins are today are so incredibly high lends support to that.

Another move was to upgrade its technology as it replaced its first-generation single cyclone with one with seven chambers. It may be no coincidence that according to one source in 2001 one of Dyson's most important patents was about to expire and in that same breath pondered: "So do you think that matters?"

In the early 2000s Dyson started to press its international expansion and increased its profitability once again, which had been dented by the reorganisation write-offs and a dip in UK sales as a result of the media commentary.

In the period post-2010 Dyson grew rapidly especially through its overseas sales and especially in the U.S. Initially, Dyson's U.S. invasion was frustrated by the difficulty in getting really good distribution and also because of the very big price premium that American consumers and retailers do not naturally take to. I recall doing some senior executive courses there around 2000 and using my Dyson case, and I also took my Dyson with me (as hand luggage! Security at the airport thought I was a spy!) on workshops for NCR in the Midwest, and for Nokia in California and Texas. No one had seen a Dyson there before!

It is always difficult for an inventor/entrepreneur to step back a bit from the job of running an increasingly complex company, but wisely in my view James moved into the pure R&D role and appointed a career professional CEO to run the business as a mature (but still highly innovative) company. This is,

I believe, one of the major drivers of this outstanding company today, coming on top of James' brilliance and the leadership of the business in its early years.

After what were perhaps some more dubious forays into the robotic vacuum cleaner and the purple washing machine (I always wondered what market research was done into the strategy to do a white good in purple), a more promising stream of products drove off the competences that started Dyson off: the hot air dryer, the bladeless air fan and also very fast moving digital electric motors were feeding the company. R&D has always been high at Dyson, making the return on sales even more remarkable as it is hard to capitalise the lot! In February 2017, Dyson announced a huge new R&D centre in Malmesbury at the former RAF Hullavington Airbase, clearly stating the group's strategic intent to be a centre of world beating technology.

A consistent theme in the Dyson story has been an ongoing series of legal battles with Hoover, Qualtex (in a battle over the Vax vacuum cleaner) and Excel Dryer, who sued Dyson over what were alleged were misleading claims about relative performance levels.

In a BBC Documentary called "Dyson at Home" James Dyson recounts his story of his second venture (after the military boat) – the wheelbarrow with the ball for a wheel – whose distribution strategy was one of the keys to his early success with the Dyson carpet cleaner. His comments reveal how he thought about his ventures – at least originally – but of course later he would be far shrewder commercially:

> I didn't really think about the money. It wasn't about that. It was about starting off with an invention and seeing whether that could be successful in the market place.
>
> At first we tried selling the product to garden sellers. I employed three or four housewives to sell to them and they were laughed away.
>
> So we had to stop that exercise. I then tried to sell through little adverts in the Sunday Times and the Mail next to the baldness and incontinence pads with little drawings of the wheelbarrow. I was absolutely astonished when the cheques kept rolling in.
>
> I had proved that if you design a product well and it really is a genuine improvement that it will sell.

We now go through this very dynamic strategic path of development more slowly and in detail in order to understand its truly fascinating trajectory.

The BBC Money Programme 1995

My italicised comments are added.
Opening commentary:

> *Throughout this historic account of Dyson's market entry, we see over and over again the influence of mind-sets that are highly defensive, especially from Hoover, who*

seems to be particularly affronted by the new upstart Dyson. Indeed, in my previous literature on strategy I have called that the "Industry Mind-Set" — "the beliefs, the assumptions and the expectations shared within an industry":

INTERVIEWER JANET TREWIN: "Not only is Dyson's new, revolutionary machine not cheap, but it's already outselling its rivals like Panasonic and it has got Hoover that has been cleaning in this market for many years on the defensive. The innovation is that neither of the (Dyson) machines have a bag."

JAMES: "Most of our competitors acknowledge that the technology is a breakthrough and that it is very interesting, which indeed it is."

MIKE RUTTER, EUROPEAN VP MARKETING, HOOVER: "Well Hoover has been in the marketplace since 1919. Since that time there have been a number of "shooting star" competitors that have made short term impact and disappeared. *Dyson is just another one of those* (my italics.)"

ADAM FORMEL, MD PANASONIC: "As far as we are concerned, from the work that we have done there are no particular advantages relative to more traditional products."

Panasonic echoes the Hoover stance

INTERVIEWER: "So it's no better?"

ADAM FORMELA: "It is certainly no better than an Electrolux product."

Only Panasonic seems to be taking Dyson seriously

COLIN DEVONSHIRE, PRODUCT MANAGER, PANASONIC: best-selling product in the UK and he "The figures are actually quite astounding: he is already the best-selling product in the UK and he is outselling all the other manufacturers by two to one."

INTERVIEWER: "The upstart newcomer threatens all the manufacturers and their multi-million-pound profits, and even the very science upon which their empires have been built for half a century, and it has thrown them into confusion."

We then go to a close up of one of the labels that used to be put on the handles of each new Dyson: "say Goodbye to the bag": This was originally at the heart of Dyson's distinctive customer value system.

INTERVIEWER: "This is the essence of the (Dyson) threat: 'Say Goodbye to the Bag.' It is a revolution, and he intends to wipe the floor with the opposition. They (*competitors*), on the other hand, say that is a transient marketing gimmick that will be swept aside by the traditional power houses. It (*the Dyson*) might look weird but Dyson says that it is 100% efficient…the dust is sucked up through the bottom in the normal way, but when it gets into the cyclone it is in effect hit by a whirling cyclone of air, revolving at speeds of up to 920 miles an hour. That separates out the dirt, flinging it against the walls of the cyclone. The clean air escapes through a chimney at the top, the dirt is left inside, and you empty the dirt and not a bag in site."

"And it is that concept that has left other manufacturers in a flat spin."

JAMES DYSON TELLS THE INTERVIEWER: "Well, I was vacuuming at home and realised that the cleaner had no suction and replaced the bag and found that although it did one room then it immediately lost all of its suck. I figured the reason for that was the bag hardly had anything at all in it and the pores of the bag had been clogged. So I looked for some alternative technologies and came up with a cyclone…I was delighted that the vacuum cleaner (my new version) worked brilliantly."

INTERVIEWER: "Dyson has stolen more than a quarter of the UK market despite the fact that the product is twice the price of most popular vacuum cleaners. Holders of the Royal Warrant, they (*Hoover*) have held the number one slot almost without break since 1922" (73 years to that point).

When I first saw this programme this was one of the most impressive things about the Dyson phenomenon: it was as if there was a rupture in the fabric of competitive space-time that profoundly influenced the forces of gravitational attraction towards Dyson and away from the traditional players.

MIKE RUTTER (HOOVER): "The bag does not clog, it does not have any reduction of suction, we have 50% more power minimum than a Dyson Cyclonic."

INTERVIEWER: "So what he is saying is wrong, so the bag pores do not clog in the bag?"

MIKE RUTTER (HOOVER): "He may be talking about technology that's from the? 1970s, but technology has moved on."

It is not clear from this whether Michael Rutter was just in public denial of the obvious advantages of Dyson or whether he was actually deluding himself.

INTERVIEWER: "It may of course not be relevant, but the bag market itself (*for the UK*) is vast and is worth about an estimated £100 million a year. The main players all have a share of it, which is why they want to see Dyson sent packing."

The Dyson case exemplifies so well the qualitative difference between the market for first time purchases and the secondary after-service market. In the latter case, where this ties the customer into a specific supplier, Porter's Forces will be so very much more attractive there because of the very low bargaining power of the buyers. Buyers will be more vulnerable to being milked (as in the Hoover bag market). Such a cosy market will also, of course, increase the threat of entry by disrupters.

INTERVIEWER: "Whilst at the start it was word of mouth that got the ball rolling it is true that Dyson has used more sophisticated marketing techniques."

ELECTROLUX: "He was offering retail, in-store people to take the product home with them and use it, which gave them the confidence in the product. So they weren't afraid to go up to people coming into store and demonstrate the product to them."

INTERVIEWER: "Is that an unusual thing for them to do?"

ELECTROLUX: "It is an unusual thing for them to do, and I feel aggrieved that I didn't think of that first."

MIKE RUTTER, HOOVER: "I think that he's a good inventor; he has been very good at marketing and he has challenged my organisation. My organisation and I, befitting my character, are responding in an aggressive fashion and we will see Mr Dyson off."

We again go back to the theme of the complacent, collusive, competitive structure:

INTERVIEWER: "Dyson approached Hoover, Electrolux and Panasonic and all the big boys with this idea and they all laughed him away."

JAMES DYSON: "I don't think that they are really interested in the technology, that's the thing that drives me on. I think that they are more interested in making money and protecting their market and making money out of bags."

INTERVIEWER: "They are complacent?"

JAMES DYSON: "I think they are complacent, yes!"

INTERVIEWER: "In Glasgow the Hoover design engineers are more traditional – they too are working on new models – with bags. They say that they are unstinting in looking for new ways to pick up the billions of dog hairs and daily debris of the world but nonetheless, Dyson came as a horrid shock."

MIKE RUTTER, HOOVER: "Hoover must respond to all challenges, for instance earlier in the New Year Hoover will be introducing new models in colours such as yellow, tropical green and strong reds, obviously to fit the fashion."

INTERVIEWER: "Is yellow significant?"

MIKE RUTTER, HOOVER: "Yellow is always significant."

INTERVIEWER: "Dyson invented the yellow vacuum cleaner? Didn't he?" (*Chuckling a bit*) "No one did a yellow vacuum cleaner before Dyson came along."

It would seem that faced with such a fundamentally challenging competitive attack of the kind envisioned by Sun Tzu in The Art of War, *Hoover's response is clutching for straws. Hoover does seem to have missed the point here: the combination of doing away with the hassle and the cost of the bags and the promises of more consistency of suction plus the trendiness of the product and its emotional value more than outweighs the price being double.*

MIKE RUTTER, HOOVER: "One is always happy to acknowledge James' inventions in those areas, but quite frankly we take that tune from things like the use of yellow in cars."

INTERVIEWER: "Hoover was happy that they knew what they were doing when they turned Dyson away. They get a dozen approaches a week for earth-moving cleaners. They know a good product when they see one and Dyson wasn't it. But now they admit unashamedly they wished they had strangled the Dyson baby at birth."

MIKE RUTTER, HOOVER: "There are two reasons for taking on new technology. The first is to put it into your product range and the second is to take it off the shelf so that no-one else can use it. We actually believe that our products beat the Dyson on all the key features. However, I do regret that Hoover as a company did not take the product off the shelf. It would have lain there and not have been used."

Which is a shocking admission of anti-competitive behaviour.

INTERVIEWER: "So what about now? Would you consider a cyclonic arrangement like this now?"

MIKE RUTTER, HOOVER: "Well, it has some benefits, he has exploited them but he has patented them. So even if he chose to go down that route we can't, so we won't."

JAMES DYSON: "Well that's nice to hear. But I think that unless they get rid of the bag they have a real problem. We believe that they can't (get around the patent)."

INTERVIEWER: "So they are stuck?"

JAMES DYSON: "It looks like it" (*chuckling*).

At that time of seeing this on TV I had mixed thoughts: strategically Hoover and the others could not rely on their conventional competitive recipes to either stop further erosion of their market share by Dyson nor to reverse his gains. But equally, Dyson could not assume that the opposition would not try something to get around the cyclonic patent. Indeed, I was sure that they would.

I also wonder whether Hoover might have been deliberately trying to get Dyson to believe that he was safe whilst they were working around the clock. On balance, I didn't feel that was the card Hoover was playing and that the threat of imitation was more likely to come from Panasonic or Electrolux. But I also had another scenario that Mr Rutter would have moved jobs or been fired, as maybe his employers had thought that he hadn't come over that well! Anyway, never assume static competitive structures, assume dynamic ones.

> MIKE RUTTER, HOOVER: "He has probably got another 18 months out of his cash cow products; at the end of that period will come the crunch. Will he make a step out of being a small, niche player to become a multi branded one? If he can then he has a chance to survive. If not, then he should do the same as he did with his other businesses and sell them and move on to another inventor-driven stream."

Again, in this game of cards, what was going on here? Was Michael Rutter sending a weak signal that Hoover could find deep pockets to buy him out? Probably not as for a start this might have attracted the Competitive Monopolies Authorities. More likely that Hoover was so rattled by the attack that they just preferred to fantasise that the threat was just going to "go away" somehow. In strategic terms, it simply was not correct to write off Dyson as a niche player (if the market is happy with just two products or at least just a few then that just brings greater economies of scale and simplicity). Even more importantly, a company with a market share of 25% (and if that were in terms of numbers sold only you might say that with the Dyson costing twice as much) is not a "small player."

Dyson's success 1993–1996 was nothing short of stunning, as he came from having no position at all in the market to having not only patents that appeared to prevent rapid copying of his bag-less technology but also a business model that was lean, focused, fresh and overall a far superior emotional appeal that in itself gave him a couple of years lead on his competitors. ***He was a honey badger look-alike!***

Studying this very case led me to create the sister technique to "fishbone analysis" of "wishbone analysis" which we see in Figure 9.1 (which we saw originally as Figure 2.5 in Chapter 2).

In this wishbone analysis, we see that there were a number of mutually reinforcing competitive advantages like no bag, premium price (signally quality and also prestige), simple product range, positive media coverage etc. In addition, I also showed some other preconditions of continued success such as the assumption that the competitors didn't imitate Dyson, and continued positive media coverage.

Even into 1997 and 1998 I felt that many of these were potentially fragile or at least could be eroded. We will return to these after the next section interpreting and evaluating the Money Programme's material.

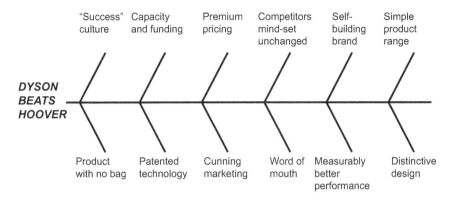

Figure 9.1 Wishbone Analysis

Some comments on the money programme

The interactive debate that was channelled through the excellent interviewer, Janet Trewin, surfaced quite graphically the industry mind-set and how it was disrupted by an aggressive new entrant Dyson in a manner rather reminiscent of the honey badger earlier in the book. Clearly, at least Hoover and to a lesser extent the other players were badly thrown by the effects of, and the implications of, his attack. They were reacting for the most part like frozen animals. But a danger ahead I felt at the time was that having scored such an overwhelming victory it might not be long before there was the onset of complacency there too.

I also felt that the other players could and to varying extends would fight back in a more strategic way than they had to date. I decided that it would be useful to run some simulations of that future.

At the time, I was running six or so of my Breakthrough Strategic Thinking courses each year and another four similar ("Mini MBA") courses in London. I ran a case study simulation of Dyson and its competitors with a huge number of Senior Executives over the next 10 years or so, probably about a hundred times with four sub-groups in each one (Dyson, Hoover, Electrolux, Panasonic or a new entrant) to get a view of their "degrees of strategic freedom/options/strategic intent/evaluation of options, plus how the new market and competitive structures might pan out.

So there were probably a hundred scenarios done in all, and four hundred competitor profiles!

I also tracked all the press cuttings of what was said about all the players.

Typically, after we had familiarised ourselves with the bases for Dyson's success, I would get the executives to then "think customer" and think customer experience and customer value. Whilst I didn't actually have the Value Optopus around that time, I did separate out for people, things like:

- Effectiveness
- Design
- Weight (many Dyson's were rather heavy)
- Status and life style
- Reliability
- The flex
- Animal hairs and dust mites
- No bag, dust disposal.

These were eight useful variables (see Figure 9.2).

After my recent trip to the new Dyson store near Marble Arch, London, I would add "fashion" explicitly to "status and life style": as much expressive as functional.

Continuing, I then encouraged the executives to draw a picture of what their end product looked like and of the target customer doing something exciting with it: this is called a "Rich Picture" (not my invention).

Finally, overlaid on that were dimensions of the more generic Optopus to think about, for instance:

- Customer segmentation;
- New areas of customer value – e.g. other products;
- Market segmentation – e.g. industrial applications.

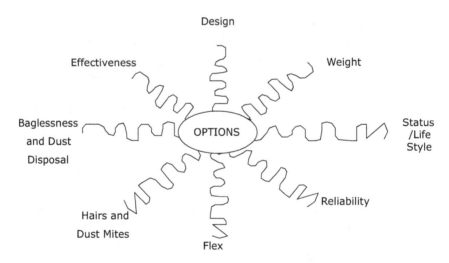

Figure 9.2 The "Value Optopus" – Dyson Vacuum Cleaner

All together, these produced a huge variety of ideas that were evaluated through the Strategic Option Grid, and the other "Deep-Dive" techniques we explored earlier in the book. Some of the more interesting ideas that came up regularly were:

- *The weight*: this was a frequent complaint by smaller people, the elderly, and some women, that most Dyson's were simply too heavy and cumbersome: this suggested "The Dyson Lite."
- *The flex*: this was the next thing that I would have put on my list after getting rid of the bag. I did studies of my own Dyson use with ergonomic principles that suggested that probably 15%–20% of the time that I spent Dyson-ing and 35% of the frustration went into moving the wire around not only to maneuvre the machine but also re-plugging it in different sockets. (I will return to this idea later.).
- *Status and life style*: more could have been made of this like special editions, the "Dyson club", the personalised Dyson (like Dell computers with colour etc.). Each could have a name too, building up emotional value and loyalty.
- *Bagless and dust*: the option of having no dust visibility and sensing devices.
- *Personalisation*: visualized as long as 17 years ago but only recently embodied in the different coloured nozzles of the cordless top of the range, V8.

A really important, if obvious, point here is that whilst Dyson majors on technology and functionality as a deliberate strategies, there is a parallel, emergent one of competing on emotional value. As owning a Dyson (with some exceptions; some have not enjoyed them) this frequently converts into a very strong emotional attachment and loyalty (see my story at the end of the chapter). So we see here a very strong link between this case study and the last chapter on emotional value.

Dyson 1999 to 2002

During this period whilst the business was still growing, I detected what I felt were some changes that I picked up as Ansoff-like "weak signals."

The first thing I spotted when I was being an alien anthropologist was the departmental retailer John Lewis that was renowned for its service around 1999. My then partner (second wife-designate) was absorbed in shopping (that and her laptop absorbed her) and I said: "Darling, do you mind if I go over to electricals and watch some vacuum cleaner buying behaviour?"

"Of course not" she replied – she was probably glad to not have me around, as our relationship reached an early peak and even by then was in "secular decline" in my opinion, as economists might say.

So without distractions, I hid behind some clothes at the edge of electricals and tuned into the discussion of a couple asking the sales guy what his take was of the Dyson versus the rest of the competition. (In those days people really talked about Dysons – it was for sure a talking point at dinner parties in middle class homes.) Many people would leave it in their hallways as they felt the design was cute or as a more obvious, status symbol. Where I lived then was a posh part of the South East and there it was just as much a part of conspicuous consumption as having a BMW in your drive.

The conversation went like this (I will make up the names):

MR SMITH: "Could we just ask you for a minute about vacuum cleaners as we know now there are more choices and it gets confusing."

MRS SMITH: "Yes, and some of the new ones are pricey."

JOE (SALESMAN): "Sure, what would you like to know?"

MR SMITH: "Well, for a start, the Dyson there, could you tell us more about it?"

JOE: "Well it's the market leader and we were the first to sell it in the UK; it has done really well."

MR SMITH: "Can I ask what those yellow things are?"

JOE: "They are filters."

MRS SMITH: "So they last forever?"

JOE: "No. They need changing at least once a year."

MR SMITH: "So how much do those cost?"

JOE: "£20 a year."

MR AND MRS SMITH IN UNISON: "Oh…"

MRS SMITH: "Well what else do you have that's good?"

JOE: "Well, actually, we are now selling the new Miele which is selling really well here; in fact last week I sold more of those than Dysons."

At that point, I retreated in shock. Interpreting what I had just heard it seemed on the surface that Dyson had either replicated the income stream of selling bags but in another form *Or* he had failed to design (at that time) lifetime filters. Either way I felt that Dyson was showing some early signs of losing its competitive and cultural edge.

The second weak signal was when I was at my then business school – Cranfield School of Management has a very large facility for Executive Development in a new building. There was a large atrium where faculty would hang around philosophising when not teaching or doing admin – not my thing! I was there to teach and when I wasn't teaching I could be somewhere else on the planet!

Anyway, on one occasion I was hanging around and overheard an MBA student saying he was at Dyson. So I asked him, "How's the business and how is James?"

The reply was a surprise:

Actually we have recruited managerially really heavily from outside and to my mind what seems to be happening is that as we are a market leader etc; then the mind-set is that we should recruit people who have already worked with big name companies. But I think that what we are getting is more and more people whose political skills are more paramount than their other skills. We seem – and it's just a personal view – to be importing the culture of the older and more mature corporation.

I thanked him for that and was very thoughtful afterwards as that fitted a possible hypothesis about some competitive decay creeping in.

There were also a number of things that worried me: increasingly the press who had been all behind Dyson were now beginning to run some critical stories about unhappy customers. In one farfetched story, *someone actually suggested that after something went wrong with his hose and his Dyson actually attacked him. He fell and was injured, so he tried to get compensation for the attack!*

Sometime around then I did some scenarios myself of Dyson's future trajectory. By that time there were a number of other cyclonics launched which challenged his patents, and I also believe that around then his major patent was due to expire. In my scenario it went:

- Over the next 18 months competition intensifies in the UK and Dyson comes under pressure.
- James decides that his cost base is too high and there are job losses.
- Some of Dyson's better talent decide to leave.

Whilst I didn't quite get the exact form of the pause in Dyson's competitive advancement, events publicly did do something rather along those very lines. Dyson's most public decision to move manufacturing to Malaysia resulted in more job losses than I had visualised and attracted some very bad media publicity, including some on primetime news. Not only were the job losses damaging to the profit and loss account, but so too was an apparent market backlash which stemmed UK sales. According to media reporting at the time Dyson's profits fell considerably (but to what extent that was restructuring costs of squeezed margin was unclear).

At the time, I felt that Dyson might struggle to get back on track and that organisationally Dyson might struggle to evolve. It seemed to me to need to move from an entrepreneurial technology-led organisation with a highly charismatic but self-taught leader that was "top-down," to one with a balanced management team led by a career CEO. Although systematic and commercial in its style, it also retained a lot of the original agility of thought, behaviour and action with James' own design and engineering spark still very much in play. I was wrong: Dyson rebalanced that mix and bounced back with a vengeance, particularly after 2010 with impressive rises in sales, and recovered its past level of super-normal profits..

Also, in its international operations, which set off initially with somewhat faltering strategies, Dyson got its act together especially in the US, the graveyard for UK companies who go there thinking as they speak English (Do they? Well yes and no), that their commercial culture is similar. For sure it's different, as are its economic and competitive structures.

One thing I did observe was that whilst there was a natural push from Dyson to look for other possibilities of exploiting technology commercially a number of these had mixed success. For instance, around 2000 Dyson developed a "concept" robotic model remote control vacuum cleaner that was designed to do an entire house, although there needed to be a manual intervention to do the stairs.

In a video of that time, James describes his wonder product and at the end claims "that this is the vacuum cleaner of the future – eventually all homes will have one." I could never afford the price (see below), but I used to take my "Roomba," a £200 competitor, to play with at Cranfield in the atrium which caused a lot of interest and amusement as the manager couldn't see who was controlling it!

I used to show that video as part of my case study simulation and ask my audience two key questions:

1   Would you be attracted by that concept?
2   Assuming it did do the job it is supposed to do, how much would you pay for it?

There was by no means a universal positive affirmation to question one, which suggested to me that it wouldn't have a market diffusion curve quite like the original bag-less DC01. And when I asked question 2 I got answers ranging from £200 (the then price of the average Dyson) to a maximum of £500. That was really interesting, as in press coverage it was suggested that the machine would be £2500! I used to say at that point:

There are perhaps three people in the country who might be conceivably attracted at a price of £2500:

1   The Queen (showing a spoof picture of her in cleaning attire with a Dyson that appeared in an article) – but of course as she has servants; it wouldn't save time, so that's doubtful;
2   Posh Spice – Victoria Beckham;
3   Myself as a demonstration model, but only if it were less than £1000.

Maybe that was just a play at the "rich" end of the market, and yes, I could see a possibility by selling it through Harrods at that super-premium price, but to me that seemed to be going unnecessarily "over the top" on the price. Indeed, well imbued with my obsession about strategic options and my philosophy of "Never, ever, go direct from problem to solution without first going through the land of 'What are my options?'" Why not sell it at something like £500 a unit initially? Even if the first 500 lost £300 each (as the total costs are £800), then the next 500 units would be £200 and then there would be break even at probably around 3000 units. The investment in entry losses would be:

$$(500 \times £300) + (500 \times £200) + (500 \times £100) = £15,000 + £10,000 + £5,000 = £30000$$

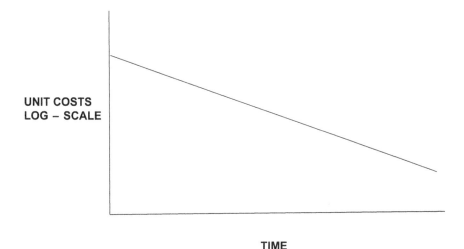

UNIT COSTS
LOG – SCALE

TIME

Figure 9.3 The "Experience Curve" – Declining Unit Costs

This is what is called the "experience curve" or the "learning curve" effect, as once figured very centrally in the strategy literature going back to the 70s and 1980s. The mathematical formulation of this was that using linear regression for many high-tech products, the unit cost declined in a straight line in proportion to cumulative volume since inception, and actually this worked on a "log scale" (see Figure 9.3).

But do you really need or want to know that? (I laugh.) At the very mention of log scale I can sense my readers' breathing getting heavier as it does when one is just about to go to sleep…that's just *Too Technical*. Well I would have spared you that were it not for the fact that where the experience curve effect is the unit cost declines faster and faster and faster so that you might be able to not only smash the break-even barrier quickly for a robotic Dyson but then achieve unit costs unthinkable at the start of production!

So, in terms of strategy had Dyson priced the robotic at initially £500 and just regarded market entry costs as the same thing really as capital expenditure the invention may well have worked! I did buy a robotic "Roomba "at the time and used to set it going at my business school at that time in the Cranfield atrium to see if anyone noticed! Whilst of novelty and amusement, it wasn't that effective but was useful for a half-hearted clean, so there was an open goal for Dyson.

The second diversification project around that time was the Dyson washing machine. This was a technology that was designed to be a lot more ecologically friendly and its other unique selling point was that it could clean a king-sized duvet. Now taking that to the dry cleaners would cost an arm and a leg, so that is a potential benefit; but what proportion of washing machine buyers would see the relevance of that benefit? How often would they use that facility and how often would they actually use it over the lifetime of their machine? Effectively I am trying to tease out the customer value-over-time curve as a dynamic and in numbers.

As an illustration let's assume that it would cost £20 to get a king-sized duvet cleaned, and you might do that twice a year over a machine's lifetime of 8 years:

$$£20 \times 2 \times 8 = £320$$

But Dyson originally marketed his machine at £1200 – which was probably £800 more than the average washing machine of that time – a differential of four times the saving. Whilst there was no doubt that there were some other benefits from a switch from a traditional machine from a customer's economic value perspective, these again seemed insufficient.

The new machine was designed in purple, which again I thought might not have been the best idea. Whilst I fully empathise with James Dyson's drive to make his products distinctive and if necessary to ignore or break the rules, there is a reason why electrical products are "white goods," as they are a part of a "kitchen" which will be designed to have a "look" that something in a purple, orange or pink might mess up. From a marketing perspective, where a male and a female couple are buying together, I believe that this is still the most common purchasing unit when it comes to the washing machine that the female would typically carry most of the voting rights!

Production was abandoned in 2014 as the machine was felt too costly to make. I suspect that the reason for that was that sales volumes were too low, and the price that it could be sold at was also around £700–£800.

A quick focus group for each product idea would almost certainly have flushed out these issues. Remember the cognitive psychologist Kahneman's warning about relying too much on intuition for strategic decision-making.

My hypothesis, which I feel plausible, was that it was James himself who was the driving force behind these strategic decisions around this time and also that this may have diverted some resources and attention away from other areas which in Dyson's later phases of development and evolution have been more successful.

Since 2005 and over the last 12 years Dyson has been making continuous improvements to his vacuum cleaner products and also has been building his research and development capability. This has spun off a number of different types of product including the Airblade – a hot air heater with rapid air movements for public toilets and ones at the workplace and in hotels and restaurants – which does seem to have been successful. Interestingly, this does seem to have spawned imitators even more quickly than his vacuum cleaners did.

Another product has been the hot/cold air fan without blades, again going back to that key capability that first brought the DC01 vacuum cleaner. At current prices, these range from about £550 to £900 whilst competitor models are more like £150 to £400 – a considerable premium. Again, and in common with Dyson's products generally, these are expensive and in some markets and applications it isn't always easy to get away with that as the differential value over other products is often lower. The main advantages here are claimed as being speed and hygiene, although there have been claims that have been disputed that these spread germs.

In addition we have seen in recent years' further product diversification through the bladeless Dyson fan which again sells at a premium price and can either blow cold in summer or hot in winter. This sells for from £300 to £450 and has a number of advantages including quietness and a facility in some to remove pollen from the air. The latter would be of very real value to someone suffering from hay fever.

In 2016 Dyson also launched a hair dryer; this was claimed to be a lot quieter – now there's a very real advantage! Also, Dyson contends that conventional hair dryers can overheat and might damage hair: the Dyson is limited to 150 degrees Centigrade. How easy it will be to translate that claim into a widespread perception of real need that someone will pay £299 for a hair dryer is not quite clear. It is interesting to look at the video reviews on YouTube, which are very positive, except for the fact that it is really expensive. Just like in the case of the Dyson washing machine that we saw earlier, I do wonder whether a cheaper price point (e.g. £250 or £300) might have generated more margin through experience curve effects. One would hope that Dyson's planners run that through a marketing, competitive and financial model to see which option gives the best broad brush NPV (Net Present Value) given the life of the patent?

Counter-balancing this premium cost is the very real appeal of superior hair look plus avoiding burning hair. Both have a potentially big emotional appeal to women and younger men who want to look good.

I interviewed my hairdresser Nicky (who runs "Nix" hairdressers, Portland Road, South Norwood) about this product.

NICKY "Oh yes, the Dyson Hair Dryer, yes we have all heard of that. I haven't used it myself but we have some very, very good hair dryers which we bought for £90."

TONY: "But a Dyson Hair dryer might save you time and thus I might be prepared to pay more. If it was better on that what extra would you spend?"

NICKY (AFTER A 10-SECOND PAUSE): "I would not expect to pay more than an extra £50. It really isn't for the business market."

TONY: "And what about the point about being able to avoid heating the hair too much?"

NICKY: "I really don't see that as a problem. I think that they are very much a gadget thing. And to sell many to the consumer market (which I do do) it has to look good, and in my opinion they don't look good, they don't look stylish."

TONY: "What do you mean, "they don't look good, and they don't look stylish?"

NICKY: "Well just look at that picture on YouTube: the end of it, see, the end of it? It looks…really Masculine, and also it's so chunky…and well the price?? It's just so, so, so expensive. What did you say? £300? There is one really top product, the GHP Professional is at least £90. [Actually the price range is £99 to ££185.] *I actually think that if Dyson had priced it at £150 then they would have a LOT more volume in the consumer market.*" [My italics.]

This is an example of how valuable it is to do a micro piece of strategic market research in order to inform strategic thinking not only about strategic positioning but also to generate strategic options. I said in reply to Nicky:

TONY: "EXACTLY! If Dyson could do some strategic cost targeting of how to get costs down to say £100 assuming sales are direct and VAT is £25, then you would have a unit margin of £25, with the price net of VAT at £125, and a return on sales of 20%, which seems pretty attractive to me; and by selling a multiple number of the machines it currently probably does it could get there through scale economies."

The other thing that I hypothesised here was that perhaps James has a strong influence on the design which has moved it away from a more female style to a more male one? I believe that it was he who came up with the colour of the (discontinued) Dyson washing machine – the Dyson mind-set at the time was "it had to be purple" – which I think would have been an extremely unlikely one for any focus group with just women on it.

It also occurred to me that in due course Dyson might design a women's model and also consider some way of personalising the design (at a premium price). Early steps have been taken to do that, as there is a limited edition model in a special case for £320 via John Lewis. Another thought (Optopus-wise) would be to have a new sales channel like "Dyson parties," as was pioneered by Avon (cosmetics) and Ann Summers (adult accessories). A women's parties channel might be a most promising line of enquiry, as it would create more emotional appeal and social pull, as well as be entrepreneurial for the casual sales force. If successful, the approach could be broadened to other Dyson products – especially to cordless vacuum cleaners and the bladeless fan.

In my recent simulation of Dyson versus the other competitors (2017), I visualized a "competitive mix" which weighted in a visual form the key ingredients by weight of emphasis of the Dyson hair dryer's current competitive positioning. My perception was that these were ranked currently as:

1   Speed of drying (38%)
2   Safety from heat (22%)
3   Image (of the brand) (20%)
4   Design (12%)
5   Style (relatively minor) of the hair (8%).

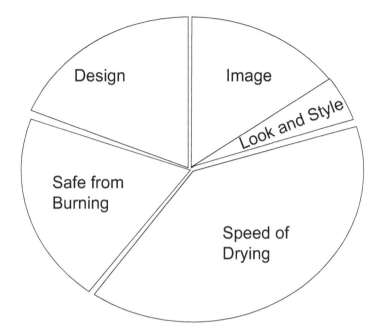

Figure 9.4 The Competitive Mix – Dyson Hair Dryer (Current)

A potential positioning ran like this:

1 Speed of drying (34%)
2 Safety from heat (14%)
3 Personalised (13%) new
4 Design (12%) (product)
5 Image (10%) (lower)
6 Look and style (of hair) (9%)
7 Fair price (8%) (new).

So here we assume that the basic product would be a lot cheaper and it would be personalised for big premium prices. Dyson could also make the benefits of the product more user focused, such as time saving and the end look, and for women, de-emphasise the technology as so fundamental a thing – the video on the web site has a picture of a spinning motor whirring around at 110,000 revolutions a minute: that sounds like a male not a female thing!

The "competitive mix" picture (or, if you prefer, "competitive pie") will be very useful indeed, not only for strategic option formulation and definition, but also for presenting the output of strategic thinking in planning documents.

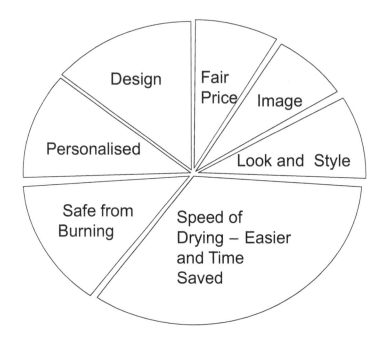

Figure 9.5 The Competitive Mix – Dyson Hair Dryer (Possible)

A very big "wake-up call" for Dyson was the entry into the market of a cordless vacuum cleaner by a new company called GTECH. GTECH does seem to have followed the kind of strategy that Dyson did originally when he entered the market. GTECH took big advertisements in magazines thus cutting out the retailer. Interestingly, going back 15 years or so ago I had identified the opportunity for cordless machines to be a number one possible target for Dyson. It had many of the advantages of the robotic but still provided for human control.

GTECH also invested in some very cunning UK TV advertising. In one advert, there was a small army of attractive young women vacuuming with their conventional machines with their rhythm following the music of Queen:

"I want to break free!!"

Then they are liberated from the wire and can move much more freely with their new GTECH cordless machines: a very powerful message.

GTECH was founded by Nick Grey, another inventor who had spent some time in sales at Vax. He started selling machines – mainly white label – around 2002, so we only saw his brand being sold direct some 10 years later. Around 2012, he did get some excellent press reviews; the Daily Mail ran an article that was used extensively to support his marketing effort entitled:

"Could this be the best vacuum cleaner ever?"

That has been quoted in so many of his adverts in the press, coincidentally in the Daily Mail (!) Here, Nick Grey was using almost the same sales strategy as Dyson in his original entry strategy. His product was very light and claimed to be far more energy efficient. Another benefit was that rather than being potentially messy on emptying the duct with a Dyson (it can easily happen, even though the dust has been compacted to some extent). The GTECH actually creates dust pellets, which is claimed to be less messy.

GTECH also reported several attempts at "industrial espionage" by key competitors that he has used to suggest that they are envious of his technologies and products. Indeed the industry is ultra-nervous about this; in March 2017 I contacted Dyson's technical helpline to ask some basic questions about the Dyson fan, and when I used the word "research" and mentioned my book it really freaked them out! I was put on hold for five minutes and then just referred to the website: understandable!

Going back to GTECH, its products were reported to be initially sold at the cheaper end of the market, and whilst Grey was initially able to get very good prices from his Chinese supplier, over time this arrangement seems to have gotten more difficult. He seems to have adjusted his strategy to have a lot more emphasis on marketing and has set more premium price points with recent prices being closer to £150 to £200 – a lot closer to Dyson's pricing.

It was in late 2016 when it came to my attention that Dyson, who had not gone for what seemed a pretty obvious opportunity, fought back with his own cordless machine. Both GTECH and Dyson were also very light, which was a major second "line of enquiry" I felt Dyson should exploit. So I splashed out and got a second Dyson (to our "Animal" cylindrical cleaner), the cordless Dyson V6. It is so light at around 2.2 kg that I will take it on my next Executive Development programme in the Middle East. Given its small size, I was impressed at is power and efficiency.

In one of Dyson's adverts there are claims that the Dyson (V6) that I have has 10 times the suction of the GTECH. Nick Grey would no doubt claim that the other cordless models waste 75% of their power whilst his doesn't. GTECH has always taken the position that he wants to have an ultra-lightweight machine rather than just going for power, so he wouldn't disagree with the fact that his uses less electricity. Indeed the literature actually suggests (Wikipedia) that over its lifetime the GTECH will save about the same cost in electricity of the cost of actually buying it! So this brings a potential ninth dimension of customer value into the equation: energy efficiency!

Why doesn't Dyson allow for home trial and send back if not happy as GTECH does with its hybrid electrical bike? Or why don't they promote at women's' parties as above?

Interestingly, whilst GTECH may have been seen as a ruthless competitor, it actually suggests to me that it might have also been *a good one* for Dyson as well. I hypothesise that Dyson Appliances, by setting such very high price premiums, is allowing GTECH to leverage that. GTECH is cheaper by a higher margin than Dyson. I appreciate that Dyson is putting out their product as being more heavyweight with a greater technological edge, power and reputation than GTECH, and they wish to be rewarded at that. But is a price of £500 inviting GTECH to attack even more ferociously? It is all a fascinating competitive dynamic, but has Dyson actually gamed all of that? Have they actually role played GTECH?

Going forward, it is clear that Dyson is advancing on a number of technical fronts, and whilst the vacuum cleaners are clearly at the core of the business Dyson is following a much more coherent and commercially grounded strategic logic than in the late 1990s/very early 2000s. That logic is to develop and exploit its competencies in rapid air flow, very fast motors, digital technology and potentially robotics.

Dyson is now reportedly spending many millions of R&D into fisheye digital camera technology for a second-generation robotic. Its pricing follows its original strategic recipes of PREMIUM pricing (with capitals) and mostly that seems to be in a fit with customer-perceived value, the perceived value of which is boosted deliberately by the message about the huge sums it is investing in that. At around £800 will that break out of the "gadget" niche? By making conventional vacuum machines so much more effective, easy and quick, will the time saving element be worth that premium, especially as it seems to take a 4 by 4-meter room about 40 minutes to vacuum?

More generally, Dyson will always be vulnerable to potential "number two" innovators in its markets like GTECH, as those very premiums create a penumbra of market space where that second wave disruptor can claim other advantages that Dyson may have neglected or chosen to ignore, and a better value-for-money proposition. I think that it is rather like top class football; it can be more important to know the spaces where the players are not sometimes, rather than where they are! This underlines the importance

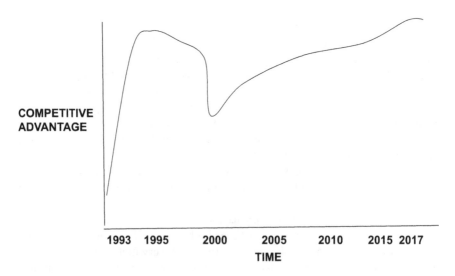

Figure 9.6 Dyson's Competitive Advantage-Over-Time Curve

of having a very clear idea of what the competitive landscape really is and where there is empty and under-occupied *competitive space* as well as *a crowd* (see Figure 9.6 later).

Figure 9.6 shows Dyson's competitive advantage-over-time curve. It is slightly simplistic, as after 2006 Dyson had multiple product lines which ought to have their own curves. With that caveat, we see the astronomic rise of the curve over the first two to three years to become dominant that is characteristic of a disrupter with an overwhelming appeal. Then after competitors try to imitate, this falls off by 2000, and then following the loss of a major patent and the disruptive move to Malaysia there is an abrupt fall, with delayed recovery through cost economics, then technology and product innovation. Arguably, competitive advantage was also diluted over 2000 to 2005 through wasted R&D on the initial robotic and also due to the unsuccessful washing machine. Were we to fully factor in the fact that Dyson was entering other countries from a weaker position, the recovery from 2010 to 2015 was less strong.

I show competitive advantage over 2010 to 2017 climbing steadily, as the R&D pays back through a wave of innovations for the vacuum cleaners, through the success of the hand dryer and the Dyson fan − although initially volumes would have been a fairly small part of the business. Whilst GTECH would have been posing an increased threat, especially after the "We want to break free" video, they were still not large compared to Dyson in the UK who had a much larger global business: but watch this space.

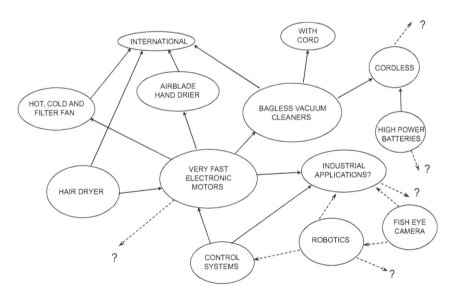

Figure 9.7 Dyson's Business Value System/Opportunities

Figure 9.7 shows the present state of play of Dyson's value-creating activities, highlighting the following:

- Its multi-product businesses that will all have different positions on the GE Grid
- The importance of Dyson's international businesses
- The potential emergence of a second division with a focus on industrial activities.

This picture also shows some dotted lines and question marks for:

- Industrial applications
- Robotics
- Very fast electronic motors
- High storage batteries
- Cordless.

All suggesting possible dynamic lines of enquiry for strategic development, maybe "stepping stone strategies" as I wrote about in my first ever article in *Accountancy Age* in 1983!

I also did an approximate positioning of Dyson's portfolio by product type as of 2017, and all were firmly clustered in the Northwest segment of the General Electric Grid, which would be very comforting based on the analysis of this case study (see Figure 9.8).

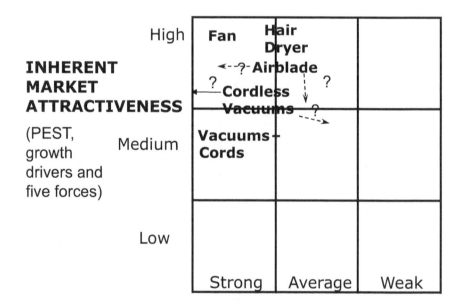

Figure 9.8 The "GE" (General Electric) Grid for Dyson Appliances – Estimated Positions 2017

Here the Dyson fan comes out as very attractive (market wise, growth drivers and competitive forces due to its strong emotional appeal to women and to younger men) and that gives them a strong positioning too relative to older competing products; and there is the patent protection. "Cordless" is a more attractive market, but we have GTECH in the frame so Dyson isn't as dominant as cleaning appliances with cords.

The fan is out on its own for the range of things it does, so it wins on both dimensions. The Airblade had a very high premium that must inhibit sales but might be strengthened. The question marks are there not as definite movements but to illustrate possible shifts. For sure, these 2017 positions are not the same as they would have been three to five years previously.

Such a positive set of GE Grid positionings is entirely consistent with the fact that Dyson enjoys a whacking return on sales of 25% per annum.

And now back to the future: the Dyson Eye (the Dyson 360)

So what is the one big thing we have missed? In late 2016 Dyson launched a robotic some seventeen years after his original attempt. This time it incorporates much more advanced guidance technology which is guided by sensors so that it can navigate its obstacles. It has some good reviews, but at £799.99 it again falls into that area of customer value which may over-rely on a premium image. At first sight that seems really expensive for almost everyone.

I wondered whether Dyson looked at the customer business case for that. If instead of spending say 30 minutes time Dyson-ing, but it still takes 10 minutes per week of management time and the value of marginal time to you (net of tax) is say £12 an hour, the utility value per annum is:

52 week × £12 per hour × 20/60 = £208.

And if we assume that you can buy a great normal Dyson for £240 then the extra cost is £560, so that's a payback period of only 2.7 years – well that's a really interesting selling point! I was surprised by that; is that message an opportunity for Dyson?

So in terms of the competitive landscape and competitive space that we spoke of, I was drawn to map this on two dimensions: quantitative-price positioning and along the bottom axis of functional-to-emotional (value positioning) (see Figure 9.9). Originally, pre-1995 we would have had the bulk of the players as low to medium price, and with more technical functionality (with a Kirby – not shown – at the top left or top middle). Post-Dyson, these would have been squashed in the southwest of the grid. Then GTECH came in and pushed into the medium space, but still more "functional," maybe towards the middle. This still left more competitive space above the southwestern pack.

I did find it difficult positioning Dyson on the horizontal aspect, as it did seem to contain strong elements of both, but probably still with a more functional emphasis. This also suggests ambiguities of its strategy, *although I am not suggesting that functional and emotional are necessarily mutually exclusive.*

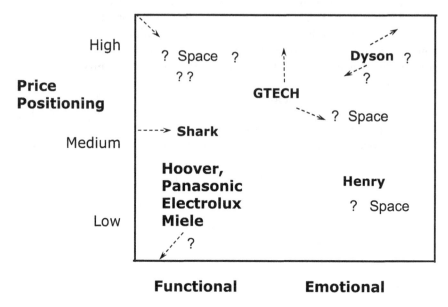

Figure 9.9 Competitive Landscape: UK Vacuum Cleaners 2017

That all sucked in a new player – the Shark – which is cheaper than a Dyson but has a strong reputation, achieving the JD Power Quality Award in the United States, where articles claim it has overtaken Dyson in the US. It advertises heavily and very aggressively and specifically targeted Dyson. The U.S. advertising body told it to refrain from its exaggerated claims relative to Dyson. This is a very real warning to Dyson that its high premium pricing creates attractive competitive space for others and also makes itself more vulnerable. The Dyson – "honey badger" – has paved the way for further disruptive competitors!

Shark is sold in the UK and thus threatens Dyson in its own pond.

Figure 9.9 shows with its question marks a number of other areas where there is competitive space, just like the gaps on the football pitch!

Reader exercise:

- Using the Strategic Optopus (Figure 3.2), or working from Dyson's core competences (Figure 5.14), or using the business value system (Figure 7.5) what are some key strategic options for Dyson?
- How could two or three of the best of these be done in a "cunning" way?
- What is their evaluation using the Strategic Option Grid? (Figure 3.3)
- For one of these, using scenario storytelling, how might this actually pan out in terms of its competitive dynamics?

In March 2017, I ran a simulation of future moves by all the key players in the industry with seven groups of seven senior executives (50 in all) via the Henley Partnership at Henley Business School. We had groups of executives imagining they were from Dyson, Hoover, Electrolux, Panasonic, Henry, GTECH and a new entrant. The brief was to draw a picture of a new product concept where there was free play with the imagination (a kind of "visual brainstorm" of the ideas as a "rich picture"). As input for them, I did a tailored value Optopus (see again Figure 9.2 earlier to flesh out more aspects of strategy development), like distribution channels, market and geographic focus and alliances. We then appraised two options on the Strategic Option Grid after a briefing by me, viewings of videos on Dyson and G Tech and a demonstration of my cordless V6 and my multi-floor cylinder model.

A myriad of options came up, including building the machine into the house (new build only, as in Finland) and also clothes drying – e.g. with a small machine that could dry a shirt that did not need immediate washing. I piloted this with my wife, and she balked at anything over £100, so that probably fails Dyson's strategic recipe, which seeks a higher (assumed by me) threshold price point. (Maybe that has been looked at and discarded). Independently, I came up with the challenging idea of combining the suction of the vacuum cleaner with the blow of the hair dryer – like a jet engine! Reverse thrust!

Another recent development was the Dyson retail outlet: there is one on Oxford Street and one in Japan. I visited the London one in 2017, a very stylish shop, very minimalistic and not unlike an Apple store. On display were the Dyson fan, the hair dryer, the robotic Dyson eye and of course the V8 cordless and upright. There was also an interesting Dyson museum with the many prototypes of the hair dryer. Interestingly there were some sinks so that people could try having their hair washed and dried with the Dyson hair dryer – a novel touch. Overall it did the job it was supposed to, but I wondered how busy that store got. I was the only customer although it was a Wednesday, unless just its presence may add sufficient value elsewhere. I did feel that it had a more masculine look. I speculated who had been on the design team.

Postscript

Sadly, our Dyson Animal carpet cleaner died in February 2017, and on the way to the recycling centre I was passing a cemetery in Elmer's End South East London and I stopped outside to take some final pictures of it – it must have been an attachment thing and Dysons do get into your heart. It tapped into emotional value.

I had mixed feelings about its death, which I felt was premature as we hadn't had it for a full six years. It was only just out of warranty. I did lobby Dyson for a replacement but they declined, which was a disappointment. To be fair I didn't wash the filter every month, maybe every three, but only half of our house is carpeted.

If it is true, as the sales lady in Curry's Bromley implied, that over and above the threat to longevity if you don't wash the filters regularly that the machine loses power (as my V6 is doing) then an option is to set up a monthly email to all Dyson holders to do a filter wash!

Postscript: in late 2017 Dyson announced a £2 billion investment in electric cars and batteries by 2020, no doubt linked to robotic technology!

Key insights and learning lessons from Chapter 9

- Dyson's success is down to multiple and reinforcing competitive advantages: brand and image, product superiority, customer emotional attachment, R&D, personal charisma, low Far East manufacturing costs, technology competences in rapid air movement, very fast electric motors, control technologies – rather like the honey badger "System of Competitive Advantage."
- This competitive advantage hasn't been static but has shifted over time, as has its business value system.
- Dyson's earlier success was greatly facilitated by competitor complacency.
- But within a couple of years these same complacent manufacturers tried to fight back with single cyclone machines causing issues for Dyson.
- The dip in performance in the early 2000s was foreseeable – and foreseen – through storytelling.
- Dyson's earlier product diversification (the robotic and the washing machine: a white good) doesn't seem to have been well prioritised; neither were positioned well on the GE Grid, the market attractiveness against competitive position was weakened and washing machines were also a very competitive market.
- Both those two innovations seemed to be demanding a premium beyond the extra value that most potential customers would pay.
- The entry of GTECH flagged up the dangers of a disrupter settling down too much and thus leaving vulnerability to new entry.
- To test the viability of a price premium, it is essential to look at the world and the real "in use" value of a customer of the product and to get their input. For the Dyson Hair Dryer, and possibly the Dyson fan, lower price points, much greater volumes and lower costs might be a better competitive mix.
- Dyson created and exploited some new competitive space in the Hoover market and transformed the competitive landscape, but that opened up new spaces and new disruptive innovators.
- Applying similar strategic recipes to other markets through related technology and capability is likely to work differently depending on variations in customer mind-sets, emotional value, relative incremental value added, competition, market scale and type and across cultures – considerable strategic complexity.
- All of this couldn't have happened to a more stable market and industry mind-set; no one is safe, even the disruptive innovators!

Reader exercise

- Where are the businesses that you are in on the GE Grid? (see Figure 9.8). What is their likely trajectory?

10 Dynamic stakeholder analysis

Introducing stakeholder analysis

Other than in the context of the multiple Uncertainty Tunnel, I haven't as yet made a very important point that many of these frameworks are equally applicable to internal organizational change, but I should now. For vector pictures, systemic models, storytelling, the Cunning Checklists, the strategy mix and tools like the Strategy Optopus and the Strategic Option Grid are all hugely applicable to change management.

But there is one particular tool that is equally relevant to both, and that is stakeholder analysis.

Stakeholder analysis is a vitally important technique/set of techniques exploring the dynamics of strategic influencing in coming to firm strategic decisions. But it is also a major tool for analysing the dynamics of implementation (Piercey 1989; Grundy 2002).

A "stakeholder" is an individual or group defined as being one who either has one or more characteristics from:

- A decision-making role
- An advisory role
- An implementing role
- A role as a user or as a victim.

It is very important to include all of these stakeholders in your analysis, so the very first step is to identify all those who might be involved over all phases of strategic decision-making and implementation. If my memory bank of all of the tools in this book were wiped clean, it would be right at the very top of those I would want to have back the most!

Overall there are two important but rather different uses of stakeholder analysis: first, there are internal stakeholders within the organisation, or a social group like family or friends; second, there are stakeholders that are external – for example customers, competitors, suppliers, regulators, media, alliance partners and also potential acquirers or acquisition targets.

I devote a whole chapter to stakeholders because very often it is their actual behaviour that is a big driver of the dynamic of strategy in the business, both in terms of formulation and implementation. It is also in my view the most uncertain and unpredictable area of strategy. Besides all of that, everything in this chapter can be used not just in a more pure "strategic" context but every day. It is also the supreme example of the cunning planning that we covered in c and 4.

Stakeholder analysis is also a huge ingredient in the Strategic Option Grid that we saw in Chapter 3.

In this chapter I cover:

- How to do it
- Stakeholder influencing and cunning planning
- Stakeholder dynamics
- Stakeholder agenda analysis
- The stakeholder influencing cycle
- Stakeholder scenarios
- Case studies on cunning stakeholder influencing
- And concluding learning points.

There is also a major case study of stakeholders at Arsenal FC.

How to do it

Stakeholder analysis is done as follows:

- First, define as precisely as you can what the issue in question.
- Second, identify *who* you believe the key stakeholders are at any phase of implementation.
- Third, evaluate *whether* these stakeholders have a high, medium or low influence on the issue in question (You need to abstract this from their influence generally in the organization.) Here it is crucial that you try to *imagine that you actually are them.*
- Fourth, evaluate *whether* at the current time they are for the project, against it, or idling in 'neutral' (see Figure 10.1).
- Fifth, consider their potential trajectories over time.
- Sixth, develop cunning influencing plans that can cope with that dynamic.

If most of the stakeholders are clustered towards the bottom part of the Stakeholder Grid then you have a mission impossible on your hands (unless the stakeholders can be radically repositioned somehow).

Another difficult solution you might find is where there is an equal number of supporting stakeholders (with lower influence), i.e. in the northwest of the picture, to those against (but having higher influence) in the southeast. This will again mean that implementation is likely to be very difficult.

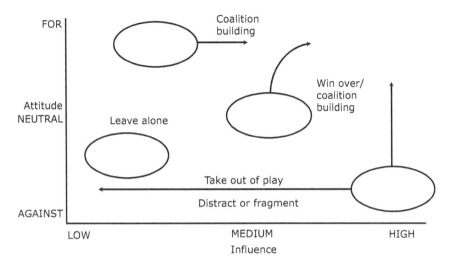

This tool is based on earlier versions by Piercy (1989).

Figure 10.1 Stakeholder Analysis

Also, where you have a large number of stakeholders floating in neutral in the middle of the picture, that very neutrality can present major problems due to inertia. Stakeholder analysis thus is very powerful in being a predictor of strategic success.

In order to estimate where a stakeholder is approximately positioned, it is absolutely vital that you look at the world from that particular stakeholder's perspective. I have found that the best way to do this is to have in effect an "out-of-body experience" or "OBE." This entails really imagining not just the world from that stakeholder's perspective but actually imagining that you really are them, and you have all of their desires (likes and dislikes), their drives (a function of personality), and their beliefs and anxieties. It is also about picturing their attitudes, their behaviour patterns and values, their thoughts, prejudices, feelings and their ambitions and agendas. Finally, it is about their mind-sets.

Rather than just ask you to hold onto this I have even drawn a new and original systemic picture in Figure 10.2.

This Figure contains no less than sixteen important sub-systems which are connected by around 30 major causal influences shown as arrows. Even here I have been forced to be selective and thus omitted the lesser influences. The arrow direction shows the predominant directions of influence – that is not to say that there aren't feedback effects the other way! I have only included in one place a double headed agenda – "thoughts" with "feelings" – as they play off each other pretty equally unless the stakeholder is very emotional with limited rationality.

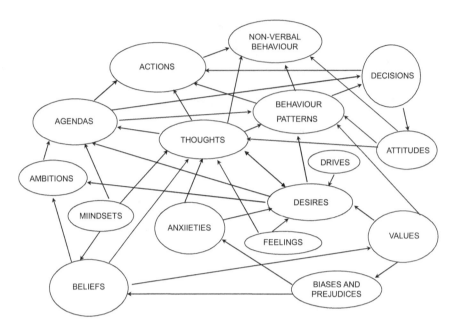

Figure 10.2 Stakeholder "Out-of-Body" Experience

Although this picture was the result of me seeing it as a bit of a play and purely from the point of view that I wanted to fully communicate my own mental map of stakeholder analysis and what was needed to fully "OBE" with another stakeholder reflecting on it, there does seem to be an awful lot more potential in it than just that. For instance, I visualize using a blank sheet for each major, named stakeholder so that managers trying to "deep-dive" into their position can do it in a far richer and more complete way. So each sheet they annotate becomes a mini map of that position. For any academic readers or master's students doing a research project, it could also be a vehicle of data collection, analysis and interpretation, especially in behavioural studies.

Another thing would be to use it to simulate stakeholder intent and gauge how that might change or develop over time.

Besides using it for other people, it also has obvious applications for the individual. One might use it to explore why they have a really difficult dilemma.

At the highest level, there seem to be three major zones of the map, namely those:

- Generated by softer factors like anxieties, mind-sets, beliefs feelings and desires right across the bottom
- Driven by thoughts and agendas to the upper left part of the picture
- Concerning action and behaviour to the upper centre and top right.

Some of the more interesting causal influences to think about here are:

- Behaviour patterns are the result of many factors, including thoughts, agendas, desires (and behind that feelings and anxieties) and also attitudes.
- Patterns drive actions, decisions and non-verbal behavior.
- Beliefs underlie mind-sets, anxieties and thoughts.

Later on we illustrate how a specific stakeholder's agenda can be mapped using stakeholder agenda analysis, which is another application of vector analysis.

To develop cunning influencing strategies, things to consider are:

- First, can new stakeholders be brought into play to shift the balance of influence or can existing layers be withdrawn in some way (or be subtly distracted)?
- Second, is it possible to boost the influence of stakeholders who are currently in favour of the project?
- Third, is it possible to reduce the influence of any antagonistic stakeholders?
- Fourth, can coalitions of stakeholders in favour be achieved so as to strengthen their combined influence?
- Fifth, can coalitions of stakeholders antagonistic to the project be prevented?
- Sixth, can the project change itself, in appearance or in substance, and be reformulated to diffuse hostility towards it?
- Seventh, are there possibilities of bringing on board any negative stakeholders by allowing them a role or in incorporating one or more of their prized ideas?
- Eighth, is the pattern of influence of stakeholders sufficiently hostile for the project to warrant its redefinition?

Figure 10.3 is a great example of one organisation where a successful repositioning of stakeholders was achieved. This was illustrated in a popular TV series called *Back to the Floor*. Besides having the good fortune to see the documentary that was made about a Strategic Turnaround at Champney's Health Resort (an up-market spa), I also managed to interview its MD on two occasions to get his story of how this turnaround was affected, especially in terms of his influencing strategy.

When it's new MD, Lord Thurso, arrived at Champney's, it was losing money at the rate of a million pounds a year on a turnover of just 10 million pounds. This was all the more remarkable considering that it had about the highest rates for any spa at that time in the UK.

Thurso didn't act immediately, even though there was an obviously swollen structure of 22 managers. Instead he spent a month talking to staff and guests and sampling some of the treatments to learn what Champney's was all about. Not only did this help him formulate his strategy and his plans, but it also showed that all staff could see that their views had been listened to, thereby also lowering likely stakeholder resistance.

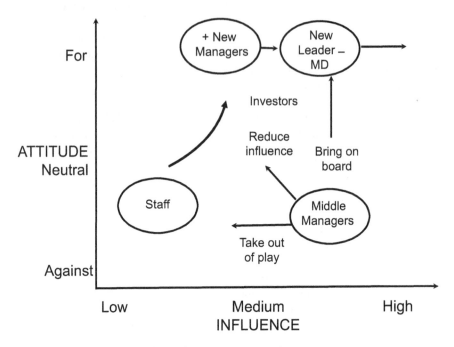

Figure 10.3 Stakeholder Analysis: Champney's Case Study

In Figure 10.3 we left the general staff in a position of neutrality, but the existing managers were fearful of the inevitable – that some would lose their jobs – and thus in a medium influence but potentially quite negative (towards a new strategy and a major restructuring).

However, he dealt with this in two thrusts: one, in a warm, positive and up-beat meeting with the general staff at one sitting when he confirmed their jobs were secure and inspired them with a vision of service unrivalled before in the UK. Next, he met with the managers in a no nonsense way, saying to them: "as in fitness, there will be no gain if there is no pain, he skilfully segmented his supporters from the potential antagonists. As a natural, highly charismatic leader, his messages proved very effective and he thus considerably enhanced his influence.

Once he had processed one by one all those senior and middle managers who were going, including his FD, he brought in a new, younger and more energetic FD and also a highly disciplined Head of Operations who might well have once trained in the army. With that in place, his own position strengthened (plus no doubt increased the owner's support). With staff support and dissidents gone all stakeholders were in favour, save for an isolated one or two. (see Figure 10.3). In truth, it was one of the most impressive examples of strategic influencing that I have seen.

When I showed this analysis to Lord Thurso he was positively beaming with pleasure. I think that to him this was just a very intuitive strategy. But I think that even if you can just "intuit" that so very naturally, it is also good to do it formally on a piece of paper so that you can consider all the factors and there is no one big thing that you have forgotten. And we are not all political geniuses, either!

Often a particular stakeholder may be difficult to position. This may be because his/her agendas might be complex. It is quite common to find that it is only one specific negative agenda which has made a stakeholder into an influential antagonist. The micro-level stakeholder agenda analysis in the next section can be very helpful here.

Where there are very large numbers of stakeholders at play on a particular issue, this may invite some simplification of the implementation. For instance, the implementation project may need to be refined, perhaps even stopped and then restarted, in order to resolve an organizational mess.

To make this all work well and smoothly you may need to set some process arrangements in place where a team project is involved. For instance, the analysis may be usefully performed in a workshop environment so as to give the analysis a reflective or learning feel. This will help to integrate managers' thinking on a key strategy. It may also be useful as well to devise code words for key stakeholders in order to make the outputs from this change tool feel safe. You may decide to adopt nicknames for the key players!

Stakeholder dynamics

Key stakeholders invariably shift over time, and early support for the decision may get diluted and evaporate. For example:

- Senior managers' support is likely to be sensitive to the perceived on-going success of the strategic project as it evolves. Any signs of failure are likely to be accompanied by suddenly diminishing support.
- Certain stakeholders may increase in influence, or even decrease in influence.
- Where the project changes in its scope or in its focus significantly, stakeholders will then change their positions.
- Stakeholders' own agendas might change due to external factors outside this particular project. For example, other projects might distract them or result in a reprioritization of agendas and of this project in particular.

It may be really useful to therefore review stakeholder positions at least several times during the lifetime of the project.

For further analysis, it is possible to examine how stakeholders may change over time (using a similar dynamic picture like the difficulty-over-time curve) by plotting:

- Their attitude over time (ranging from "against" through to "for") (Figure 10.4)
- Their influence over time (ranging from "for" through to "against") (Figure 10.5).

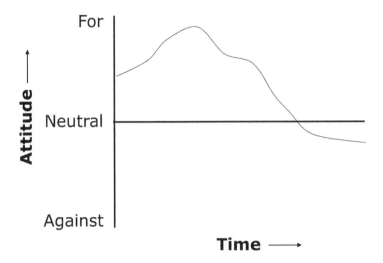

Figure 10.4 Attitude-Over-Time Curve

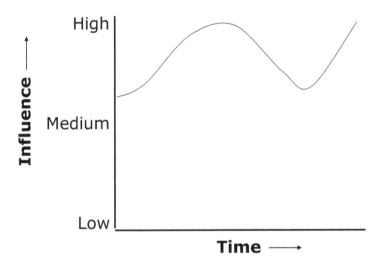

Figure 10.5 Influence-Over-Time Curve

One thing to watch with stakeholder analysis is that you do not make fixed and rigid assumptions about stakeholders' attitudes. Using the grid over many years leads us to believe that often managers have a pessimistic bias, assuming that certain stakeholders will be against. In fact, they are often in neutral due to overload of existing agendas or due to perceived resource constraints.

When confronted with positioning of themselves as "against" they are often slightly surprised. The lesson here is that often many organizational agendas are actually more fluid than is perceived. This is actually good news for strategic thinkers who may feel there is little real chance of their ideas being implemented.

Stakeholder analysis is useful:

- At the very start of a strategic process especially during the "plan for the plan"
- At the strategic options stage
- When performing detailed planning during mobilization of implementation
- Mid-way or at the latter stages of implementation
- After implementation to draw out the learning lessons.

Stakeholder analysis is also particularly useful helping develop an effective communication strategy. Here it will help, finally, to identify which stakeholders to communicate with, when, how and with what message.

The key benefits of stakeholder analysis are that:

- It deals effectively with the political issues associated with strategy.
- It encourages mental agility and the ability to take a variety of perspectives on an issue (through the out-of-body experience) simultaneously.
- It defuses organizational politics and makes particularly sensitive issues discussible.

Stakeholder agenda analysis

Stakeholder agenda analysis now helps you to go down a level deeper – to the agenda of a specific individual, distinguishing between positive agendas (or 'turn-ons') versus negative agendas (the 'turn-offs') – see Figure 10.6. This particular example was taken from the case of when my step daughter wanted a party with disco in our garden and summerhouse (and drinks) for around 45 teenagers for her sixteenth birthday, a truly strategic project if there ever was one.

In order to facilitate a decision on whether or not, and if positive on what scale and with what provisos we asked her for a position paper to put her case. She more than obliged and presented us with one as her cunning influencing plan – a masterpiece!! We don't have the space here for the whole thing but to give you a taste of it she said:

> There are several reasons as to why I should have a Halloween party; one being that I have not had a party in a long time; secondly it expands my socializing skills and allows me to interact with people I wouldn't normally have a chance to interact with; and thirdly the actual organising of the party will permit me to improve my organisational skills.

Another reason as to why I should have a party is that it will enforce the equality and the independency of women and display that the many feminist movements have made a difference.

By having a party at home there is no danger of me getting drunk as it is a controlled environment where you would be able to monitor what is going on. I have not had a party in a long time and I believe that parties are an enriching activity and allow us all to have fun with friends and family.

Secondly, as you know I find it difficult to socialize at times with certain people and a party provides a ground for me to talk to people. Plus, it does make me *more popular*, and I am aware that this is not the strongest of reasons to you but it *really means something for me to be seen to be popular* among friends – even if it is only for a short period of time.

A party gives a base for conversation: I can talk to people I wouldn't normally engage in conversations with. This will sanction me to become *more socialized* and increase my confidence, which I know is very important in today's society; for example, in job interviews I must be confident but not arrogant and a party will let me do this.

Along with this a party gives me the opportunity to "play the hostess," which may be beneficial for the future.

The party will require organization, and as I'm sure you know I really need to improve my organisational skills. I'm not necessarily extremely disorganised but I still lack in organisational skills. Organising a party will involve sending out invites, keeping an up to date list on who is coming, decorations and refreshments. On top of this something I know you will be pleased to have done is we will *have* to clean the house from top to bottom. I promise both me and Basty will help and do the majority of it since we are the ones who want the party. I understand that parties require a large amount of organisation and I think it will be good practice for me to organise a fairly large event.

I think we can agree that there are several (if not many) reasons as to why we should have a Halloween party. Also, I believe that it would be in our *best interest* to have a party as there are many benefits for all of us.

Thus, a party should take place. Moreover, a Halloween party will likewise display a woman's creativity because a costume will need to be thought of.

In conclusion, there are evidently many, many reasons as to why this Halloween party should take place. Firstly, there are the personal uses and the benefits to feminism. As a family unit, we should promote the important cause that is feminism because even in today's society, despite the efforts of many courageous women, inequality is still present and therefore we must do everything in our power to amend this inherited discrimination, including having a *Halloween party*.

I think that not only was Fran's influencing strategy cunning, it was more than that, most stunning. And if a fifteen-year-old girl can step so comfortably into the shoes of a cunning influencer then why do most managers fail to come up with a more than average influencing strategy? That's so sad!

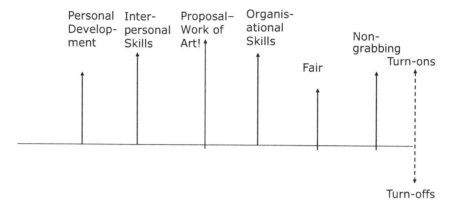

Figure 10.6 Stakeholder Agenda Analysis – Halloween Party

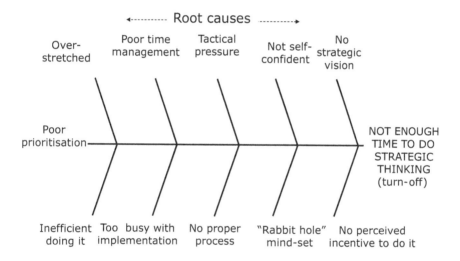

Figure 10.7 Fishbone Analysis – Diagnosis of a "Turn-off": "Not Enough Time to Do Strategic Thinking"

Most commonly, instead of having all of the agendas being positive turn-ons, invariably there are a number of turn-offs that need to be dealt with. A first step in doing that is to do a fishbone analysis (see Figure 10.7) to diagnose why a turn-off exists. For example, in Figure 10.7 I use this picture to deep-dive why a senior executive struggled to put real effort into strategic thinking, such as due to poor time management, not having a process and no real self-confidence. If you were to struggle with this, you might find my Figure 10.3 on the out-of-body experience helpful in doing that which looks at all kinds of useful things like mind-sets, anxieties, drives, beliefs etc.

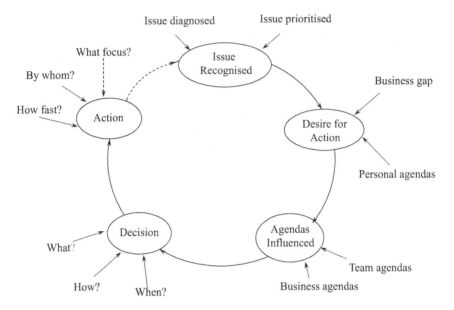

Figure 10.8 The Influencing Cycle – The Influenced (1) of (2)

Besides being applied at a macro-level on the bigger strategic issues stakeholder agenda analysis can be used on projects, for meetings generally, and for even drafting a simple letter or email, or making a telephone call.

The strategic influencing cycle

Besides things like the stakeholder attitude-over-time curve and influence-over-time curve and using vector analysis and systemic modelling of stakeholder agendas, we can also look at strategic influencing as a dynamic cycle as we do in Figures 10.8 and 10.9.

Essentially this is a refinement of the "AIDA" model from marketing that breaks down demand creation and capture into:

- Awareness
- Interest
- Desire
- Action.

So that for potential demand to be funnelled into realised sales you have to go through all four steps of that process and very often there is leakage and you only end up with a fraction of what you hoped for at the beginning. Similarly, when one is seeking to influence stakeholders they have to be made aware

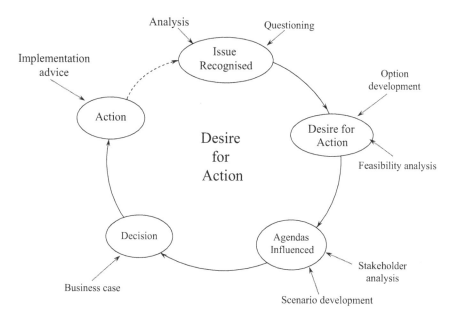

Figure 10.9 The Influencing Cycle – The Influencers (2) of (2)

that there is an issue, to have thought about it, to have an interest that is shared amongst stakeholders about it. Then there has to be not just a decision but also a follow through action, too.

That is all a torturous process, and any influencer has to hold the hand of all stakeholders throughout that process. They have to be good therefore at helping them diagnose and prioritise the problem, to evaluate solutions, make the decision and help them to actually do it (see Figure 10.9).

These figures are not only good for understanding how complex a particular stakeholder influencing process might be, but also how long it will take and how persistent you will need to be, all dynamic aspects. But in addition to this there may also be complex interdependencies between stakeholders. To cope with that complexity systemic thinking again comes to our rescue, particularly through Figure 10.10.

A stakeholder interdependency model of this kind can be done for a very specific influencing issue or it can be done as a more general sociometric of patterns of "who influences whom" in an organisation or a team.(the latter is more challenging) as this may vary across issues but may still be helpful where there are definite stakeholder clusters or cliques, or where there is a forceful or dominating personality. In Figure 10.10 I show the directions of influence as strong as double headed lines and more moderate ones as single lines, plus with the arrows showing who is influencing/being influenced by whom.

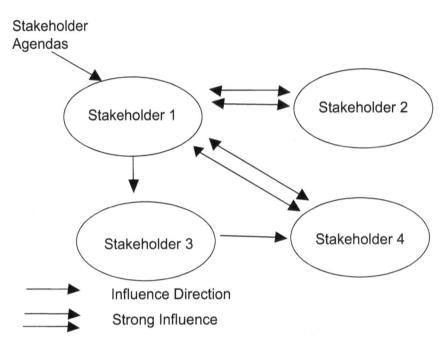

Figure 10.10 Stakeholder Networks

Stakeholder scenarios and the case study of Arsenal FC

Of course, this all points strongly to stakeholder scenarios as being a useful technique for exploring what might happen in terms of stakeholder decisions and actions. For here we would effectively role-play the interactions between the various stakeholders, probably throwing in some real and transitional events in the course of that, and keeping the Uncertainty Tunnel in our heads.

Arsenal, with its back to the wall:

> For instance right now (Spring 2017) my football team, Arsenal, has been having the most torrid time for 20 years. After losing over two legs 10–2 to Bayern Munich in the Champions league which totally knocked their self-confidence up until 16 April excluding the FA Cup since their first loss to Bayern they lost three and drew one of their matches.

Other aggravations have been that their two top players Sanchez and Ozil have not signed new contracts and were reported to be seeking moves with a lot more money causing uncertainty which seems to have unsettled the team. On top of that, the manager Arsene Wenger who has been there for a remarkable 20 years, hasn't yet signed a contract for next season even though at least at one point he was offered one.

After a disastrous 3–0 loss against Crystal Palace away last Monday that I watched in person – though in the Palace crowd as that's where the tickets were – their performance was excruciatingly embarrassing. After each goal, the Arsenal team was isolated with slumped body languages as if all they could smell was Doom! That loss and the results of the recent weekend's games elsewhere *put them in seventh place* (a fall from second only months ago) and no real chance of Champions league football, the first time in nineteen seasons.

At the Palace game Arsenal fans were crying "you are not fit to wear the shirt." There has been a lot of campaigning for "Wenger Out" and leading football pundits have been virtually pleading for Wenger to go. Media coverage has been extremely critical.

Meanwhile Arsene Wenger has repeatedly said, "I have made my decision and will communicate it later." But we can't wait that long; we want to sense the future!

So what are some possible stakeholder scenarios here at that time?

1   Arsenal loses either away at Middlesborough or next week at Manchester City in the semi-final of the FA cup (or both), and Wenger then resigns or at least says he is going at the end of the season (they passed the first test last night!).

2   Same as scenario 1, but Wenger gets fired and a replacement – temporary or permanent – is installed (that's what usually happens in football and would have happened by now if Arsene had not been so successful in his earlier years with Arsenal when he was ahead of other Premier league managers).

3   Arsenal's results stabilise and they limp through to the end of the season; Wenger signs a one-year deal signalling the search for a new manager.

4   A "cat dead bounce," where the market bounces back after it looked dead: Arsenal players pull their finger out and win all premiership games with one draw and finish fifth and win the FA Cup. A director of football is found and the playing organisation is changed and there is a clearing out of players including more recent mistakes. There is better leadership on the pitch.

5   Arsene Wenger moves to be director of football at the end of this season and a new manager is found too.

6   As in scenario 4, the next season is a disaster and Wenger goes, followed by a new manager (as at Manchester United) who messes it up again. Arsenal is no longer a top flight club.

To flesh these out into real scenario stories we would have to visualize what would happen vis a vis the two players, Messrs Sanchez and Ozil, going or not and changes in dressing room politics where there have been suggestions of difficulties. Quite a little soup! We would also have to model another level of stakeholders at board level. At Arsenal there is complex interplay between directors with different equity stakes and interests, and arguably the issues here have been as much a cause of the club's problems as they have at the player-manager performance level. We see at Arsenal many of the issues that big Corporate Groups face with a multi-level political reality.

Finally, we would need to look at all the possible new managers from the pool of those who are in between jobs, have signalled that they might like a move, are falling out with their owners or who specialise in turnarounds. Is a Cunning Plan to offer Sam Allardyce, who is 90% of the way to turning around Crystal Palace, the job? He comes from Bolton, Lancashire, as I do and we are the same age. Should I see if I can broker a deal here? 5% agent's fee of a year salary would easily buy a pool for the garden that my step kids have been angling for!

But now look at: www.arsenal.com/the-club/corporate-info/the-arsenal-board.

We glean that 66.6% of Arsenal is owned by an American, Stan Kroenke, and 30.5% by a Russian, Uzbek Usmanov. Its directors are:

- Both the two key owners and also Josh Kroenke (relative)
- The Chairman, Sir Chips Keswick
- Its CEO Ivan Gazidis
- Ken Friars, who has done almost all jobs at Arsenal; he is clearly a steady hand
- Lord Harris of Peckham.

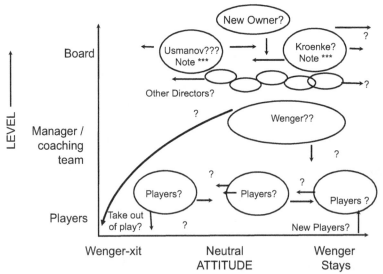

Important Note * above,- these two positions are illustrative – could be other way around! -Excludes Fans**

Figure 10.11 Arsenal Stakeholder Map, Spring 2017

All of these players would need to be positioned in the stakeholder mix; see my Stakeholder Map in Figure 10.11, which also shows the possibility of ownership change!

Figure 10.11 looks like a somewhat peculiar mix (e.g. a U.S. and a Russian owner???). The least we can take from this picture is the overwhelming impression of uncertainty and complexity at three levels, and one wouldn't want to be starting from here.

I then used Occam's razor to cut through this to a year's time with a new manager in place and a new ownership structure to give a clear steer on Arsenal's future strategy in terms of competition, players and organisation and in terms of its financial strategy (See Figure 10.12). As we said before, sometimes it is best to time travel to the future and to work backwards from that to define your strategy.

Whilst scenarios 1 to 6 don't suggest what is actually going to happen, taken together they do give a pretty good range of possibilities so that "big surprises" are far less likely.

I then visualized, a map of the different domains of stakeholders from top to bottom in the organisation with the horizontal axis being those for Wengxit, or Wenger stays, or those neutral. The vertical dimension is the player, the managerial level and the Board/Ownership level.

I found populating this even with the skimpy information that is available most interesting. To see the dissent at player level and even the next level up whilst Arsene Wenger puts a brave face on the situation, he must be wondering

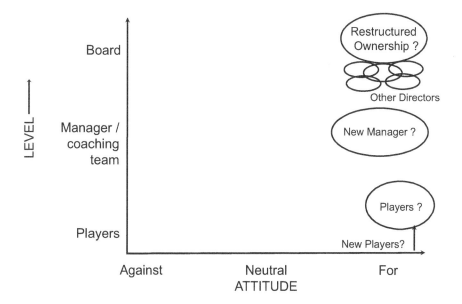

Figure 10.12 Arsenal Stakeholder Map – Early Summer 2018: Vis-à-vis a New Structure

whether to relax his interest and his commitment when so many seem against him; so his position is vague. We can't easily know where the top echelons are, but given the range of their backgrounds and interests I can imagine some spread. In the corporate world, a situation like this screams out for the possible intervention by a new owner. Will Kroenke or Usmanov want to cash in chips that may well lose a lot of their apparent value in the next two to three years?

I sent a copy of this case to Ivan Gazidis, CEO; I received only a letter of acknowledgement.

The outcome:

> Arsenal went on a run of league wins but missed Champions League qualification for the first time in 20 years but surprisingly beat Chelsea in the FA cup, putting Wenger as the all-time winner of that competition. Kroenke decided that he should be offered a two-year contract and that was approved by a still divided board. Wenger was to stay on but with changes in the management structure and coaching staff and mount a serious attack on winning the league. Meanwhile, Arsenal's star player Sanchez said he wanted a transfer to Manchester City.

Case studies on cunning stakeholder influencing

We end on two really interesting case studies on influencing that was very cunning in the past, both set in or after the Second World War:

Case Study 1 – Cunning Influencing Strategy of Pykrite in the Second World War

This first case study is from the History Channel and tells the story of a new and cunning technology which was invented during the Second World War:

> "It is a very special kind of ice called Pykrite. Pykrite is ice mixed with wood slurry; the effect is to double the tensile strength. It is as strong as concrete.

The British General Lord Louis Mountbatten took up the cause and went to see the British Prime Minister at his country home. (Figure 11.4) where Mountbatten was going to try to sell his idea to Admiral Ernest King, Chief of the U.S. Navy.

During one session of the Frontenac conference Mountbatten brings into the room two blocks of ice and puts them on the table. Suddenly he takes out his revolver and fires at the normal ice and it splinters. Everyone is confused by what Lord Mountbatten is up to.

Then he takes the piece of Pykrite and fires his revolver at it. The bullet ricochets off it and it goes into Admiral King, nicking his leg.

Admiral King isn't phased by this and he even seems impressed:

> *Although this project never seemed to get full follow through (maybe because it was felt that the war was being won by more conventional methods or even through the possible deployment of the nuclear bomb) that doesn't detract from not only the brilliance of that novel idea but even more so for the way in which Mountbatten engaged both Churchill and Admiral King!*

Case Study 2 – Cunning Influencing Strategy from Just after the Second World War – Roosevelt versus Churchill

The following was from the BBC's brilliant series on "Planet Oil" (part 2):

> Both President Roosevelt and Winston Churchill emerged from the Second Word War with their sights set firmly on the Middle East. They both realized how crucial oil had become in the modern world. Saudi Arabia was the biggest producer of oil and they both wanted it for themselves. (2016)

In a shamelessly transparent move, Churchill made frequent visits and showered the Saudi King with gifts. He arranged to ship a one-off gold plated Rolls Royce to the King, a real gift with a regal cause.

Roosevelt on the other hand, used the heart and not the wallet. He had done his homework. He had studied the man and his culture. He travelled great distances to see him despite his ill health. He showered him not with expensive gifts but with poignant ones such as his own wheel chair as one polio sufferer to another. This wasn't the time for extravagant gifts or gestures it was about winning hearts and minds.

> *What a brilliant cunning influencing plan based on a highly accurate out-of-body experience of the Saudi King.*

Key insights and learning lessons from Chapter 10

There are a number of really important learning take-aways from this chapter:

- Stakeholders are diverse and it is crucial to know who all of these are.
- They can be internal or external to the organisation.
- And can be analysed at a variety of levels: as groups of them and as individuals or at a very "deep – dive" level of agendas.
- To do the latter effectively you need to do the out-of-body experience.
- Their positions are continually shifting and changing so the analysis has to be very dynamic: these shifts can be napped pictorially.
- Much of organisational uncertainty is due to them, so it is even more vital to explore this in depth.
- Stakeholder analysis is a vital ingredient in the Strategic Option Grid;
- It needs a lot of cunning and creative input.
- Strategic influencing is a complex process and requires multiple and diverse skills.
- Stakeholder scenario story telling is another powerful technique that will assist, coupled with stakeholder maps and an understanding of stakeholder interdependencies.
- Besides its obvious strategic applications, dynamic stakeholder analysis is an everyday technique that can resolve the thorniest management issues.

11 Dynamic strategic planning and implementation

Introduction

This book is primarily about the dynamic substance of competitive strategy. But we must also cover the process, which of course is vitally important, too. So in this chapter we also look at the inputs and processes, and the dynamic outputs of strategic planning.

In this chapter we therefore look at:

- Getting started – dynamic inputs (with the "plan for the plan")
- Planning processes (strategic workshops, facilitation and other aids, steering team behaviour, and the "strategic audit"
- Dynamic outputs ("from-to" analyses, implementation projects, and business cases).

Getting started – dynamic inputs

As we said in Chapter 2, the first step of any planning process is to define the key strategic issues facing the organisation. This will help you very much to determine the focus of any planning review and will help to avoid it becoming dominated by analyses, or by a forest of tactical objectives, or by overly detailed forecasts.

A planning review might take different forms such as:

- A regular strategic review that updates and changes a strategic plan that was there the previous year: an "incremental mode"
- A more thorough going review of the whole strategy again as part of a regular planning cycle basis – an "evolutionary mode" – where there are big environmental/other shifts
- A more urgent and fundamental review caused by abrupt change or crisis: "revolutionary mode."

Alongside the Strategic Issues analysis, we also need to do a Strategic Gap analysis (see Chapter 3). This needs to be framed in a dynamic way which looks at not just changes already impacting *but future ones, too.* So we will have to incorporate things like:

- Future market changes
- Future shifts in competitive intensity
- Future entrants and disrupters
- Future shifts in the business value system.

This will give an initial agenda with a set of aspirations that provides a plan for the plan. Logically we now need to organize this in terms of planning activities, inputs, processes, people and finally interdependencies. This means formulating a "plan for the plan."

The "plan for the plan" (Figure 11.1) is a document laying out the detailed steps, timings, resources for the plan. This should be done by the coordinator of the process who might be the Strategic Planning Director, the Finance Director or even the CEO himself/herself. It is a great idea to display this in a flow diagram, with the boxes containing the individual work-packages or "modules" of the process. To fully flesh these out, identify these items in the following order:

- Outputs (start to plan the process by working backwards from what you want as specific outputs: what is it that you want to get out of this phase? These are the flows of data, or insights, or decisions from the conclusion of the work-package)
- Processes
- Inputs
- Interdependencies (for instance, the marketing work-package might require input from the environmental analysis module, or from the competitive analysis module)
- People to be involved.

For instance, you might have, from a marketing module, things like the marketing and brand strategy, marketing breakthrough projects, implications for technology strategy, some L&D programmes on customer service or a competitor intelligence overview.

By defining the outputs you can then design the process to be really lean. For instance, if the core of the process was two, one-day workshops, then the first workshop might be used to analyse three marketing breakthrough areas. As an illustration, there might be inputs from four position papers – one on the market environment, one on market intelligence, one on key competitors and also one on the major key account strategies.

There is also a behavioural advantage to this targeting of outputs; as I found in research into strategic behaviour years ago (Grundy 1997b), where that is done it is an enabling factor in smooth team dynamics.

You would also need to look at *who might be the best to contribute* to that in terms of: knowledge, analytical skill, creativity, cognitive style, preferred team role style and political influence, and also their roles in the decision-making process.

Workshops or stretched meetings must all have a planned process and targeted outputs *and be guided by some "Key Strategic Questions" so that the debate doesn't get lost.*

Next, you will need a set of background planning assumptions that identify trends and continuities as well as potential uncertainties and discontinuities – drawing from the scenarios (see Chapter 1 [the environmental and competitive tools], Chapter 2 [the Uncertainty Tunnel and Uncertainty Grid] and Chapter 7 [scenarios and the Tesco case].

You will also need to consider time-scales for the planning horizons, for instance:

- Over what period would you be expecting to recoup any long term investment decisions that are contemplated?
- How much uncertainty might fog the plan and even with scenarios after about when does this turn just too cloudy to plan meaningfully?
- Should the environment change viciously how easy is it to be able to manoeuvre around that in time and what warning are you likely to have? How sticky is your strategy?

In the Tesco case, top management became heavily committed to both Non-Food and the Dot.com strategies over 1997–1999, but with some foresight the cannibalisation of the former by Dot.com of Non Food and of Food too (foreseen in 1996!) would dilute and then destroy value beginning around 7 years into the future, from around 2002-ish onwards. This was potentially foreseeable and might have been factored into capital plans.

Planning processes

These break down into:

- Running and facilitating strategic workshops
- Strategic behaviour in teams
- Hypothesis testing and killer strategic questions
- Evidence-based planning and strategic position papers
- Testing and the strategic audit.

Running and facilitating strategic workshops

As I said earlier, Strategic Workshops need detailed planning of what the desired outputs will be and also the key objectives of the workshop. The workshop needs to be broken down into key activities with estimated timings. Each of these also needs to be focused on a number of Key Strategic Questions to provide a direction and scope to the debate. For instance, in a Brand Strategy Workshop these might be:

- What is the current positioning of our brand vis a vis customer needs and also our competitors? (30 minutes)

- What are the options for achieving one or more strategic breakthroughs with that (Brand Optopus)? (25 minutes)
- How attractive are these (Strategic Option Grid)? (25 minutes)

It is wise to break down any group of managers of six or more into two or more sub-groups so that the discussion unit isn't too unwieldy. Each group should have a balance of skills, experience, and cognitive and role styles (maybe get them to do Belbin psychometrics from the internet).

There should also be a proper facilitator whose role is not to contribute to the content of the debate in a creative way or an expert way but in terms of process and to highlight obvious confusions, ambiguities, gaps in thinking, possible "lines of enquiry" etc. They should be impartial, and if they have a personal opinion to address they must signal that they do so not as a facilitator, and once expressed they must step straight back into the facilitator's role again.

Another job is to monitor the level of debate and (quite separately) its difficulty, value-added and the energy-over-time curve. That's all on top of monitoring the balance of input so no one is over-dominant or being a passenger, and intervening in that where necessary.

I would add to that the imperative of heading off the wrong kind of political play. A trusty way of doing this is to brainstorm the "P" behaviours at the start – we don't want to be "political," "pedantic," "procrastinating," "personal," "protective (overly)," "pointed," "poisonous" or even "p…d off": somehow the humour of being able to gently behave along those lines seems to protect from

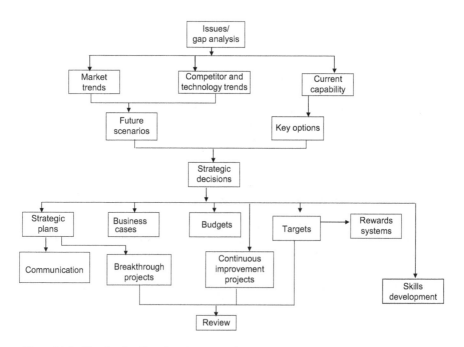

Figure 11.1 Plan for the Plan for a Strategic Planning Process

politics. My wife recently added a very good one to the list: "perverse." Other fun ones might be:

- Panicky
- Paranoid
- Pathological
- Patronizing
- Perfectionist
- Pernicious
- Preconceived
- Prejudiced
- Provocative
- Provoking
- Psychotic
- Punishing
- Pushy.

These "P" challenges can be brought by any of the participants and also by the facilitator. As another possibility in reserve I typically carry two football cards – yellow and red – as a deterrent against inappropriate behaviour. Whilst this may seem extreme, even having them on your desk is a sign of who is the boss! It also adds to the humour that this is an event with a difference. I always add to that by showing a picture of an Apache helicopter and of a man with his head down a rabbit hole to suggest that we need to be in higher mental space and to avoid rabbit hole thinking and discussions!

Other possible facilitator approaches are to:

- Call one longer session or the whole thing an "end of the world" exercise with stretching outputs which you have to imagine you will have to attain to "Save the World."
- Get the teams to draw a "rich picture" of the situation, which is a drawing, like a cartoon, of what is going on and between who.
- Have out-of-body experiences of key stakeholders or use the Stakeholder Analysis Grid to develop cunning influencing or negotiation strategies.
- Do a scenario storytelling exercise, or one with alien thinking.
- Choose a sub-set of the most relevant Cunning Checklists from Chapter 4 and apply these to the issue.
- Get real time data by going on Google to provide evidence of stimulus generally.
- Ask the question: "what is the one big thing that we forgot?"
- Create a kind of "war room "environment with a Panorama across the room with different flipcharts and high-level pictures of important output.

Ideally, the Strategic Planning Director/Manager should be facilitating strategic workshops, although quite frequently they lack facilitation skills; training here is a must, and preferably specialist training in strategy facilitation. I have trained staff in the strategy departments of some of the very biggest companies in the world – e.g. in banking, oil and telecoms – and their staff have been hired more for their analytical skills rather than their creative or facilitation skills. There can be quite a skills gap.

Indeed, the role of the Strategic Planner can be a lot more than putting together the plans for other people, but to get them to become strategy coaches and also to be able to do a constructive critique of the strategies that line managers come up with. They can also train line managers in strategic thinking. This model of being a strategic planner is much more that of conductor rather than pianist or lead violinist!

Strategic behaviour in teams

It is well known that managers often resist thinking in uncomfortable ways about their strategies as can be found in Argyris's seminal work (1985), which suggested that defensiveness was the most acute the brighter that they were. Some years ago I researched the way that behaviour during strategic debate impacted on strategic thinking (Grundy 1997b). I studied the debates of a top strategy team within BT that dealt with technology strategy by studying them as a fly-on-the wall observer of their behaviour with one another. After playing back my initial results of their behavioural patterns, I also did some experimental research with some strategy sessions (recorded) with me as facilitator and using a cut down Strategic Option Grid.

The results were very powerful and led to the following conclusions:

• Their Personal and Strategic agendas were inextricably tied up together (I subsequently called these the "PASTA" factors), but they could be separated out from each other and then dealt with more effectively through stakeholder analysis.
• Without using analytical models, very bright individuals (as in this team) were at sea as they lacked shared mental maps, and long and focused enough attention spans and structure in their ideas, with resulting poor strategic output.
• By intervening through a combination of facilitation and visual tools, and a narrower, clearer agenda with key strategic questions, this largely dissolved. Team harmony was transformed into the kind of "flow" described in Chapter 3.

Here are two of my models from that research: the System of Strategic Behaviour and the Dynamics of Strategic Behaviour models.

To get optimal flowing team interaction it needs to be focused on very clear value-added tasks with very clear outputs, as in Figure 11.2. There needs to be no distraction from extraneous organisational influences, and appropriate strategic leadership, vision and facilitation, which I call "meta-behaviour." In Figure 11.3 we also see the effectiveness of strategic debate

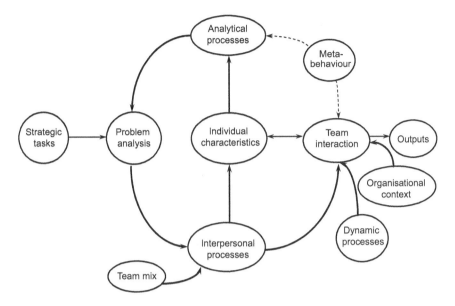

Figure 11.2   Strategic Behaviour and Team Working

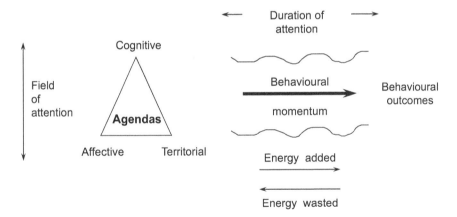

Figure 11.3   Key Dimensions of Strategic Behaviour

and behaviour very much tied into the narrowness and duration of the attention of the group.

Hypothesis testing and asking killer questions

One of the most useful and dynamic ingredients of issue-based strategic planning is to use hypothesis testing and asking killer questions. This really invites deeper thought and in the swirl of management, thought especially at this depth is no bad thing! For example, one hypothesis might be:

> *As a result of Brexit, eventually the European Union will either modify itself or come apart in a domino effect.*

The challenge here of course would be to assemble the weight of evidence for or against that hypothesis.

Or from the Tesco case in Chapter 7 one might have hypothesised in 2010 that:

> *Tesco might be about to decline just as was Marks and Spencer over 10 years before.*

A "killer question" is one that usually the facilitator might throw in to provide a new line of enquiry of a challenge to the mind-set or assumptions. Examples might be:

- If there are no great acquisition targets smaller than us what about a larger, reverse takeover? Or,
- If we time travelled to the future and discovered that this strategy actually worked what did that look like and how did we ever get there?

Evidence-based planning and strategic position papers

Evidence-based planning and strategic position papers both help to avoid the subjective. This helps avoid the trap of falling into assumptions, like "we think X is about to happen" as this is balanced by thinking along the lines of "here's the evidence for some different views on a topic or dilemma, and these are the kinds of strategic options that might be suggested to flow out of this."

A great vehicle for operationalizing this is through doing a Strategic Position Paper for a business area, or for a particular strategic opportunity or threat. Such a paper is maybe at least three to five pages of carefully reasoned thoughts which might cover

- The strategic issues
- Current position, objectives and gaps
- Strategic options
- An initial evaluation, further key questions/lines of enquiry data needed etc.

Such a paper is not meant to be definitive and it is iterative. It is useful to circulate it around key stakeholders to stimulate thought, ideas, debate and refinement. Another vitally important benefit is that it encourages inclusiveness and ownership.

Testing and the strategic audit

As we said in Chapter 3, it is also crucial to go through a "Challenge and Build" process of refining strategic options and plans through the process. That means checking these out for resilience. Existing strategies and projects can be audited using the Strategic Option Grid and its "deep-dive "techniques like the Uncertainty Grid. Or if you want to go further you can build some tailored checklists (or apply some generic ones) to your own business to test out by ratings what score you give your strategic position and performance.

My most sophisticated version of this strategic audit process (for assessing strategic health) is made up of around 180 questions that deal with corporate, business and functional strategies, and the strategy process too. I have a taster version if you care to contact me! (see www.tonygrundy.com).

At Scottish Water, for example, the process rapidly identified three areas of gaps that had the opportunity for strategic breakthroughs, one in particular having a very, very large financial potential. Not bad for a day's work!

I believe that there is huge potential for complex organisations doing a focused "strategy audit," especially to check that they are not being left behind through the pace of external strategic change, and maybe also to trigger bigger but more timely strategic reviews than might have happened otherwise.

Dynamic outputs

We now cover:

- "From–to" analyses
- Vision and strategic breakthroughs
- Project managing implementation
- Economic value targeting.

From–to analyses

In FT analysis, you create in effect a multi-gap analysis with the left hand characterising one extreme and the right hand another, for example:

FROM – TO
Very High Cost Base – Very Low Cost Base
Low Flexibility – High Flexibility
Low Value-Added – Very High Value-Added

You rate where you are (or were) on a scale of 1–5, left to right, and also where you are targeted to be in the future, and maybe also write in the strategic actions to close the gap. This is a very powerful way of distilling a Plan.

Vision and strategic breakthroughs

Other potential outputs could be vision and strategic breakthroughs. "Vision" is a very popular notion – I think appealing as it fulfils a strong symbolic role and is also aspirational. A "vision" I usually describe as being "a picture of the future, either of the organisation or environment, or both." The organisational vision can be twofold: the competitive vision that is outward facing and the organisational vision that is all about the feel of the internal organisation.

The more symbolic role is for me akin to it being like the fairy at the top of the Christmas tree that just finishes the whole thing of. That is not a stupid thing to think as it may be best to add the "vision" once you have the main tree sorted out – otherwise you could easily end up with the wrong fairy on top!

"Vision's" role as came through very powerfully from six CEO's that I interviewed (Grundy 2014) i.e. to screen new strategic ideas as they come up. I guess that this I very much similar to my own definition of "what is it that we really-really-really want?" – reminiscent of the Spice Girls pop group that we saw in wishbone analysis!

Arguably more important than "vision" is the set of strategic breakthroughs that has crystallised through the planning process. A "strategic breakthrough" is a strategy that will make a major contribution to either a) the competitive advantage of the business, or b) to its financial performance or c) to its capability, or d) any combination of these. The idea comes from the Japanese philosophy of "Hoshin," which simply means "breakthrough."

Examples of such strategic breakthroughs for Dyson (see Chapter 9) would have been the cordless, the Airblade, the fan, the hair dryer, its U.S. strategy, its massive new R&D centre, etc.

The rule of thumb is that you can typically only really attempt a maximum of three breakthroughs over a particular time period, say of 1–2 years, otherwise you are likely to spread yourself too thin like the three-foot Hadrian's wall that we saw in the *Blackadder* story of the Cunning Plan back in Roman times in Chapter 3.

In the words of Sun Tzu (1910):

> When the front is prepared the rear is lacking. When the rear is prepared the front is lacking. Preparedness on the left means a lack of preparedness on the right. Preparedness on the right means a lack of preparedness on the left. *But preparedness everywhere means a lack everywhere!*

So strategy is all about choice and whilst there may be many strategic options with good scores (as in Chapter 3) it doesn't mean that you have to go and do all of them, and certainly not now and all at once! In sound strategic management there may be an opportunity stream greater than the need of the organisation and its capacity to implement them well. I am beginning to feel, as my brain is in the flow that a systemic model is coming on...

Figure 11.4 shows a best practice, strategic option generation process in a group with a stream of strategic opportunities including:

- Evaluation by the Strategic Option Grid
- Screening by the strategic vision and key strategic objectives
- Position papers.

And as outputs:

- As actual strategic breakthroughs ("go" decisions)
- Or, as contingent strategies "might do's"- (depending on conditions lining up)
- As part of opportunities for the future
- Or as "Don't do's."

Actual "Go" decisions will clearly need to be matched according to capacity and resources and also relative implementation difficulty, plus financed and evaluated economically.

Project managing implementation

Project management provides a critical linkage between any strategy and its implementation (Grundy and Brown 2002). Many senior managers seem reluctant to link these very closely. My suspicion is that this is because they lack firm commitment to actually implementing the strategy in a targeted way, presumably as that ties them down and commits them. If they don't deliver then they will

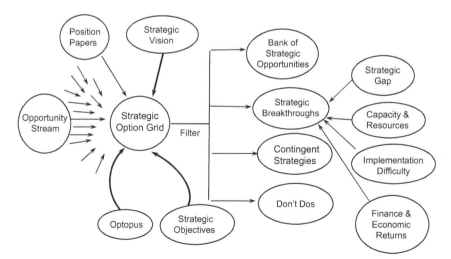

Figure 11.4 The Strategy Opportunity Process – Supply *v.* Demand

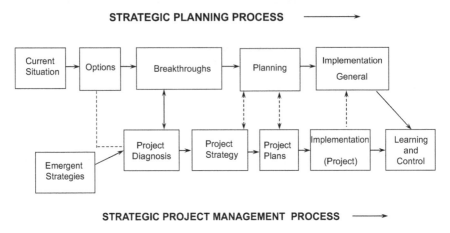

Figure 11.5   Strategic Planning Process and Links to Project Management

have failed, and failure is something that they would fear. So left to their own devices they will prefer to leave actual action vague – and this is one of the very most important reasons why so many strategies fail to be implemented well.

Plans, by their nature, need to be quite broad, and this may not allow space for sufficiently detailed thought about strategy implementation. We know that this whole area is complex so it makes sense to take a lot of this detailed thinking out of the strategic plan itself into the project planning and management system, just as you see in Figure 11.5.

Indeed where the strategy involves (as it so often does) significant change, then that triggers the need to look at all the dynamics ("harder" and "softer") that that brings into the equation, including all those "over-time" curves from Chapter 5 and the stakeholder material from Chapter 9. That implies "change projects" and that of course brings you back to Strategic Project Management.

This also enables emergent strategies to be swept up. Between the deliberate and emergent processes there is therefore a strong dialectic. In its more developed form, this Strategic Project Management process takes quite a lot of the thinking load from the strategic planning process, such that much of the strategic plan becomes:

a) A more general definition of where to compete, how and with what capabilities.
b) A summary of the strategic projects that together mobilise the strategic breakthroughs.

Although I first taught these principles twenty years ago to senior managers at Cranfield, many of my readers might consider this novel, the suggestion that every project should have its strategy and needs to go through parallel steps that a company strategy should!

Economic value targeting

Finally, besides implementation there is also the issue of the economic value of strategies and strategic projects to be addressed. We have already looked at three techniques for assisting with that. First, there is the business value system which helps to identify the interdependencies which impact in or influence the economic value; we also have the value-over-time curve. The third analytical technique is the "Uncertainty Grid," which allows all the assumptions that impact on economic value to be probed so that the sensitivity analysis can be much more targeted towards the things that are most important and most uncertain. In Chapter 8 we also discussed how to evaluate the "intangibles." Finally, scenario storytelling is a process for testing and resilience-testing value, especially where value is "contingent."

Key insights and learning lessons from Chapter 11

- Define your strategic issues and get a feel for the "Strategic Gap" before doing the "plan for the plan."
- Depending on the business context, define the planning horizon, and establish common strategic assumptions.
- Strategic Workshops need a lot of planning e.g. careful choice of those providing inputs, breaking down into groups, key strategic questions, other process catalysts, mindfulness, monitoring and management of group dynamics, attention to distillation of output into a position paper.
- Behavioural interaction needs managing through for example agreeing the "P" behaviours that you want to avoid, facilitation, using stakeholder analysis and getting the right people there.
- Outputs need to dynamic too, through strategic breakthroughs and projects and from–to change management.
- There also needs to be a careful targeting and evaluation of the economic value added by strategic breakthrough projects, rather than a purely qualitative assessment.
- Implementation should be project managed, all projects should have a strategy and much of the detail of the overall strategy in terms of implementation can go into project plans.
- Position papers can be of great help in evolving the cunning side of plans, and in moving forward towards a strategic plan, in sharing of ideas and ownership.

Reader exercise

- For a strategy you or your team is working on, what are two big things you have forgotten?

12 Lessons and conclusions

Having a Cunning Plan every day – strategic thinking in everyday life

In this chapter we return to the dynamics of cognition by looking at strategic mindfulness, cunning and the strategic unconscious mind. I then cover some final very humorous illustrations of cunning ideas and planning in everyday life to stimulate you to think about wider applications. Finally, I suggest how to develop strategies at you might consider to be at a more tactical level called the "Mini-Strategy Process."

Strategic thinking and strategic mindfulness

> *Sometimes inner mental stillness is needed to generate a truly dynamic stream of ideas.*
>
> *– Tony G*

Introduction

In my earlier book called *Demystifying Strategic Thinking – Lessons from Leading CEOs*, I researched how CEOs actually did strategic thinking and identified eight major aspects of that. Interestingly, from the CEO perspective only two of the eight dimensions that seemed important to them were actually about the more traditional aspects of planning. The vast majority were more about the softer aspects such as intuition, creativity, storytelling, visualisation and modelling.

The other thing that they consistently said was that they tried to maintain an inner state of calm and focused their attention very carefully as if in a state of strategic alert, of reflective detachment, and "strategic mindfulness" (see Figure 12.1). According to one CEO, in this state you are open to new strategic thoughts on a 24/7 basis.

This is a rather different model from the more scientific approaches to planning that are predominant in many conventional strategy texts. Relatively few that deal sufficiently with the more "cognitive," "behavioural" or "process" factors, one rare exception to that being Mintzberg et al.'s excellent *Strategy Safari* (Mintzberg et al. 1998). In Grundy (1997b), I contended that in strategic debate,

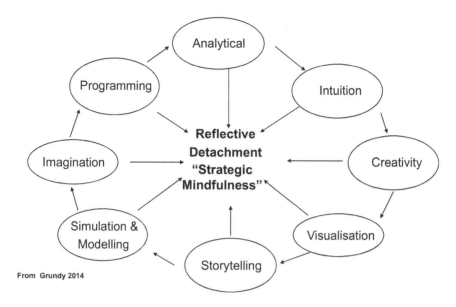

From Grundy 2014

Figure 12.1 The Wheel of Strategic Thinking

managers blend three key elements: strategic thinking, strategic innovation and strategic influencing. To be a really good strategic manager you therefore need to be very good at all three, and very, very few are: *all three are processual*.

The control of one's cognitive dynamics can greatly help cunning planning in everyday life. Not only does that facilitate a steam of inventive strategic ideas but it also helps to do that without such uncontrolled excitement that you lose all sense of grounded-ness. Of course, here I will be looking at the individual level and at group level we need other things such as group analytical processes, facilitation and basic ground rules.

After we have looked at my new model for that I will look at how my own mind used playfulness as a catalyst for cunning strategic planning in everyday life – fasten your seatbelts for that! We end with how my readers can think and manage strategically in a different way in the future.

Cunning and the strategic unconscious mind

The original spark for this book came out of a random conversation I had at one of the business schools I teach at in Spring 2016, as I was just saying that each day I was having at the very least one strategic thought and on a good day I might have three to five! (It is a good thing to keep track of these too in your diary. That helps you to track your cunning practise)!

These thoughts can occur not so much at your desk but anywhere; it may be when you are driving, mowing the lawn, at the gym or even in the middle of a challenging yoga posture! Indeed, when I work from home I often break off and do something quite mundane and suddenly think a brilliant strategic idea.

When I started recording my Cunning Plans I realised just how many I was having – sometimes several a day! I was Multi-Cunning! Some were really micro, as they might have to do with some very specific opportunity or way of dealing with a family or non-work issue. So they don't have to be life threatening.

Indeed, as I was writing this very morning I had to put down tools to drive three miles to my hairdressers, "Nix." It was a wonderful, warm spring day with no clouds. I started to have a stream of disconnected cunning ideas about approaching Dyson, changing my own business brand slightly, a business school opportunity, interviewing some CEO's for the book, helping one of my executive development channels to be a lot more cunning by training them myself! That's five! I added a sixth process cunning idea: that if I am ever need ideas I just jump in my car and go for a cunning drive and drive aimlessly until I have at least one really cunning idea!

I then had the idea of the "strategic unconscious mind," which is that portion of your mind that works on strategic ideas without your being conscious of it; that promptly got added into the "Cunning Checklists." So my stream of *seven cunning ideas* was a product of it being a nice day, that I was in the "flow" and my rational mind was switched off and I allowed new ideas to surface through strategic mindfulness: *a total of seven cunning ideas in fourteen minutes – one every two minutes!* At this rate, I could advise the President of the United States!

This new and cunning idea of the strategic unconscious mind did not evaporate, and the next day I thought it would be really useful to do a "deep-dive" into it. The output is Figure 12.2, which is a descriptive model of how I had observed how my mind worked when it was formative phase of arriving at a Cunning Plan. (I have left out the second phase of iterating the Cunning Plan to become a stunning plan and also all the further work that is needed to bring into being a more targeted and implementable strategic plan). So we are dealing here with the far less conscious side of mental processing and its interface with the more rational mind up top.

As a practitioner of advanced meditation techniques for 20 years I am skilled at stilling the mind and concentrating it. I also do some more extreme forms of yoga like Bikram and Kundalini where you really need to have 99% concentration plus – in balance and acute sensations which you guys would feel as "pain." We are taught in both forms of yoga, particularly the latter, to transform that pain into a pure sense of persistent willpower. So I have a natural advantage of sustained concentration!

But lots of people find ways to still the mind through music, dance and sports, so your potential for keeping concentration and your cognitive flow is probably a lot better than you think. We all can accomplish it if we try and are disciplined.

> *Sometimes inner mental stillness is needed to generate a truly dynamic stream of ideas, and when one idea starts it seems to pull others in as if through a magnetic force.*

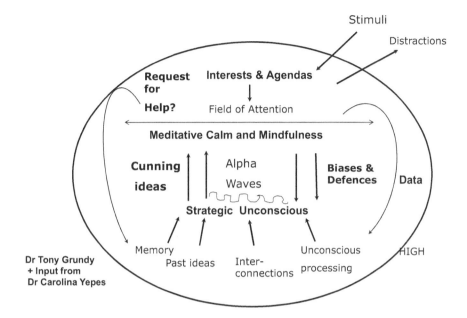

Figure 12.2 Cognitive Dynamics and the Strategic Unconscious Mind

Returning to Figure 12.2 we see that:

- When there is a stillness of attention and a meditative calm then alpha brain waves can kick in so that any thoughts that do occur are in a natural flow.
- To activate subconscious strategic thought, I might "send for help" to my strategic unconscious either to help sort out a strategic problem or dilemma or to just come up with strategic ideas, as I did in the drive to the hairdressers.
- My attention is filtered at some interests and agendas but these are kept sufficiently fluid to avoid missing insights.
- I need to wrestle with distractions but when I am in a general state of strategic mindfulness then I am still "open."
- When in a state of flow my strategic unconscious mind, I imagine, although I don't directly observe this, that it sometimes recycles past ideas, searches my memory banks for possible solutions or processes that might lead there, and makes interconnections.
- I am calm on the surface of my awareness so that I don't filter what comes up (biases and defences) and then at some point I will surface one, two or even more cunning or stunning ideas. I can also revisit these by breaking off and effectively "saving" the results so far, so I can reactivate the processing.

I ran my original model through with my wife, Dr Carolina Yepes, who is a clinical psychologist (some say "my minder"!) and specialises in cognitive processing. She added the bits on bias and defences plus some other fine-tuning.

Carolina did say, however:

> It makes sense that you have managed to optimise the smooth and natural flow of thoughts from your unconscious mind through that practice of mental calming. But I guess it still all depends on what is in there to get the results! (Your mental processing capability.)

Tony:

> Well, I guess that's true and it's something that we all take for granted: the processing capability. It's probably a bit like my laptop that crashed a week ago, and I had to have everything reinstalled; all the software and data. Not only is that all well structured in an immense filing system on my laptop, but also there is, and this is according to its brain surgeon, Ali (of Norwood Net), a truly vast amount of data there. My laptop (now clear of viruses and redundant programmes causing it to run at a snail's pace) is now uncluttered and not being caused to run in a zig-zag and convoluted way. It processes smoothly and easily and without delay. Similarly (after 30 years strategizing and 20 years of meditation practice) when I am thinking strategically in a mindful way with smooth cognitive flow, my mind is totally orchestrated and the whole mental organisation just purrs along.

So my conclusion on all that is that although the rational – at both conscious and unconscious levels – is necessary in order to think really effectively strategically to reach fullest creative potential, this is insufficient without adding the condition of full mental flow as well.

And, on a lighter note: letters from a strategist

I now turn to two ideas that came to me in a very playful way that actually shed a refreshing perspective on some deep, political issues: Donald Trump's somewhat idiosyncratic policies and also the way in which we in the UK have become conditioned to think about Brexit. Humour is much underrated as a vehicle for strategic thinking; when in that mode, although some ideas are often quite crazy, there are often ones that really are not.

From time to time I do send these letters to famous people as a random holiday, for example:

- My three applications to be Coach of the England Football team.
- My three other applications to be CEO of the Football Association (now those were actually plausible!).
- A letter to Prince Charles on his marriage to Camilla as conducted by the same registrar that I and my second (ex) wife also enjoyed – we brought

a cardboard cut-out of the former England Manager as a "witness" to the wedding. I suggested to Prince Charles that as the Queen wasn't coming to his wedding he could do a cardboard cut-out. Prince Charles's PA wrote in thanks saying that Prince Charles was "highly amused" by the suggestion.

- After seeing hoards of overseas non-UK visitors in a very long queue at Heathrow, and my brandishing a real Red Card (bought from the referees association) for bad customer service at Border Force, I wrote to the (then) Prime Minister Tony Blair, to suggest that to improve Britain's competitiveness I could have a new role as "Minister for Red Cards" to improve customer service throughout the public and private sectors. My letter was forwarded to the Home Office where it was submerged in mist.

- A letter before the fall of Baghdad to President Saddam Hussein suggesting he and his son Uday (who coached the Iraqi football team) fly out Michael Jackson's plastic surgeon to disguise them, then flee over the border and apply for the CEO of the Football Association as I did not get short listed (and they needed a Dictator to sort them out). This would then have avoided many casualties for the Iraqis. I never actually posted that one! But the reality was that one way of waging that war was to show Mr Hussein an alternative way out than certain defeat against "Shock and Awe."

Letters to the world from deepest Croydon

My first letter takes the policy of the new president to stop all illegal immigration from Mexico by building a wall and then charging the Mexicans for the cost and looks at the alternative options and business models for doing it. *I would stress that my letter doesn't for one second imply that I am in support of such a wall!*

DONALD TRUMP
PRESIDENT ELECT, UNITED STATES OF AMERICA
725 FIFTH AVENUE,
NEW YORK, USA
14 November 2016
Dear President (Elect) Trump

My future role as Strategic Planning Director, Special Projects

I am writing to you on a most historic day: the earth is the closest to the moon since the start of the Cold War. Hopefully we will get through to 12pm without a threat that we should all fear a surprise attack from Mars. Those cunning aliens might attack from the moon just when they are closest and we are mesmerized by its light. You must know that!

It is nearly a week since your amazing political coup that has reverberated around the globe. No doubt when in office you will not flinch from making promised changes. As a Corporate Strategist myself now for nearly 30 years I know all too well that it is one thing to commit to a strategy, but another thing to do it. And it is another thing to do that in a cunning way.

Many are impressed by, and indeed, fearful of many of the projects that would deliver your strategic goals. When I toss and turn in the night I can see why. May I therefore offer my services (just as Nigel Farage did) to guide you through this precarious process.

After having had published twenty books and been an academic at many leading business schools and through my consulting advice globally I propose you consider engaging my services in a new role (see above) to help you deal with these enormous challenges, like deporting millions of illegal aliens in hours (are you going to rely on Uber?).

I will skip the problem of extra-terrestrial threat which no doubt the Pentagon and the CIA has briefed you on: follow the advice of the great film *Mars Attacks* 15 years ago that the Chief of Staff gave the President: "We should Nuke them! – and Nuke them now!).

Instead let's look at your splendid notion of building a wall to keep the Mexicans out. Left to their own devices, contractors will build an ugly monstrosity that could come back to haunt you both in a second term and after you get kicked out for invading Mongolia or somewhere like that. It won't be revenue generating, and I really don't think the Mexicans will want to pay for your two thousand long mile long garden wall: what's in it for them without force of arms?

A way around that can be found, I believe, by combining two Cunning Plans (my forte):

1   Generate revenue streams from advertising on opposite sides of the border, by making it a tourist attraction like the Great Wall of China or by staging competitions to see which Mexicans can surmount it or tunnel beneath that – there has to be betting revenue there;

2   To fund it this the cost could be securitized by issuing stocks that carry rights to these revenue streams, and then sell these to Mexicans so that, yes, you could still say they are paying for it without having to threaten to nuke them too!

Once you have vanquished the Mexicans, I can help you prioritize other ventures. We should surely promise to stimulate global growth with new walls not only around the Globe (Scotland/England) but perhaps even on the moon (we really don't know where those Martian critters are hiding there). When we chat over brandy and cigars I will fill you in on a very savvy economist, John Maynard Keynes, who had some interesting theories of "economic multipliers" that work when you throw money around. Just think about U.S. GDP after we have conquered Mars too.

Wouldn't you like to have someone truly independent advise you instead of the White House cronies?

Take a while to think about it, Mr President.

Very best wishes,
Dr Tony Grundy
Director
(with address)

Ps I could probably cope with $1.25 million a year and a nice penthouse in the White House, plus a CIA chauffeured car (as I struggle to drive on the wrong side of the road – oh, and a GREEN CARD please – and I know you love guns. Mine's an MK 23 .45 Heckler and Koch automatic pistol and a Heckler and Koch 9mm submachine gun please, with loads of ammo to practice out of the penthouse window). You can never be too ready given those U.S. Special Forces.

Sadly I didn't hear a reply: maybe he or the CIA didn't find my requests for the firearms acceptable, or maybe someone else got that job (a relative?). It does seem that I wasn't the only one in the UK trying to get jobs in his team.

My second letter sprung from the Cunning Plan prompt of "Can you reframe what the problem is really about?" In this case, turning a threat to an opportunity!

THE HON THERESA MAY
PRIME MINISTER
UNITED KINGDOM
10 DOWNING STREET
LONDON SW1A 2AA
24 December 2016
Dear Ms May,

Some interesting thoughts on turning BREXIT from a problem to an opportunity – the idea of "BREXMAS"

Hello Theresa:

First to introduce myself, I am a leading Strategy Consultant and Business School academic.

I thought of writing to you as I felt I could help you with one of your biggest challenges: how we think of Brexit.

It seems you are settling in well after assuming power in the rather unusual circumstances of constitutional change in the UK. Now have you have done the necessary culling of certain ministers who certainly required pruning and have had the time afforded to ride over economic turbulence through the UK Stock Market's surprising buoyancy, this may afford the thinking time to turn Brexit from a problem into an opportunity.

Actually, it is not totally unusual for me to offer to help governments think about their strategic options. For example I once offered to be Tony Blair's "Minister for Red Cards" – to rid the UK of the often terrible customer service that afflicts both the private and public sector – e.g. To challenge those aspects of the UK which diminish our comparative economic advantage as a nation e.g. the often horrendous queues at inward passport control at Heathrow.

More recently, adding to my credibility even more, I offered to become Donald Trump's special strategic adviser and more specifically suggested some most interesting ideas for making his new wall idea with Mexico not only self-funding but a major tourist attraction! I am awaiting his response-maybe I was over-ambitious in my salary needs or the fringe benefits-including various Special Forces' weapons to have fun with during quieter moments at the White House.

Whilst I was working out at the gym just before Christmas I suddenly had an idea for turning the whole Brexit issue from a problem to an opportunity. After all doesn't "Brexit" make you think of "Brexmas?"

Instead of us having all of our lavish celebrations just once a year (i.e. Christmas), after Brexit is actually implemented then that would be a real opportunity to make this into a huge cultural festival which would then be celebrated annually!

After 30 years as a leading strategic thinker I have come to recognize a great strategic idea when I see one!

At each annual celebration to mark the event there would be an extra Bank Holiday and all kinds of spectacles that would generate a huge extra influx of tourists. It would be a major British cultural happening that would draw the attention of the world to a celebration of political, economic and cultural independence. *It would be a huge boost to morale in the country and be a historically important, unifying force*. I don't know if you are Keynesian but on that day, do think of the economic multiplier effect that the benefits of a second mini Christmas plus the overseas spend might bring!

Definitely something to chew on: I would be happy to provide strategic input to a Brexmas working committee of likeminded people like James Dyson, Richard Branson, Alan Sugar and Jackie Gold.

Keep on the good work Theresa!
Very best wishes
Dr Tony Grundy
(with address)

I received a polite letter thanking me for my suggestion, which no doubt was binned!

I thought that the matter was dead until lo and behold a yellow envelope with a letter from Theresa May herself arrived some four months later during her surprise election campaign asking for my help. It turned out she was only after my vote! I couldn't help replying (edited):

Hello Theresa:

I wrote to you some time ago re Brexit suggesting…*the Idea of Brexmas*… .

I wondered whether our letters have "crossed" – unless some mean-minded civil servant did not pass on my letter to you … Do please find a moment to read my "Brexmas idea" – that could be wheeled out as an idea mid-campaign. It is most cunning!

I have had personal contact in the past at Ministerial level on … and confess I wasn't too impressed in terms of the calibre generally. I had to quote from Blackadder at one point. (I believe that minister's throat was dealt with quite surgically by you on taking power.)

If I could … seed your thoughts maybe I could be your new Minster for Cunning Planning to help the UK to steer through the mid to latter stages of the Brexit assimilation process …

Changing tack, a year on from that business school visit I was invited to do a day-long workshop there on the topic of "Demystifying Strategic Thinking" which proved extremely popular; there were 50 senior executives attending. I had during the day illustrated my habitual use of strategic thinking on things like using the Strategic Option Grid to screen and evaluate potential candidates for a longer-term relationship and also to run scenarios for what might go wrong when my wife went to Colombia to see her family for 10 days whilst I held the fort.

So it was not a surprise when I got the question:

"Is there anything or any area in your life, Tony, where you would not do strategic thinking?"

To which I replied:

"No, I really don't think so. Actually, the only regret that I have is that I did apply strategic thinking to one very important marital thing once and then proceeded to partly ignore it, and paid the consequences."

One of the more localized issues that I applied it to was an everyday project of our family getting a dog and the integration process. This project graphically illustrates the applicability of dynamic strategic tools on everyday issues and the impact of uncertainty. May it inspire you to join the "At least once a day, Compulsive Cunning Club."

Not only does this bring out that there are always many options for how you implement the strategy but also to search for options which are cunning. It also demonstrates the rather false dichotomy which is often made between "operational" and "strategic" as if there is a kind of Cartesian dualism between very tangible matters of operations and ones that are much less tangible.

Before we ever had a dog when we moved to our house in Croydon we got a cat-flap fitted for Millie. Anyone who has had cat litter will know why that's worth doing, as not only is litter smelly and horrible looking but it is messy and costs £50 a year!

But the only place we could fit one in the back of the house (Millie must never get run over) would require fitting a cat-flap to a massive plate of patio glass at a cost of £300!

So when the dog project began we had a legacy of a cat-flap.

Introducing Max

Fast forwarding to 2015, we got a nine-year-old dog, Max. He was rehomed after his owner had died. We thought that it would be less difficult than getting a puppy, as puppies are renowned to be like babies; you can't leave them that long and a lot of training is required. Damage happens.

We did try to reduce risk of piloting having a dog by getting one from the "Borrow My Doggy" website, but honestly that isn't the real thing!

We got Max from a rescue home after his owner had died: he just looked at us and said: "Take me home." We did.

After we got Max he got very upset at being left, as he must have been constantly with his previous owner. In late spring new fox cubs were born underneath the decking. *That was a transitional event of dramatic proportions* (Chapter 7).

Max is a mixed breed Jack Russell terrier and it is in his DNA to catch foxes. This was combined with his "separation anxiety" and whenever we went out he crashed through the cat flap, breaking several different ones at a cost of £80, he can shift obstacles weighing 30 kilos with his nose, and he has even tried to dig through the kitchen tiles to get out! I estimated that at our initial rate of losses the cost per annum was around £1,000 a year!

We were in crisis; my wife said: "Tony, we have talked so much but we really haven't done your Strategic Option Grid to generate more options and to evaluate them." So I set to work with that, the Optopus and the Cunning Plan and along with Google including the amazing video that has gone viral: "Houdini Hound" which could worm his way through a cat-flap. I identified 17 options for solving the problem which gave us real hope, including:

- Get a smaller dog, and send Max back to the rehoming centre.
- Get a bigger dog, so that there would be no way that it could get through.
- Get a second dog so that they could both keep each other company (but what happens if Max still escapes?).

- Don't have a dog at all (rehome him e.g. through the organisation "Cinnamon").
- Get a new pane of dog sized glass (expensive).
- Put him in a dog cage (cruel).
- Fill the hole and annoy our cat Millie.
- Maybe ship a virtually indestructible, "bullet resistant" high tensile plastic and steel cat-flap from the U.S.! (Google "Catwalk" it is true!). Unfortunately they don't ship to the UK.
- Ask family in Florida to buy one and then ship it out to us (a bit of a burden on them though).
- Get a doorway dog gate like a giant child gate; again it was thought Max would out jump it.
- Bite the bullet and replace the cat-flap with a dog-flap, possibly costing £400 of damage and also potentially impairing the value of our home. Whilst potentially attractive, when he's escaped into the garden even though we have tall defences, Max has an amazing vertical take-off facility and can still get over tall fences. Even if he didn't his barking would be bound to upset the neighbours.
- Install some special noise emitters in the garden that would be unpleasant and stop him from going through: that assumed a) they would work and b) that Max would sense them before he went out as he stuck his head through, and that this would be an effective deterrent to try some special dog comforting herbal treatments that would make him sleepy; we would have to administer that sooner as he might panic as soon as we shut the door.
- Install a door to our kitchen (this had been taken off by the previous owners to give a more spacy feeling). But wouldn't Max just attack it as he had one of the doors in the kitchen that was now protected by the ironing box?
- Block the cat-flap when we went out, annoying all other stakeholders as we would have to block and unblock this each time and Millie would not be free to roam; this was part of our solution as a transitional measure but we had to pile around 60 kilos of my weights into an old chest which Max would gnaw at, and in his efforts to get out his paws managed to scratch our stone tiles.
- Hire a dog therapist (which we actually did for £335!).
- Try to get him to realise he needs to be at home, as that's his job to be its "CBO" ("Chief Barking Officer").

And on my last proof read before printing I suddenly saw the light. Yet another option is to overfeed him on a special very bulky diet–unethical? Or, we could get him a very posh suit (a heavily padded Bouncer Dog Uniform) to wear on duty when we are out. Of course that would make it impossible for him to break out–QED! I would go with the second plan. Figure 12.3 actually shows a tailored "Optopus" representing the degrees of freedom that we had here.

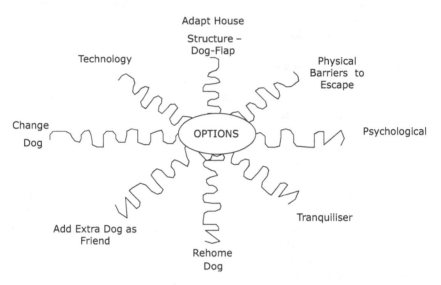

Figure 12.3 The "Max-opus" – Lines of Enquiry for Solving the Problem of Our Escaping Dog, Max

Options / Criteria	Option 1 Bullet Proof Flap	Option 2 Dog-Flap	Option 3 Sedatives	Option 4 Dog Therapist
Strategic Attractiveness	★★★	★★	★★★★	★★★
Financial Attractiveness*	★	★★	★★★	★★
Implementation Difficulty	★	★	★★	★
Uncertainty and Risk	★★★	★	★	★★
Acceptability (to Stakeholders)	★★	★★	★	★★★
Scores	9 1/2	6 1/2	9 1/2	9 1/2

Score: 3 = very attractive, 2 = medium attractive, 1 = low attractiveness.

Figure 12.4 Max's Strategic Option Grid

Figure 12.4 shows the Strategic Option Grid that we did to try to make up our minds; it shows just how and why we had such a dilemma. Three of the best candidates actually had the same score!

So we went eventually for a very humane strategy – the last one – which involved around four months of operant conditioning with an arithmetic sequence that began "leave him for five minutes" then 10 minutes then 15 minutes. After half an hour gaps were established I took him up to five and a half hours! We were able to not move the chest with the weights for many months over summer, but then it rained heavily, and that's when a second phobia kicked in – so we then had to use the chest again. We lost two more cat-flaps in the process (seven gone now). This did turn out to be more laborious and difficult than we imagined and also riskier (we did have some damage!).

Just when we thought we had it beaten we went out for a meal for just two hours and he was gone again: there had been no rain, no foxes, nothing; no excuses. On the last occasion for no apparent reason and after an absence of just an hour and a half he had gone, *and actually he was gone, entirely*. I shouted for him then used the dog whistle (probable range a third of a mile) – nothing! Eventually he surfaced tail between his legs, filthy as if he had got stuck somewhere! He had gone for a short walk before that.

The Max difficulty-over-time curve is drawn for you in Figure 12.5. In recent times, he seems to be thinking that I should not go to work or go out ever without him so he barks wildly even if I pick up my bag or shoes or seem to be sneaking out: maybe the one big option we missed was: "Maybe they do dogs at Harley Street." We bought a supersonic device that mutes his barking from Amazon that humans can't hear!

This interesting and humorous strategic project illustrates that there are often as many ways (strategic options) to do a strategic project as to do an entire

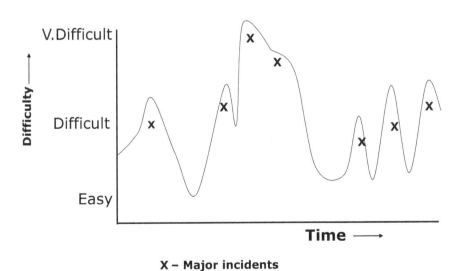

X – Major incidents

Figure 12.5 Difficulty-Over-Time Curve – Max the Dog

business strategy! Also, you have to integrate the strategic, operational, financial and stakeholder analysis and to focus creatively and relentlessly on getting a result that "you really-really-really want" (the "vision").

It also illustrates the effects of interdependencies (e.g. between projects over time), the impact of the environment (foxes in our garden) and the interplay of these which can wreak havoc on economic value through the value and cost drivers. In addition, it highlights the fluidity of the whole process of turning a strategy into a sustainable reality. Right now we have a mix between a deliberate strategy which works unevenly and one that is in submergent mode. Dynamic strategy is far more than a set of frameworks and formulae: *it is a style of very open and at times playful thinking which is truly "anti-sticky."*

Strategy is not only dynamic but it is also non-linear as the volatile difficulty-over-time curve in Figure 12.4 demonstrates. And that belies the fact that that curve is a function of a whole bunch of other things such as Max's:

• Anxiety-over-time curve
• Engagement with us as a family-over-time curve (and vice versa)
• Claustrophobia-over-time curve (and its flipside, the freedom-over-time curve).

So we are all playing games with each other and not just a human game but an animal one. And whilst we can't banish uncertainty from the equation it is residual – 80% can usually be dissolved or modelled in some way – even though some is truly "wicked."

More profoundly it, emphasises the importance of behaviour in being one of the main bearers of uncertainty. In fact, if I jump into my "thinking helicopter" now it leads me to hypothesise that Max still doesn't feel sufficiently looked after and cared for and doesn't get the exercise and freedom that he craves. Maybe his anxiety is inherent and he will never recover from the trauma of losing his past owner, nor of being in a rehoming centre … what if we were to do a regime of two, 40-minute exercise bursts each day – one in the morning and one late afternoon/early evening? Maybe our "competitive mix" has not been rich enough and deep enough and through his crazy barking he is trying to tell me that!

Complex issues come up every day. A useful approach to finish on is the Mini-Strategy Process (Figure 12.6) in six steps:

• Diagnosis: fishbone
• Strategic objective: start of the wishbone
• Strategy generation: wishbone the alignment factors
• Prioritisation: "AID Grid"
• Implementation: difficulty-over-time curve
• Support: Stakeholder Analysis Grid.

So that's all tools we have seen (apart from "AID")

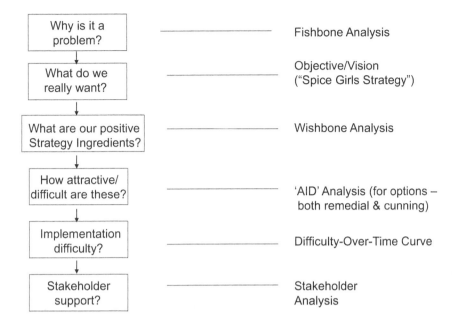

Figure 12.6 Mini-Strategy Process and Tools

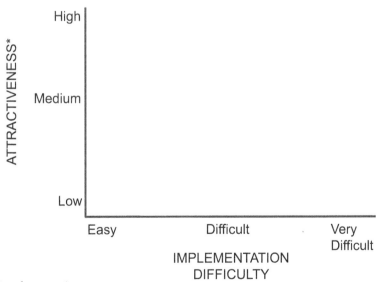

* Benefits minus costs

Figure 12.7 "AID" Analysis – The Attractiveness/Implementation Difficulty Grid

Very briefly, the "AID" (the Attractiveness and Difficulty Grid) (see Figure 12.7) is a cut down version of the Strategic Option Grid with just "attractiveness" plotted against "implementation difficulty." You simply plot all solutions to the fishbone root causes and any elements of a new and better strategy to transcend the problem on the "AID." The total set of solutions can then be tested in the aggregate as a single difficulty curve, or broken down individually.

The AID analysis can be used very dynamically through plotting the possible trajectory on the grid.

Reader exercise

- Using the Mini-Strategy Process, find a problem and work through the whole process, or if an opportunity from the wishbone onwards (can be like the Max one, or smaller, at work or outside). *Remember to be as cunning in your thinking as you possibly can. Revisit* Chapter 4, *"The Cunning Checklists"*.

Summary of our journey

My proposition throughout this book was that conventional strategy with rare exceptions had become too static and rigid in its time perspective. In Chapter 1 I looked at some of the most familiar strategy techniques like SWOT, PEST and the Competitive Forces and identified their more static limitations and began to suggest ways of getting around this.

In Chapter 2 I then looked at what agile philosophy could bring to the process in terms of allowing a good deal of flexibility into the planning process to avoid it being too set-piece. We also looked at how the actual forms of strategy – "deliberate," "emergent," "detergent" etc. – can morph as well so that the dynamically evolving context can be coped with. We looked at the special case of "contingent strategy," which has a major role to play in dynamic strategy and highlighted that much must change in conventional planning processes to accommodate that. Finally, we looked at how cognitive inflexibility can make us vulnerable to cognitive bias and strategic deception and how to be alert to that.

In Chapter 3 our focus was very much on strategy as a Cunning Plan. In conventional planning most plans are very average and also lack flexibility so are not resilient in the face of competitive dynamics. To be superior plans do need a strong element of cunning and invariably this means thinking ahead of the opposition. Being "cunning" relies on being able to think obsessively about options – not just about What, but also the How and the When of strategy. To generate these in a truly rich way we turned to the Strategy "Optopus." We then explored the engine of dynamic competitive strategy, the "Strategic Option Grid," illustrating both with a number of examples. In Chapter 4 we added into that creative mix no less than 101 questions from the Cunning Checklists.

Chapter 5 took us back to Chapter 1 themes by showing you how more dynamic versions of the earlier tools such as the market attractiveness-over-time curve and competitive advantage-over-time curve could remedy the weaknesses of the more conventional, static models. We covered the "systemic" models of strategy including the "system of competitive advantage" with the honey badger and Metrobank. In Chapter 6 we saw how taking an "alien" perspective was particularly powerful, with some colourful stories on its effectiveness in banking, the fitness industry and in pubs and bars.

In Chapter 7 we turned to another crucial ingredient in the dynamic strategy mix with scenarios from fascinating illustrations of the Second World War, the North Sea Oil and Gas industry, and from Grocery Retailing and the volatile and graphic story of Tesco and its extraordinary strategic trajectory.

In Chapter 8 I then looked at the dynamic dimension of "emotional value," which is about how customers are themselves complex and dynamic absorbers of value and how they experience and feel that value plays a huge role in competitive advantage. In Chapter 9 (which is closely related) I then looked at the evolution of Dyson Appliances over a 22-year period and how Dyson Group has created an amazing formula for creating and capturing what is for the large part an emotional market. But I also highlighted that this is *increasingly contested competitive space and the shifts in the competitive landscape, but it can nonetheless still be possible to find new competitive space.*

Chapter 10 dealt with the dynamic political dimension of strategy which arguably is the tail that wags the strategic dog. In Chapter 11 I grounded all of these thoughts in extensive although concise thoughts and pointers in the art of dynamic strategic planning. In this final chapter I looked at strategic mindfulness, the unconscious strategic mind and some humorous examples of Cunning Plans.

An important message to my readers is that there are some very quick returns from experimenting with some of the dynamic strategic tools in this book that grab you. Try a few out and work hard at their practice so that you begin to truly reprogram your strategic mind. Then maybe move onto others one at a time. *Like yoga or meditation, practice and persistence are critical*. But there is also a message to be much more mindful how you are trying to think strategically: are you in System 1 – quick thinking (think of that as Red), or slow thinking with System 2 (Blue) or the more agile thinking System 3 (Purple)? What do you find that works for you?

Key insights and learning lessons from Chapter 12

- Strategic thinking can be done 24/7 through being strategically mindful.
- Mindfulness can be of the external world or of your inner cognitive flow.
- You can be truly prolific and have not just one "Cunning Plan a day" but even more.

- You can get your strategic unconscious mind to serve you.
- The more still the mind is the better the cognitive flow, the more chance of surfacing Cunning Plans and not losing them to everyday distractions.
- Applications can range from deep economic and political problems down to very domestic problems and dilemmas like our escapologist dog, Max!

Reader exercise

- What do the tailored Strategic Optopus and the Strategic Option Grid tell you about an important everyday dilemma in your life?

A final story – the one big (hot) thing I forgot

Whilst writing this book I had an accident that was strategic. I was making a cup of tea in the kitchen. I planned to go into our garden to write a bit more of my book and make a fire in our chimney. I was in a bit of a rush, as once lit it would take 30 minutes to get going and I only had a two-hour slot.

I was at the kitchen sink and hadn't put all the dishes away from dinner, so whilst I thought I had already made a cup of tea I couldn't actually see it anywhere, which I thought odd. So I put some more water in the kettle and when turning my elbow I destabilised the very large, very full and very hot mug of tea that I had already made that was hidden. It was my very best mug: the one with "I Love Strategy" on it in bold red letters.

It took probably, due to the strength of gravity on our planet, around a tenth of a second to reach my foot with a lot of momentum. Besides the substantial blow, it efficiently emptied most of the scalding contents onto my foot, penetrating my sock and causing excruciating pain.

I screamed and stuck my badly injured foot in the kitchen sink and ran cold water over it for 10 minutes to minimise the continued burning.

My strategy mug lay on the floor unbroken. It will be a reminder of four key strategic lessons going forward:

1   Always be mindful, and especially strategically mindful.
2   Never neglect your strategy.
3   Never forget to ask yourself: "What is the one big thing that you have forgotten?"
4   Things that look profoundly static and safe always have the potential to go "Dynamic"!

And added by my good friend in Israel, Mike Emery:

5   "Don't throw tea on my foot in the future!!"

A further twist in the story: after this accident, a few days later I developed a foot infection, and when I saw my doctor he wondered whether I had broken a small bone in my foot. I went the next day to a hospital in Sevenoaks, Kent for an X-ray. As I was checking in at the minor injuries reception I was explaining how the accident had happened. As I simulated the twist that sent the mug crashing down on my foot for the nurse I noticed something red – another mug over in my right vision. I was in mid-sentence and froze.

I hobbled over and was astonished at the similarity to **my mug**; it was virtually identical. It was a very large white mug,– the exact same size with red writing on it – not "I LOVE STRATEGY" but "I LOVE TEA" – it was the sister product. And it too had been perched just like mine. It was similarly totally full and scalding hot. Was that a sign from the Universe??? It was a hell of a coincidence. It did seem to be one of Igor Ansoff's weak signals (Ansoff 1965) that you should ask: "What is that about?"

The moral:

> In a dynamic, complex and uncertain world, be strategically mindful – or else!

From Tony G

Tony's website is www.tonygrundy.com. Feel free to contact him there or direct via tony.grundy101@gmail.com.

Bibliography

Ansoff, H.I. (1965) *Corporate Strategy*, McGraw–Hill, New York

Argyris, C. (1985) *Strategy, Change and Defensive Routines*, Wiley, Chichester

Barney, J.B. and Clark, D.N. (2007) *Resource-Based Theory-Creating and Sustaining Competitive Advantage*, Oxford University Press, Oxford

Berger, P. and Luckmann, T. (1966) *The Social Construction of Reality*, Random House, New York

Bywater, H. (1925) *The Great Pacific War*, Applewood Books, Carlisle, MA

Csikszentmihalyi, M. (1975) *Beyond Boredom and Anxiety*, Jossey-Bass, San Francisco, CA

Davidson, D. (1967) "Truth and Meaning", *Synthese* (17) pp. 304–323

Day G.S., Reistein D. J. and Gunter R.E. (1997) *Wharton on Dynamic Competitive Strategy*, Wiley, Chichester

De Geus, A. (1998) "Planning as Learning", *Harvard Business Review* (March–April), pp. 70–74

Ghemawat, P. (1991) *Commitment: the Dynamic of Strategy*, Free Press, New York

Grant, R.M. (1991) "The Resource-Based Theory of Competitive Advantage: Implications for Competitive Advantage", *Californian Management Review* 33(3) (Spring), pp. 114–135

Ghemawat, P. (1991) *Commitment: the Dynamic of Strategy*, Free Press, New York

Grundy, A.N. (1993) *Implementing Strategic Change*, Kogan Page, London

Grundy, A.N. (1994) *Breakthrough Strategies for Growth*, Pitman Publishing, London

Grundy, A.N. (1997a) "The Strategy Mix and the Industry Mind Set", *Journal of General Management*, 22 (4), pp. 16–30.

Grundy, A.N. (1997b) *Harnessing Strategic Behaviour*, FT Publishing, London

Grundy, A.N. (2002) *Mergers and Acquisitions*, Capstone, Mankato, MN

Grundy, A.N. (2003) *Shareholder Value*, Capstone, Mankato, MN

Grundy, A.N. (2006) "Rejuvenating Michael Porter's Five Forces Model", *Strategic Change*, 15 (5), pp. 213–230

Grundy, A.N. (2012) *Demystifying Strategy*, Kogan Page, London

Grundy, A.N. (2014) *Demystifying Strategic Thinking – Lessons From Leading CEOs*, Kogan Page, London

Grundy, A.N. and Brown, L. (2002) *Be Your Own Strategy Consultant*, Thomson Learning, London

Grundy, A.N. and Brown, L. (2003) *Strategic Project Management*, Thomson Learning, London

Grundy, A.N. and Brown, L. (2004) *Value-Based HR Strategy*, Butterworth Heinemann, London

Hamel, G. and Prahalad, C.K. (1994) *Competing for the Future*, Harvard Business School Press, Cambridge, MA

Husserl, E. (1980, 1982, 1989) *Ideas Pertaining to a Pure Phenomenology and to a Phenomenological Philosophy*, Books 1–3, Kluwer, Dorrdrecht

Janis, I.L. (1972) *Victims of Groupthink: A Psychological Study of Foreign Policy Decisions and Fiascos,* Houghton Mifflin, Boston

Kahneman, D. (2013) *Thinking, Fast and Slow*, Penguin, New York

Lewin, K. (1936) *A Dynamic Theory of Personality*, McGraw Hill, New York

Mintzberg, H. (1994) *The Rise and Fall of Strategic Planning*, The Free Press, New York

Mintzberg, H., Ahlsrand, B. and Lampel, J. (1998) *Strategy Safari*, Simon and Schuster, New York

Mitroff, I.I. and Linstone, H.A. (1993) *The Unbounded Mind*, Oxford University Press, Oxford

Morgenstern, O. and Von Neumann, J. (1944) *Theory of Games and Economic Behaviour,* Princeton University Press, Princeton, NJ

Ohmae, K. (1992) *The Mind of the Strategist*, McGraw-Hill, New York

Piercey, N. (1989) "Diagnosing and Solving Implementation Problems in Strategic Management", *Journal of General Management*, 15 (1), pp. 19–38.

Porter, E.M. (1980) *Competitive Strategy*, Free Press, Macmillan, New York

Porter, E.M. (2011) *The Price of Everything*, Amazon.com

Quinn, J.B. (1980) *Strategies for Growth: Logical Incrementalism*, Richard D Unwin, Homewood, IL

Spender, J.C. (1980) Thesis. Manchester Business School

Spender, J.C. (1989) *Industry Recipes*, Blackwell, London

Stalk, G. (1976) "A Study of Escalating Commitment to a Chosen Course of Action", *Organizational Behaviour and Human Performance*, 16, pp. 27–44

Stalk, G. (1997) *Wharton on Dynamic Competitive Strategy*, Edited by G.S. Day, D.J. Reibstein and R.E. Gunther, John Wiley & Sons, Chichester.

Stalk, G. and Hout, N. (1990) *Competing Against Time: Time-Based Competition: Reshaping Global Markets*, Simon & Schuster, New York

Straw, B.M. (1976) Knee-deep in the Big Muddy: A Study of Escalating Commitment to a Chosen Course of Action" *Organizational Behavior and Human Performance*, 16(1), pp. 27-44.

Sun, Tzu (1910) *The Art of War*, Lionel Gate, London

Tovstiga, G. (2010) *Strategy in Practice*, Wiley, Chichester

Tversky, A. and Kahneman, D. (1974) "Judgement Under Uncertainty: Heuristics and Biases", *Science*, 27, pp. 1124–1131

von Neumann, J. and Morgenstern, J.V. (1944) *Theory of Games and Economic Behaviour*, Princeton University Press, Princeton

Wack, P. (1985a) "Scenarios: Uncharted Waters Ahead", *HBR* (September–October), pp. 73–85

Wack, P. (1985b) "Scenarios: Shooting the Rapids", *HBR* (November–December), pp. 139–150

Index